VENICE PAST AND PRESENT.

There is a glorious city in the sea!
The sea is in the broad, the narrow streets,
Ebbing and flowing; and the salt sea-weed
Clings to the marble of her palaces.
No tread of men, no footsteps to and fro,
Lead to her gates. The path lies o'er the sea,
Invincible; and from the land we went,
As to a floating city—steering in,
And gliding up her streets, as in a dream,
So smoothly—silently—by many a dome,
Mosque-like, and many a stately portico,
The statues ranged along an azure sky,—
By many a pile in more than Eastern pride,
Of old the residence of merchant kings;
The fronts of some, though Time had shattered them,
Still glowing with the richest hues of art,
As though the wealth within them had run o'er.

Samuel Rogers.

AT VENICE.—*The Piazza.*

OH, beautiful beneath the magic moon
To walk the watery way of palaces!
Oh, beautiful, o'ervaulted with gemmed blue,
This spacious court! with colour and with gold,
With cupolas, and pinnacles, and points,
And crosses multiplex, and tips, and balls
(Wherewith the bright stars unreproving mix,
Nor scorn by hasty eyes to be confused);
Fantastically perfect this lone pile
Of oriental glory; these long ranges
Of classic chiselling; this gay flickering crowd,
And the calm Campanile.—Beautiful!
Oh, beautiful!

Then, at once,
At a step, I crown the Campanile's top,
And view all mapped below. Islands, lagoon,
An hundred steeples, and a million roofs,
The fruitful champaign, and the cloud-capt Alps,
And the broad Adriatic.

ARTHUR HUGH CLOUGH.

PIAZZETTA OF SAN MARCO FROM THE GRAND CANAL.

THE

QUEEN OF THE ADRIATIC;

OR,

VENICE PAST AND PRESENT.

By

W. H. DAVENPORT ADAMS,

Author of "Buried Cities of Campania," "Records of Noble Lives," &c.

Sea-girt City! thou hast been
Ocean's child, and then his Queen.

SHELLEY.

BOSTON:

D. LOTHROP AND CO., 38 AND 40 CORNHILL.

DOVER, N.H.: G. T. DAY AND CO.

1869.

PREFACE

———o———

Neptune saw Venice on the Adria stand
Firm as a rock, and all the sea command :
"Think'st thou, O Jove," said he, "Rome's walls excel?
Or that proud cliff whence false Tarpeia fell?
Grant Tiber best—view both, and you will say
That men did *those*, gods *these* foundations lay."

Translated by JOHN EVELYN, from the Latin of Jacopo Sannazaro, for which the Venetian citizens presented him with 6000 golden crowns.

OWING to the vivid interest which attaches to the history of Venice, and the magnificent architectural monuments which adorn the ancient city, it was thought that a book purporting to be at once a record and a description—a manual for the young student, and a series of sketches for the general reader—might prove acceptable to the English public.

With this view the present volume was compiled, and it is believed that in its own limited sphere it stands almost, if not quite, alone ; that an account of the "relics" and "sights" of Venice, and a summary of its annals, are not to be elsewhere obtained in so portable a shape. The original authorities on Venetian history seldom come within the reach of the ordinary reader, who, indeed, will have little leisure, and perhaps less taste, for the weighty tomes of Muratori. Even Mr. Hazlitt's work is a formidable undertaking; Mr. Hallam glances only at certain features and crises of Venetian policy; and in Dr. Dyer's elaborate "History of Modern Europe," the annals of the "Queen of the Adriatic" are necessarily interwoven with those of other nations. Indeed, I suspect that Venice was best known to English readers through the poetry of Byron, the works of Cooper, Mrs. Ratcliffe, and Schiller, and the dramas of Shakspeare and Otway, until Mr. Ruskin taught them how to admire the wonders of its architecture, and made them reflect on the surprising story of its rise and fall.

For nearly fifteen hundred years Venice was a sovereign power. For two-thirds of that long period she exercised a decided influence on European policy. The wealth of the East was gathered in her treasury; her fleets were found in every sea; her colonies were numerous and thriving; her fortunes, in spite of many checks, seemed with every generation to flourish more greenly. Her merchants were princes, and her princes were heroes, and a long succession of great men raised her to a position of supreme celebrity.

> "Genus immortale manet, multosque per annos
> Stat fortuna domus."

There came a remarkable and a fatal change. She was gradually stripped of her colonies, her enterprise decayed, her commerce shrank into nothingness, her heroic spirit waned, she lost her independence, and became the vassal of a foreign power. So eventful a history, however weakly and imperfectly told, can scarcely fail to arrest the attention, to impress the fancy, and arouse the judgment.

Venice has given to Art, Science, and Literature no unworthy gifts. We can never be ungrateful to the city which bred a Titian, a Bellini, and a Tintoretto, a Marco Polo and a Friar Paul, an Aldus Manutius, a Goldoni, and a Canova! In every field of knowledge as of enterprise she has shone conspicuous, and her triumphs in peace are not less renowned than the victories of her sword. What we owe to the Venetian architects and sculptors a great critic has shown us; what we owe to her commercial achievements may more readily be inferred than precisely stated.

In the following pages I have touched lightly on most of these subjects. I have sketched the history of the once mighty State; I have rapidly summarized the annals of her art, literature, and science; I have described the manners and customs of the Venetians; have dwelt on the noble deeds of their nobler spirits; and described the glorious structures which perpetuate the memory of their old renown. This I have sought to do with all honesty and exactness—with faithful reference to the best authorities; and though I must be judged by what I have accomplished, and not by what I have attempted, I trust the following pages will secure the approval of the judicious public, and command the attention of the gentle reader.

W. H. DAVENPORT ADAMS.

PART THE FIRST.—HISTORY OF VENICE.

I. Introduction.

II. First Period of Venetian History.

III. THE SECOND PERIOD.

PART THE SECOND.—THE FINE ARTS, LITERATURE, MANNERS, AND CUSTOMS OF VENICE.

I. The Fine Arts in Venice.

II. Science and Letters in Venice.

III. Glimpses of Venetian Life.

PART THE THIRD.—PUBLIC BUILDINGS AND MEMORABLE PLACES.

I. Memorable Places.

II. The Churches of Venice.

III. Public Buildings of Venice.

Part First.

THE HISTORY OF VENICE.

—o—

Like the water-fowl,
They built their nest among the ocean waves,
And where the sands were shifting, as the wind
Blew from the north or south.

Rogers.

I.

Introduction.

> Glory and Empire! once upon these towers
> With Freedom—godlike Triad! how ye sate!
> The league of mightiest nations, in those hours
> When Venice was an envy, might abate,
> But did not quench her spirit.
>
> BYRON, *Ode on Venice.*

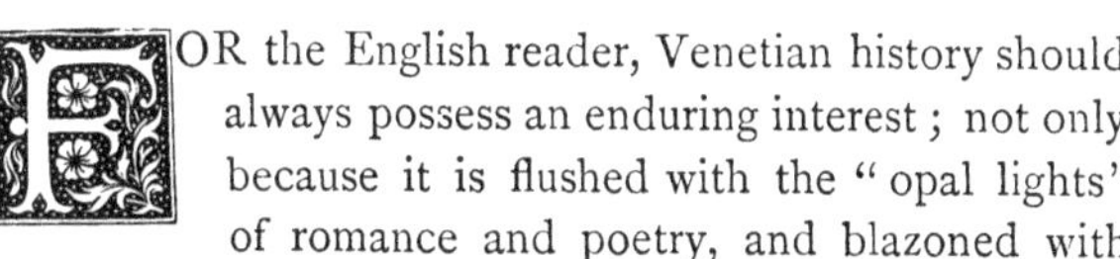

FOR the English reader, Venetian history should always possess an enduring interest; not only because it is flushed with the "opal lights" of romance and poetry, and blazoned with names which the world has agreed to enroll on the record of the ages; not only because certain of its incidents have inspired the genius of Shakspeare, and Otway, and Mrs. Radcliffe, and Byron, and Rogers; not only because of its marvellous phases of change, its quick growth, its surpassing glory, its rapid decadence, its prolonged agony, and final awakening to life and light in our own time;—these are things which appeal only to the imagination and the feelings: but it has higher claims on the consideration of the thoughtful. The two note-worthiest features in its policy are precisely those which should have the greatest attraction for Englishmen: First, the fervent religious spirit which characterized every action of the Venetians in their day of greatness, and whose decline wrought also the decline of their power and prosperity; second, the grand and persistent struggle which, for generations, they maintained against the temporal authority of the Church of Rome. There are many particulars in which Venetian history may be compared with our own. Venice rose to power through her commerce and her colonies, and was great through her maritime resources rather than her military strength. The individual citizens of Venice were more religious in their character and dealings than her Government. She had a sincere interest in the peace and prosperity of her neighbours; yet her interference was always regarded with jealousy, and she never found faithful allies. Other points of similitude, and many of contrast, might be adduced; but it is sufficient to state generally, that, both in a commercial and religious light, the annals of Venice offer an important field of study for any Englishman who regards with anxiety and interest the future of his country.

In the following pages, our restricted limits will confine us to the merest summary—a skeleton, which it would need an abler hand to clothe with flesh and blood. Yet, so deep is the charm which like a magical light surrounds the history of the Queen of the Adriatic—so full are her annals of touches of heroism, devotion, and grandeur, and even of the highest pathos and the most solemn gloom—that we are not without hopes the reader may be induced to follow with some degree of interest the rapid sketch we have attempted.

Mr. Ruskin has justly observed that the existence of the Venetian state may be regarded as broadly divided into *two periods:* the *first* of nine hundred, the *second* of five hundred years; the separation being marked by what has been called the "Serrar del Consiglio,"—that is, the final and absolute distinction of the nobles from the commonalty, and the establishment of the government in their hands, to the exclusion alike of the influence of the people on the one side, and the authority of the prince on the other.*

The independence of Venice endured thirteen hundred and seventy-six years (A.D. 421–1797)—from the foundation of a consular government on the island of the Rialto, to the declaration of Napoleon Bonaparte that the Venetian Republic had ceased to exist. The First Period of this long history was that of its rise and maturity, when its people were governed by the ablest and worthiest man whom they could find among them, as their Doge and leader; when commerce and enterprise, and those heroic virtues which at first commerce and enterprise so surely nourish—endurance, daring, and patriotism—gave them a foremost place among European powers; and their exertions were guided by the genius of their greatest princes, Pietro Orseolo, Ordelafo Faliero, Dominico Michieli, Sebastiano Ziani, and Enrico Dandolo.

The Second Period (A.D. 1418–1797) was that of the decay and fall of Venice—adding another to the grand historic instances of the mutability of states and empires. It was stained with crimes, intestine conspiracies, and

* Ruskin, "Stones of Venice," i. ch. 1, 2, 3, 4.

unjust wars; it was characterized by religious lukewarmness and commercial dishonesty; it was controlled by a dark, oppressive oligarchy, whose instruments were the secret torture and the bravo's knife. It was the ruin of a great people accomplished by their own hands, worked out by their own insincerity, lack of enthusiasm, greed of gold, and insensibility to the nobler motives of human affairs.

The most curious phenomenon in all Venetian history —and this fact the reader, at the outset, will do well to comprehend—has justly been stated, by an eloquent writer, as "the vitality of religion in the private life of Venice, and its deadness in public policy."* When other European states have awoke at the voice of enthusiasm, chivalry, or fanaticism; have had their crusades, their St. Bartholomews, their Pilgrimages of Graces, their Bannockburns and their Crecys, their sieges of Antwerp, their Lutzens—evidences, even if sometimes disastrous ones, of a certain earnestness of faith and warmth of blood; Venice, from first to last, has stood "like a masked statue," impenetrable in her coldness, and only roused by the touch of a secret spring. That spring was her commercial interest—"the one motive of all her important political acts, or enduring national animosities." You might wound her honour, and Venice forgave; insult her religion, and Venice smiled; but rival her in her commerce, and Venice bared her sword. She estimated her conquests by the addition they made to her wealth: if an enterprise offered no material gain, she checked it with the cold question, *Cui bono?* And therefore Venice fell—as Holland fell, as every principality,

* Ruskin, *ut ante*, p. 6.

and state, and empire *shall* fall, which consults only its own selfish interests, and never strikes a blow for God and human freedom!

The traveller about to explore a new and untrodden region, ascends, if possible, to the summit of some commanding eminence, whence he may mark the course of streams, and the winding valleys, and the dense forests, and thus, instructed as to the nature of the country, map out his future path. Some such procedure is advantageous in the study of history; and before we commence our connected narrative of Venetian annals, we shall put before the reader, in chronological order, their leading events, to serve as landmarks in his rapid journey. By looking back at these, he will be able to trace the road he has gone, and recall the principal features of the region through which he has travelled.

CHRONOLOGICAL LIST OF THE DOGES OF VENICE.

Date.	Doge's Name.	Duration of their Reign. Years.	Remarkable Events.
697.	PAOLO LUCA ANAFESTO	20	Concludes with the King of the Lombards a treaty which defines the limits of the two states.
717.	MARCELLO TEGALIANO	9	
726.	ORSO	11	Re-establishes the Exarch of Ravenna in his sovereignty—Bishopric of Keima erected (733)—Orso killed in a tumult.
	MAESTROS DELLA MILIZIA (ELECTED ANNUALLY).		
737.	DOMINICO LEO	1	
738.	FELICE CORNICULA	1	
739.	DEODATO ORSO	1	
740.	GIULIANO CEPARIO	1	
741.	GIOVANNI FABRICIACO	1	Has his eyes scooped out, and is deposed.

THE DOGES RE-ESTABLISHED.

Date.	Doge's Name.	Duration of their Reign. Years.	Remarkable Events.
742.	DEODATO ORSO	13	Fixes the seat of Government at Malamocco — Receives from the Emperor the title of Imperial Consul — Extends the territory of Venice—Is killed in a sedition.
755.	GALLA	1	Has his eyes put out, and is banished.
756.	DOMINICO MONEGARIO	8	Two tribunes associated with him—Has his eyes put out, and is driven from Venice.
764.	MAURIZIO GALBAIO	15	Takes as his colleague his son Giovanni.
779.	GIOVANNI GALBAIO	25	Takes as his colleague his son Maurizio—They throw the Patriarch of Grado from a tower—Are excommunicated and driven from Venice.
804.	ORBELERIO	8	Takes as colleagues his two sons—They have an interview at Thionville with Charlemagne—War with Pepin, King of the Franks, who conquers most of the Venetian territory—The three Doges deposed.
812.	ANGELO PARTICIPAZIO	15	Charlemagne restores to Venice all the conquests made by his son—The seat of Government transferred to the Rialto—The relics of St. Mark transported to Venice, and a Cathedral and Ducal Palace founded.
827.	GIUSTINIANI PARTICIPAZIO	2	Associates with himself his brother Giovanni.
829.	GIOVANNI PARTICIPAZIO	8	Suppresses an insurrection headed by Orbelerio, a former doge — Is himself deposed, and thrown into the convent of Grado.
837.	PIETRO GRADENIGO	27	The Venetian fleet is annihilated at Otranto by the Saracens—Is assassinated by conspirators.
864.	ORSO PARTICIPAZIO	17	Defeats the Saracens—Enlarges the territory of Venice.

Date.	Doge's Name.	Duration of their Reign. Years.	Remarkable Events.
881.	GIOVANNI PARTICIPAZIO II.	6	Seizes upon Commacchio and Ravenna—Abdicates.
887.	PIETRO CANDIANO (5 months).		Perishes in a sea-fight against the Sclavonians.
887.	GIOVANNI PARTICIPAZIO II. (6 months).		Is made a second time Doge.
888.	PIETRO TRIBUNO	23	Descent of the Huns, who are defeated by the Venetian fleet.
912.	ORSO PARTICIPAZIO II.	20	Abdicates the dogeship, and retires into a monastery.
932.	PIETRO CANDIANO II.	7	The Brides of Venice, loss and recapture of (932)—Aggrandizes the Venetian territories by his conquests.
939.	PIETRO BADOUER	2	
942.	PIETRO CANDIANO III.	17	His son, having revolted, is banished from Venice, but recalled on his father's death, and elected Doge.
959.	PIETRO CANDIANO IV.	17	Is killed in a riot.
976.	PIETRO ORSEOLO I.	2	Quits Venice secretly, and retires to a convent.
978.	VITALE CANDIANO (14 months).		
979.	TRIBUNO MEMMO	13	Dies in a convent, worn out by the factious strife of the Caloprinis and the Morosinis.
991.	PIETRO ORSEOLO II.	18	Rebuilds and fortifies Grado—Conquers the coast of Dalmatia—Receives the Emperor Otho III.—Famine and plague in Venice in 1006.
1009.	OTHO ORSEOLO	17	Thrice driven from Venice by the factions, and thrice established on the throne.
1026.	PIETRO CONTRANIGO	6	Is deposed, and confined in a convent.
1032.	DOMINICO ORSEOLO	1	Abdicates, and retires to Vienne
1033.	DOMINICO FLABENIGO	10	
1043.	DOMINICO CONTARINI	28	Restores Grado to Venice.
1071.	DOMINICO SILVIO	13	The Venetian fleet annihilated—The Doge deposed.
1084.	VITALE FALIERO	12	Assumes the titles of Dukes of Dalmatia and Croatia.

Date.	Doge's Name.	Duration of their Reign. Years.	Remarkable Events.
1096.	VITALE MICHIELI I.	6	Leads the Venetians on a Crusade, and defeats the Pisans.
1102.	ORDELAFO FALIERO	15	Recaptures Zara, defeats the Huns, and dies in the arms of victory.
1117.	DOMINICO MICHIELI	13	Destroys the Saracen fleet off Jaffa, and devastates the Greek Islands.
1130.	PIERO PALANO	18	Defeats the Paduans—Killed at the siege of Corfu.
1148.	DOMINICO MOROSINI	8	Conquers the island of Corfu.
1156.	VITALE MICHIELI II.	17	Makes peace with the Pisans—Conquers Pera, Trau, and Ragusa—Dies in a popular tumult.
1173.	SEBASTIANO ZIANI	6	Besieges Ancona, and protects the Pope, Alexander III., against the German Emperor—The Seignory, Senate, and Grand Council established.
1179.	ORIO MALIPIERI	14	Equips a fleet for the Holy Land—Abdicates, and retires into a monastery.
1192.	ENRICO DANDOLO	13	Distinguishes himself at the siege of Ancona—Fourth Crusade.
1205.	PIERO ZIANI	24	New expedition to the Holy Land—Capture of Modon, Coron, and Candia.
1229.	GIACOMO TIEPOLO	20	Equips a fleet to deliver Constantinople, and defeats the Imperial armada.
1249.	MANICO MOROSINI	3	
1252.	RAINIERO ZENO	16	
1268.	LORENZO TIEPOLO	7	First war with Genoa.
1275.	JACOPO CONTARINO	4	Abdicates, after an inglorious reign.
1279.	GIOVANNI DANDOLO	10	The religious Inquisition established.
1289.	PIERO GRADENIGO	21	Second war with Genoa—Defeat of the Venetians at Curzola—*Il Libro d'Oro*, or Golden Book of the Nobility, commenced—The Council of Ten instituted.
1310.	MARINO GIORGI	2	Sixth revolt of Zara—Conspiracy of Tiepolo.
1312.	GIOVANNI SORANZO	16	Papal interdict removed.

Date.	Doges' Name.	Duration of their Reign. Years.	Remarkable Events.
1328.	FRANCISCO DANDOLO	11	Treviso and Bassano annexed to the Venetian territories.
1339.	BARTOLOMEO GRADENIGO	4	Subdues the revolted Candiotes.
1343.	ANDREAS DANDOLO	11	War with Hungary—The Doge defeats King Louis of Hungary at Zara—War with the Genoese.
1354.	MARINO FALIERO	1	Conspires against the republic, and is beheaded.
1355.	GIOVANNI GRADENIGO	1	War with Hungary and Austria.
1356.	GIOVANNI DELPINO	5	The Venetians lose Istria and Dalmatia.
1361.	LORENZO CELSI	4	Petrarch flourishes—Insurrection of the Candiotes.
1365.	MARCO CORNARO	2	The Candiotes again revolt.
1367.	ANDREA CONTARINI	15	War of Chiozzia against Hungary, Genoa, Padua, and Aquileia—Siege of Chiozzia by the Genoese—Defeat of the Genoese and salvation of Venice by the Admirals Pisani and Zeno—Peace of Turin (1381).
1382.	MICHELE MOROSINI (4 months).		Venice visited by the plague, which carries off the Doge and 20,000 persons.
1382.	ANTONIO VENIERO	18	War against Carrara and Milan—League against the Turks—Climax of Venetian prosperity.
1400.	MICHELE STENO	13	Vicenza, Padua, and Lepanto are annexed to the republic.
1413.	TOMASO MOCENIGO	10	Conquest of Friuli and part of Dalmatia—Victory over the Turks.
1423.	FRANCISCO FOSCARI	34	Ravenna annexed to the republic—Constantinople relieved by the Venetians—The Emperor Frederick III. visits Venice—Deposition of the Doge.
1457.	PASCALE MALIPIERI	4	
1462.	CRISTOFO MORO	9	War against the Turks, who seize upon Negropont.
1471.	NICOLAS TRONO	2	War against the Turks.
1473.	NICOLAS MARCELLO	1	The Venetians defeat the Turks at Scutari.

Date.	Doge's Name.	Duration of their Reign. Years.	Remarkable Events.
1474.	PIERO MOCENIGO	2	Venice conquers Cyprus.
1476.	ANDREA VENDRAMINO	2	The Turks devastate Friuli.
1478.	GIOVANNI MOCENIGO	8	Peace with Turkey—Venice loses Negropont, Lemnos, and Scutari—Rovigo annexed to the republic—The plague visits Venice.
1485.	MARCO BARBARIGO	1	
1486.	AGOSTINO BARBARIGO	15	League of Venice, the Pope, and Duke of Milan against France, and defeat of the allies at Fornovo—First printing-press established by Aldus Manutius (1488).
1501.	LEONARDO LOREDANO	20	League of Cambray against Venice.
1521.	ANTONIO GRIMANI	3	Venice joins the Holy League against France.
1524.	ANDREA GRITTI	14	Venice joins France against her former allies—War with Turkey.
1538.	PIERO LANDO	7	Council of Trent.
1545.	FRANCISCO DONATO	7	The Bellinis flourish.
1553.	MARCO ANTONIO TREVISANI	1	Titian flourishes.
1554.	FRANCISCO VENIERO	2	Tintoretto flourishes.
1556.	LORENZO PRIULI	3	Venice is terribly devastated by pestilence and famine.
1559.	GARMINO PRIULI	9	Hostilities against Rome, through the claim of the Pope to present to the vacant Venetian benefices.
1567.	PIERO LOREDANO	3	The Bull *In Cæna Domini*, launched against Venice, is proscribed in all the territories of the republic—Burning of the Arsenal.
1570.	LUDOVICO MOCENIGO	6	War with Turkey—The Austrian and Venetian fleets, under Don John, win the battle of Lepanto—Loss of the isle of Cyprus—Visit of Henry III. of France to Venice.
1576.	SEBASTIANO VENIERO	2	Receives from the Pope the rose of honour.
1578.	NICOLO DA PONTE	7	The Rialto Bridge commenced, and fortress of Palma Nuova constructed.
1585.	PASQUALE ACOGNA	10	The name of Henry IV. of France inscribed in the *Libro d'Oro*.

Date.	Doge's Name.	Duration of their Reign. Years.	Remarkable Events.
1595.	Marino Grimani	10	The republic quarrels with Pope Paul IV.—Fra Paolo writes his "History of the Council of Trent."
1606.	Leonardi Donato	6	Reconciliation of Venice with the Court of Rome.
1612.	Marco Antonio Memmo	4	War with Austria.
1618.	Nicolo Donato (3 weeks).		
1618.	Antonio Priuli	5	Conspiracy of the Duke of Ossuna.
1623.	Francisco Contarini	2	War with Mantua and the Valteline
1625.	Giovanni Cornaro	5	The Council of Ten remodelled.
1630.	Nicolo Contarini	2	Peace with Spain and Austria.
1632.	Francisco Erizzo	13	Beginning of the war of Candia.
1645.	Francisco Molino	10	War of Candia.
1655.	Carlo Contarini	1	Candiote war continued.
1656.	Francisco Cornaro (a few days).		
1656.	Bertuccio Valiero	1	Candiote war—The priests re-established in the Venetian States.
1657.	Giovanni Pesaro	3	Candiote war.
1660.	Dominico Contarini	14	Candia abandoned to the Turks.
1674.	Nicolo Sagredo	2	
1676.	Ludovico Contarini	7	Owes his elevation to a revolt of the populace, who force the Grand Council to annul a preceding election.
1683.	Marco Antonio Giustiniani	5	The republic joins Germany and Poland in a war against the Turks.
1688.	Francisco Morisini	6	Conquest of the Morea.
1694.	Sylvestro Valiero	6	Peace of Carlowitz, which confirms Venice in the possession of the Morea.
1700.	Ludovico Mocenigo	9	Neutrality of Venice in the great war of the Spanish Succession.
1709.	Giovanni Cornaro	13	Rapid decline of the republic, which loses the Morea—Peace of Passarowitz.
1722.	Sebastiano Mocenigo	10	Trieste founded as an Austrian port to ruin the commerce of Venice.
1732.	Carlo Ruzzini	2	
1735.	Ludovico Pisani	7	Venice declared a free port.
1741.	Piero Grimani	11	Venice joins Rome, Genoa, and Sicily against Tunis and Algiers.

Date.	Doge's Name.	Duration of their Reign. Years.	Remarkable Events.
1752.	FRANCISCO LOREDANO	10	A Venetian elected to the Papal throne in the person of Clement XIII.
1762.	MARCO FOSCARINI (10 months).		
1763.	ALVIZIO MOCENIGO	16	War against Barbary.
1779.	PAOLO RENIERO	9	Attacks upon the Council of Ten and Inquisition of State.
1783.	LUDOVICO MANINI	9	The French Republic wages war against Venice, which surrenders to Napoleon Bonaparte—Treaty of Campo Formio—The Ionian Islands annexed to France, and Venice to Austria.
1848.	DANIELE MANIN (17 months).		Venice revolts against the Austrian despotism; elects Manin as her president, and afterwards as dictator; and gallantly endures a protracted siege—Is compelled to surrender to the Austrians, under Radetzky, after maintaining her independence from 23rd March 1848 to 24th August 1849.
1857.			Venice annexed to the new kingdom of Italy.

II.

First Period of Venetian History.

She looks a sea Cybele, fresh from ocean,
Rising, with her tiara of proud towers
At airy distance, with majestic motion,
A ruler of the waters and their powers.
And such she was: her daughters had their dowers
From spoils of nations; and the exhaustless East
Poured in her lap all gems in sparkling showers.
In purple was she robed; and of her feast
Monarchs partook, and deemed their dignity increased.

BYRON, *Childe Harold.*

THE VENETIAN TERRITORY.

HE north-eastern angle of Italy, comprising the fertile territories between the Alps and the Adriatic coast, was known in a remote antiquity by the name of Venetia, from its inhabitants, the Veneti, or Heneti. According to a popular tradition, this brave and warlike race, whom the Romans found it no easy matter to subdue, sprung from Antenor and his followers, an Asiatic tribe of Paphlagonia, who, after the fall of Troy, had established themselves among the Euganean hills. Of all the Gauls, the Veneti most stoutly resisted the conquering arms of

Rome; and, after their submission, were always numbered among its boldest subjects. In the Augustan age, Venetia united with Istria to form the Tenth Region; and was recognized as bounded on the north by the snowy barrier of the Alps, south by the river Po, east by the Adriatic, and west by a line drawn from the Po to the Adige. Thenceforward it formed a part of the Roman Empire, until that colossus was laid in ruins by its own inherent weakness and the attacks of the barbarians.

The history of modern Venice dates from the invasion of Attila, in the fifth century of the Christian era. The Sword of Mars, as that most terrible of conquerors was named, gathered in Italy a dreadful harvest; and, as he advanced, literally fulfilled his threat, that where his horse once trod the grass should never grow. Fertile plains and smiling valleys were transformed into dreary wildernesses, and thriving cities converted into silent and gloomy wastes. The maritime districts were in turn exposed to a similar calamity; and all who could escape the onrush of the barbarian horde, collected their "household gods" and betook themselves for shelter to the marshes of the Venetian coast (A.D. 421–52).

DESCRIPTION OF THE LAGOON OF VENICE.

It is a poetical exaggeration to speak of Venice as rising from the bosom of the ocean; the lagoon which surrounds her is not a lake, but a low level shore; an immense delta more or less inundated by the river-waters which descend from the glaciers of the distant Alps, and, especially, by the influx of the Adriatic.

The Romans designated under the name of *Paludes Gallicæ*, or Venetia Maritima, the whole extent of marshy littoral lying between the mouth of the Isonzo and the embouchures of the Savio. To this region a few words only are given by Herodotus; but Strabo describes it more explicitly. "The country of the Veneti," says the old geographer, "abounds in rivers; the Adriatic, subject to periodical tides like the ocean, encroaches upon the land, and forms there vast breadths of saline marshes; so that the inhabitants, like those of Lower Egypt, display great ability in directing and moderating the course of the waters by canals and dykes. Certain portions of their country are well adapted for cultivation; others, nearly always submerged, are useful for navigation; a few of their towns are wave surrounded, like islands; others are only washed on one side by the Adriatic; while, finally, those situated inland communicate with the sea by rivers."

Scymnus* of Chios, in a treatise of Geography anterior to the great work of Strabo, had said, when speaking of Venetia:—"The Veneti inhabit the sea, and their country, disposed along the shore in the form of a semicircle, includes fifteen towns and a million and a half of souls." Servius, the ancient commentator upon Virgil, furnishes numerous details in reference to the territory of the Veneti, and the rivers and canals which traversed it. The historian Procopius also loves to describe "the industry

* Scymnus (Σκύμνος), of Chios, wrote a *Periegesis*, or description of the earth, referred to and quoted by Stephanus and other writers. He also wrote a Periegesis, in about one thousand iambic lines, which was reprinted at Leipzig by Fabricius, and at Berlin by Meincke, in 1846. See Dr. Smith's "Dictionary of Greek and Roman Biography," *sub nom.*

of the sailors of the lagoon, who, after having loaded their boats at ebb of tide, wait in patience until the flow comes to raise and carry them outside the narrow straits." But the most complete description now extant of the condition of Venetia Maritima previous to the foundation of the city of Venice, is that of the senator Cassiodorus,* prefect of the palace in the reign of Vitigès, fourth king of the Visigoths, about 538. It is contained in a letter which he addressed to the magistrates of the Venetian Isles :—

"Your navigation possesses this advantage, that at need there is always open a secure channel; for when the fury of the winds closes the sea against you, the rivers offer a most agreeable highway. Your ships, thus sheltered, approach the land in safety, and cannot perish, however often they touch the ground. From a distance, and when the bed which bears them cannot be discerned, one would say they were sailing over the meadows. It is upon these lands, intersected by a multitude of canals, and whose surface is alternately covered and laid bare by the waves, you have perched your dwellings, like aquatic birds; at first sight they appear terrestrial; then, by a sudden change of aspect, they are transformed into islands, and one fancies oneself in the midst of the Cyclades."

It is now our purpose, with the exactness of modern science, to present a complete and accurate picture of the Venetian lagoon.†

* Magnus Aurelius Cassiodorus was born about A.D. 468, and died about A.D. 560. The work referred to in the text is his "Variarum (Epistolarum) Libri xii.," included in Garet's edition of his complete works, reprinted at Venice in 1729.

† Galibert, "Histoire de Vénise, pp. 6–10.

Everybody knows that the Mediterranean, penetrating inland through the channel of Otranto, forms, between Italy on the west, and Dalmatia and Albania on the east, a vast gulf, named the Adriatic Sea, 500 miles in length and 100 miles in breadth, with a superficial area of 42,000 square miles. If, from the extremity of this gulf, where the city of Venice is situated, it were possible for the eye to embrace the whole of the immense basin formed on the north by the Alps and Apennines, it would be easy to explain the existence of the low and marshy lands which fringe the northern margin of the Adriatic. In fact, all the waters of these two important mountain chains expand towards a common point. These are—the Isonzo, the Livenza, and the Tagliamento, descending from the Julian Alps; the Piave, the Musone, the Brenta, and the Adige, fed by the snows of the Tyrol; and finally, the Po, swollen by all the waters of the Alps and Apennines, which, arriving at the western angle of the Adriatic Gulf, roll with them the soil and débris they have had no time to deposit during their impetuous course. On debouching in the sea the fury of their descent is lost, the waters grow shallower, and the tardy current then divides into multitudinous arms, which combine to form the deltas and swampy plains abounding in this peculiar region.

This region, of a very irregular outline, is surrounded by a belt of lands, shutting it in on every side. Its western limit is the littoral of the continent, which describes a bold curve from Brondola to the mouth of the Brenta, at Isola, where the Sile and the Piave pour out their tributary waters; on the east, or seaward side, a long chain of low-lying plains, stretched between the two extremities of the arc described by the mainland, forms its chord, and completes the enclosure of the lagoon. This chain of narrow and elongated islands, exactly resembling the belt which bars the entrance of the Zuyder Zee in Holland, bears the generic designation of *Lido* ("the shore"); it is situated between the basin of the lagoon and the open sea, like a dyke against which the billows of "the stormy Adriatic" break furiously but in vain. Its length exceeds ten leagues; its breadth seldom reaches half a mile. The maritime littoral thus produced by the combined action of the sea and the rivers is, in great part, defended by piles of sand-hills or *dunes;* at certain points, however, it is protected against the violent effort of the waves by artificial works, of which the most important are the famous *murazzi* (sea-walls) in the island of Pelestrina. But this kind of causeway, whose general direction is nearly due north and south, is not continuous; it is interrupted at intervals by gaps or cuttings called *porti* (ports), through which the lagoon communicates with the external ocean.

The lagoon, thus enclosed, extends along the shore of the Adriatic between 43° 10′ and 45° 3′ N. latitude, and 29° 47′ and 30° 20′ E. longitude (from the meridian of Ferro). Its length is 32 geographical miles from south-west to north-east; that is to say, from the modern mouth of the Brenta to that of the ancient Piave or Sile; in breadth it varies from 4 to 8 miles. Its superficial area is computed at 172 miles. It is divided into three distinct portions, according to the different degrees of immersion each of them undergoes. The first consists of actual marshland, the substratum being a wet clay, which is covered with aquatic plants and grasses. The surface, never rising more than a few inches above the height of ordinary tides, is nearly always on a level with the water, but only entirely covered during the equinoctial gales. To this portion of the lagoon the

AN ISLAND IN THE VENETIAN LAGOON.

Venetians give the special name of *barene.* Next to the *barene* come the *velme:* the *velme* (from *velma*, mud) are also marshes, but less elevated; wholly inundated at the flow, they are dry at the ebb. Their soil is sandy and completely barren, while they are furrowed in every direction by canals almost always full of water. Finally, we meet with the *fondi*—spaces more or less extensive, where water is never wanting, even in the extraordinary ebb-tides of winter. In these different portions of the lagoon land always dry rises elevated above the highest tides, having been successively conquered by the industry of man. For hither, at different epochs, came emigrants from terra firma, to find an asylum against oppression where they might live in peace, though by the sweat of their brows; content to struggle with the sea as a less dangerous enemy than the freebooting warrior or marauding noble; and, in due time, it was from the artificial union of a great number of these insulated communities that Venice sprung into existence.

As the level of the waters rises and sinks four times daily, the lagoon changes its aspect with each alteration; at low tide it spreads before you in one vast tract of mud, relieved here and there by a few clumps of algæ or rushes.

"We see
Stretched wide and wild the waste enormous marsh,
Where from the frequent bridge,
Like emblems of infinity,
The trenchèd waters run from sky to sky."

The undulating lines of the canals trace the most capricious meanders; the small Venetian boats glide unperceived between their raised banks; you catch sight only of the rower who stands upright to guide his shallow skiff, and seems to be toiling across a muddy plain. The tall spires, white walls, and leafy trees of the farms, villages, and towns, rise above the dreary wild, like palm-oases above the sandy depths of the desert. But at high tide the spectacle is changed: the waves, pouring over the narrow channels which seek to confine them, slowly spread over the entire surface of the lagoon. When they have reached the summit of their ascending scale, they remain for awhile immovable, like a sheet of solid silver, forming an immense lake which is scarcely curled or crisped by the sea-breezes. Venice then shines forth in all her radiant and mysterious beauty, and the spectator feels the truth of Howell's saying—"It is the water, wherein *she lies like a swan's nest*, that doth both form and feed her." One might say that she had been softly and silently cradled on the bosom of the lagoon by some genius of the ocean. The radiant description of Shelley, at such a time, does not seem too highly coloured :—*

"Underneath day's azure eyes,
Ocean's nursling, Venice lies;
A peopled labyrinth of walls,
Amphitrite's destined halls,
Which her hoary sire now paves
With his blue and beaming waves.
Lo, the sun upsprings behind,
Broad, red, radiant, half-reclined
On the level quivering line
Of the waters crystalline;
And before that chasm of light,
As within a furnace bright,
Column, tower, and dome, and spire,
Shine like obelisks of fire,
Pointing with inconstant motion
From the altar of dark ocean
To the sapphire-tinted skies;
As the flames of sacrifice
From the marbled shrines did rise
As to pierce the dome of gold
Where Apollo spoke of old."

Such is the general aspect of the lagoon. Let us now

* Shelley, "Lines written among the Euganean Hills."

examine the phenomena which have produced, and concurred to prolong its existence.*

Before arriving at their embouchure, nearly all the rivers we have mentioned divide into a great number of arms, whose radiations form all over the shore-lands of the gulf a multitude of deltas, most of which are marshy. Having to traverse the muddy tracts of the lagoon before they can gain the open sea, they excavate for themselves a passage of greater or lesser depth to the *port* where outflows the burden of their waters. The openings of the so-called *ports* are simply the old or present embouchures of the rivers, and the main trunks of the labyrinthine canals the ancient beds of fluvial currents.† Thus the Grand Canal (*Canale Grande*), which cuts Venice in two, was originally an arm of the Brenta, starting from Lizza Fusina, and discharging its waters at the port of San Nicolo.

The ocean and the river-waters arrive in the lagoon, as we see, from diametrically opposite quarters, although they all quit it by the same issues. The sea, during the flux, pouring into the canals and sweeping inland, encounters the rivers as they descend in an adverse direction; the latter, retarded in their onward march, break with difficulty the compact array of the billows, with which in time they mingle and are confounded. But at the moment of the reflux, all the waters having the same direction, and mutually combining the forces which impel them towards the open, dash themselves confusedly through the narrow channels, and plunge like war-horses

* Galibert, "Histoire de Vénise," *ut antè.*

† See Sir C. Lyell, "Principles of Geology," 9th edit.

into the depths of the Adriatic. Nearly all these rivers, descending, or rather abruptly falling from the lofty Alpine valleys, have a brief course and a rapid flow. Swollen by numerous affluents, they are subject to sudden floods, and in their furious course carry down with them the débris of all the different soils they traverse. A portion of this detritus they deposit in their own bed, whose level they are incessantly raising; another portion is transported to their embouchures, where it is piled up in more or less considerable *bars*. The narrow islets of Lido are evidently only accumulations of mud and sand formerly raised by the joint action of the sea and the rivers.

These canals, invariably more or less filled with water, even at the greatest neap-tides, serve as constant modes of communication between the city, the sea, and the land; and are, what M. Galibert happily calls them, the essential and vital organs of Venice. Therefore, in all times, the Venetians have carefully and skilfully maintained those intact which nature has created, have also excavated artificial passages, and favoured by every scientific device the circulation of the waters in their lagoon. And but for the indefatigable labour of generaation after generation, Venice must long since have lost its insular position, and, like old Ravenna, the proud Queen of the Adriatic would have become an inland city.

As these canals are lost to the eye for several hours each day, their navigation would be almost impracticable if there existed no means of distinguishing their course and direction, and boats would be constantly running aground. The exact channel is, therefore, indicated by long oaken poles planted at intervals along their borders, and rising four or five feet above the ordinary high-water mark. Guided by these, the boatman makes his way securely through the worse than Dœdalian labyrinth. They bear various appellations, according to their num-

A BEACON IN THE VENETIAN LAGOON.

ber, form, and size; as *mee*, or *mede* (from *meta*, a goal or boundary); *paline* (little posts); *gruppi* (fascines); *pennelli* (pennons or streamers); and *fari* (lighthouses); and appear to have been introduced at a very remote antiquity.

It is, then, this narrow area of inundated land, whose situation, limits, and peculiarities we have briefly described, which became the cradle of the great Venetian republic, the theatre of its commercial and military activity, the seat of its power and government.*

On the island of the Rialto,† which had long served as a port for Padua, a church, dedicated to St. James, had been founded as early as 421, and a consular government appointed to watch over the infant colony.‡ But it was not until 452 that the storm of Aquileia by the Goths, and the flight of the northern Italians, caused the neighbouring islands to be peopled, and the sands of Grado, Caorlo, Heraclia, Torcello, Pelestrina, Chiozzia, and Spinalunga to be speedily covered with houses. Thus were laid the foundations of a new state, whose very obscurity and poverty favoured the growth of its independence. Each island annually elected a tribune to administer its affairs, who was in turn controlled by a general council; and, as the repeated invasions of the Norsemen depopulated the various towns of Italy, this insular republic increased in prosperity and numbers. In 697 it had attained to such dimensions as to render

* Owing to its peculiar position, the climate of Venice is singularly mild. To the north it is sheltered by the distant barrier of the Alps, while warm airs are poured into it from the bosom of the Adriatic. Longfellow ascribes the beauty of the Venetian dialect to the advantageous local situation of the city. "Sheltered in the bosom of the Adriatic," he says, "it lay beyond the reach of those barbarous hordes which ever and anon with desolating blast swept the north of Italy like a mountain wind. Hence, it grew up soft, flexible, and melodious, and unencumbered with those harsh and barbarous sounds which so strikingly deform the neighbouring dialects of the north of Italy." The Venetian pronunciation is remarkably soft and pleasant; the sound of the *sch* and *tsh*, so frequent in the Tuscan and southern dialects, being changed into the soft *s* and *ts*.—LONGFELLOW, "Essay on Italian Language and Poetry."

† That is, *Rivo alto*, the deep stream; afterwards abbreviated into Rialto.

‡ The first foundations of the Paduan settlement were laid, according to Sabellico, at noon, on the 25th of March.

necessary the government of a single competent authority. For this purpose a general assembly, convoked at Heraclia, determined upon the election of a Duke, or Doge, who should rule for life, assisted by a council of state, whose members should be nominated by himself.

ELECTION AND POWERS OF THE DOGE.

The first person raised to this illustrious dignity was *Paolo Luca Anafesto*, and the powers conferred upon him were so unlimited as to be almost despotic. He was authorized to declare war or make peace ; he convoked the ecclesiastical synods, and virtually appointed all the prelates ; he nominated the judges and tribunes ; he summoned or dismissed the general assembly ; and the public revenues were placed at his disposal. Our own Plantagenet sovereigns, in fact, never enjoyed such absolute power ; and it was found, during the reign of the third Doge, Fabriciazio Orso, that it enabled its possessor to crush all the liberties of the people. A ruler for one year, under the title of Maestro della Milizia, was then elected. Five of these annual chiefs ruled in succession ; but the experiment appears to have failed, and the office of Doge was restored.

PEPIN, THE LOMBARD.

The history of Venice for the next half century is a history of struggles between the people and their princes. In one of these civil broils, the intervention of

Pepin, King of Lombardy, son of the famous Frank Emperor, Charles the Great (A.D. 804), was invited, and with the usual disastrous results. The Lombard king availed himself of the opportunity to secure his own aggrandizement. He attacked and stormed several of the Venetian towns; Chiozzia and Pelestrina surrendered to his arms; but, acting on the advice of Angelo Participazio—one of those great men to whom a free state often gives birth in the hour of public difficulty—the Venetians threw themselves into the island of the Rialto, where they destroyed the bridges, and offered so desperate a resistance, that Pepin retired in discomfiture.*

Participazio was now elected Doge (A.D. 812), and directed all his efforts to secure the future independence of his country by providing for the defence of the Rialto. He planted his subjects on the sixty islets scattered around it, connecting them with each other, and with the central island, by bridges; he founded a cathedral and a ducal palace on the site which they still occupy; and, in a word, created the modern VENICE.

RELICS OF ST. MARK.

The reign of his son and successor, Giustiniani, was distinguished by the consecration of the new city to St. Mark the Evangelist (A.D. 829). It became possessed of certain relics of the saint by a pious fraud. The Caliph of Egypt was building at Alexandria a new palace, and decorating it with the spoils of the Christian churches. As it was feared that the body of St. Mark would share

* Hazlitt, "History of the Venetian Republic," i. 79.

in the general desecration, two Venetian merchants, named Buono and Rustico, who were then trading in the Egyptian port with ten galleys, bribed the chief priest of the temple to hand over to them the apostolic remains for transference to Venice, where they would rest in eternal security. It was necessary to conceal the contemplated theft from the Christian population, and for this purpose the body of St. Claudia was deposited in the linen shroud previously occupied by the Evangelist.* Such, however, was the superior sanctity of the latter, that the disturbance of his remains filled the church with a rich celestial odour, and attracted crowds of curious devotees to satisfy themselves of the safety of the holy treasure. They did not detect the change which had been effected. Meanwhile, to prevent all chance of inquiry, the Venetians placed their prize in a large basket stuffed with herbs and pork, and as it was borne to the place of embarkation, the porters cried loudly, "*Khanzir! Khanzir!*"—"*Pork! Pork!*"—which was amply sufficient to keep every Mussulman at a safe distance. When on board the ship, it was wrapped in a sail, and hoisted to the yard-arm. During the homeward voyage a terrible storm would have destroyed the vessel and all its crew, but for the timely appearance of the saint, who ordered the captain to furl his sails, thereby proving himself a better navigator than the Venetian.

Our fathers did not welcome the arrival of the captured eagles of France, after the field of Waterloo, with greater exultation than the people of Venice the relics of

* See the quaint account of this transaction given by Leo Antonio More in his "Description of Africa" (London, 1600; bk. vi. pp. 301, 302).

the blessed Evangelist. They abandoned themselves to processions, and prayers, and banquets, and public holidays. A commercial fair was instituted in honour of the saint. Crowds of pilgrims flocked from far and wide to pay their homage. The winged "Lion of St. Mark" was blazoned on the standards, and impressed on the coinage of the Republic.* "Viva San Marco!" was the gathering-cry of its citizens, and the battle-shout of its warriors. The Lion became the theme of many political symbols. Thus: it was represented with wings to show that Venetians could strike with promptitude; sitting, as a sign of their gravity in counsel—for such is the usual attitude of sages; with a book in its paws, to intimate their devotion to commerce; in war time, the book was closed, and a naked sword substituted.† An ambassador from the German emperor once profanely inquired what country produced so singular a species of lions? The reply was happy: "That which produces Spread Eagles!" It is sad to relate that the Evangelist's ring was stolen in 1585, and that though his body was deposited in a mysterious receptacle known only to the Doge and certain special custodians, named *Provveditori*, it long ago disappeared. Eustace, an English traveller, accuses the Doge Carossio of having sold the precious relic.‡ At all events, its present depository is unknown.

* Evidently borrowed from Daniel's vision of the four great beasts: the first of which was like a lion, and had an eagle's wings (Daniel vii. 4).

† A. de la Houssaye, "Histoire du Gouvernement de Venise," p. 568.

‡ Eustace, "A Classical Tour in Italy," i. 171.

THE BRIDES OF VENICE.

The next one hundred years, though favouring the rapid growth of the Republic, were marked by few noteworthy incidents. In 856, the opulence of its capital attracted thither on a visit the Emperor Louis II., and in 906, during the dogeship of Pietro Tribuno, it excited the cupidity of the Huns, who made a descent upon the Adriatic coast, but were promptly attacked by the Venetian fleet among the intricate channels of the Lagoon, and completely destroyed. The year 932 was signalized by the remarkable event celebrated in song and story as the loss and recapture of "the Brides of Venice." It is a curious illustration of the manners of a stormy and stirring time. A custom had long prevailed that every year, on St. Mary's Eve, twelve young maidens, whose portions were provided by the state, should be publicly united to their lovers.* Gondolas, trimly decked with flowers and flags, and blithe with music, bore the bright procession, on the auspicious morning, to the church of San Pietro. The sea-rovers of Trieste, not ignorant of the custom, had this year concealed themselves, during the night, in an uninhabited locality, named Olivolo, and so soon as the glittering cortège and the beauteous brides had entered the cathedral, they leapt from their hiding-places, burst open the

* Such is the common account, but there seems good reason to believe that on this occasion *all* the brides of Venice were married, so that there was but one marriage-day each year for the nobles of the whole nation, to the intent that all might rejoice together. Each maiden brought her dowry with her in a small *cassetta*, or chest; they went first to the church, and waited for the youths, who having oome, mass was celebrated, and the bishop preached and blessed them. The bridal costume was white; the hair fell loosely over the shoulders, interwoven with threads of gold.

sacred doors, poured in among the dismayed multitude with flashing swords, seized the weeping, shrieking virgins, and carrying them to their barks, hoisted sail for Trieste. "Now," exclaims the poet,—

> "Now hadst thou seen along that crowded shore
> The matrons running wild, their festal dress
> A strange and moving contrast to their grief;
> And through the city, wander where thou wouldst,
> The men half-armed and arming—everywhere
> As roused from slumber by the stirring trump;
> One with a shield, one with a casque and spear;
> One with an axe severing in two the chain
> Of some old pinnace. Not a raft, a plank,
> But on that day was drifting. In an hour
> Half Venice was afloat. But long before,
> Frantic with grief and scorning all control,
> The youths were gone in a light brigantine,
> Lying at anchor near the arsenal;
> Each having sworn, and by the Holy Rood,
> To slay or to be slain." *

The Doge (Candiano II.), who was present at the festival, arose in a storm of indignation, summoned the people to arms, and leaping into a few vessels hastily put at their disposal by the Corporation of Trunk-makers, the hot pursuers plied their oars lustily in search of the ravishers. They overtook them in a creek still known as the *Porto delle Donzelle;* Candiano led the attack, and the Venetians fought with such fury that not one of the sea-rovers escaped their swords. The brides were brought back to the city in triumph, and in the evening of that eventful day the nuptial rites, so strangely interrupted, were celebrated with unusual pomp.†

* Rogers, "Poems: Italy."

† M. Sanuto, "Vite," pp. 459-462; Sabellico, Decade i., lib. iii., p. 56. The story has been made the subject of an Opera by Benedict.

In memory of this event, a solemn procession of twelve young women took place yearly, and was attended by the Doge and the priests, to the church of Santa Maria Formosa, in the trunk-makers' quarter. The tradition runs, that when the Doge Candiano had proposed to reward the latter for their prompt assistance, this *andata* was all they would accept. "But what," said the Doge, "if it should rain on the anniversary?" "We will give you hats," replied the trunk-makers, "to cover your heads; and if you are thirsty we will give you drink." To commemorate both the question and the reply, the priest of Santa Maria was wont to offer the Doge, when he landed, two flasks of malmsey, two oranges, and two gilded hats; the latter adorned with his own armorial bearings, those of the Pope, and those of the Doges.

> "Ever to preserve
> The memory of a day so full of change,
> From joy to grief, from grief to joy again,
> Through many an age, as oft as it came round,
> 'Twas held religiously."—ROGERS.

The Marian Games—*La Feste Delle Marie*, as they were called—were observed with great splendour down to 1379, the epoch of the disastrous war of Chiozzia.*

* It was usual to elect twelve maidens, two for each of the six divisions of the city; and it was then determined by lot which *centrade*, or quarters of the town, should furnish them with dresses. As this involved a great amount of competition, the dresses were of the costliest description, and frequently the jewels of the treasury of St. Mark were borrowed to enhance their splendour. The twelve maidens, thus gaily attired, then went in their galley to St. Mark's, where they were joined by the Doge and Signory; after which they visited San Pietro di Castello to hear mass on St. Mark's Day, January 31st; the next day passed in procession through the streets of the city: and, on the 2nd of February, repaired to the church of Santa Maria Formosa. The festival attracted such a

They were then discontinued, and though at a later period again revived, soon lapsed into oblivion.

EXPANSION OF THE REPUBLIC.

Meanwhile Venice continued its rapid march along the difficult road which leads nations to wealth and power, and becoming conscious of its resources, felt the impulses of that desire of aggrandizement and extension which invariably accompanies the rising prosperity of a free state. Its people grew impatient of the narrow limits within which Nature had seemed to confine them. As a poet cannot rest content with singing for his own behoof, but would fain make the whole world auditors of his song, so the Venetians longed to spread the renown of their valour abroad, and call upon the nations to admire their greatness. Were it otherwise, indeed, a state forced in upon itself would speedily decay, as the fire dies to which the freest access of air is not permitted. Expansion is one of the conditions of power, and when an empire ceases to throw out new branches, and strike its roots in fresh ground, the day of its ruin is not far distant.

PIETRO ORSEOLO.

The first conquests of Venice were accomplished under its great Doge, Pietro Orseolo II. (A.D. 991–1006). He prepared a powerful fleet, and having received the

throng of visitors from all parts of Italy, that special police regulations were drawn up for the preservation of order, and the Council of Ten were twice summoned before it took place.

great banner of St. Mark from the hands of the bishop, set forth on an expedition that resulted in the subjugation of the Dalmatian coast. It was, however, rather a triumphal procession than a military campaign, for every town voluntarily yielded him submission, and solicited to be adopted among the children of the Republic. Only the islands of Curzola and Lesina offered any resistance, and these were carried by the sword. The victor then returned to his capital, covered with glory, and was solemnly proclaimed Doge of Venice and Dalmatia (A.D. 998). The new territory was provided with a simple form of government; a Count or Podesta, chosen from the principal Venetian citizens, being appointed to rule over each town, and an annual tribute demanded for the treasury of St. Mark.*

In this same year of triumph the Emperor Otho III. visited Italy. He was drawn to the Venetian capital by the fame of its prince, and the reports of its wealth and splendour. With a strange affectation of mystery he entered it secretly, with six companions, attired in pilgrim guise, and was entertained in a private apartment in the ducal palace. His visit lasted four days, and seems to have been utterly unknown to the public. On its termination, the Doge convoked the General Assembly, reported all that had taken place, announced some gracious concessions made by the emperor, and was rewarded for his prudence and secrecy by the thanks of his people.

Orseolo was not enraptured with military display. He

* Daru, "Histoire de Venise."

addressed himself to the extension of Venetian commerce, raised his country to the proud position of the Arbiter of the Seas, and secured it a voice in the European council. He rebuilt and refortified the town of Grado, and adorned the capital itself with many splendid buildings. His renown spread far and wide, and kings and princes sought alliance with his family. His second son, Othone, was betrothed to the sister of the King of Hungary; his eldest, Giovanni, wedded the niece of the Emperor of the East. A reign of great splendour, and an administration characterized by the highest sagacity and moderation, was fated, however, to close in darkness. Venice was visited in 1006 by famine and pestilence, and the epidemic numbered among its victims Giovanni Orseolo and his imperial bride. The Doge survived the cruel blow little more than a twelvemonth, and expired in 1008, at the early age of forty-seven. In a comparatively brief career he had accomplished the work of many lives, and history justly enrols him in her list of worthies as "Orseolo the Magnificent."

WAR WITH HUNGARY IN THE EAST.

Still growing in opulence and power, Venice was eagerly sought as an ally by the Byzantine Empire, while the worldly policy which her rulers steadily carried out, impelled her to share in the great religious movement of the Crusades. For a while she hesitated between her desire to remain on amicable terms with the Court of Constantinople, and her unwillingness to see other European nations establishing a naval supremacy in the Levant. At length, in 1098, she determined to join the warriors of the Cross, and a fleet of two hundred and seven vessels set sail from the Gulf, under the command of Giovanni Michieli, son of the Doge. It had arrived off Rhodes, when a Norman and Pisan armada, secretly bribed by the Greek emperor, suddenly attacked it. Though Venice and Pisa were professedly at peace, the Venetian admiral readily accepted the challenge. A fierce fight ensued, but St. Mark protected his children, and the mercenaries were defeated with a loss of twenty ships and four thousand prisoners.*

The share which the Venetians took in the Crusades was not conspicuous for enthusiastic devotion to the interests of the Cross. They were careful, however, that their own interests should not suffer, and though liberally rewarded by the Crusading leaders, showed both alarm and distrust when the exertions of the Genoese were similarly recompensed. From this epoch, indeed, dates the long rivalry between Venice and Genoa, which afterwards culminated in so many horrors. But the Republic had no leisure at present to address itself to the prosecution of this new quarrel. The conquests of King Stephen of Hungary in Croatia demanded its attention, and its forces were despatched to chastise the Croatian towns which had opened their gates to the Hungarians. The Doge Faliero displayed both capacity and energy. He blockaded the important city of Zara, and defeated the Hungarian army which had advanced to its relief. Zara surrendered, and Faliero

* Hazlitt, "History of the Venetian Republic," i. 285–6.

returned to Venice, laden with booty and prisoners (A.D. 1116).*

These disasters did but stimulate King Stephen to renewed exertions, and in the following year the rival hosts again met under the walls of Zara. The struggle was sanguinary and protracted; the tide of battle ebbed and flowed with changing fortune; yet it is probable that victory would have crowned the banner of St. Mark but for Faliero's headlong courage. At the head of his troops he dashed into the heart of the mêlée, and was stricken down by a mortal wound. Deprived of their leader, the Venetians fell into confusion; a total rout ensued; and few were the fugitives who succeeded in escaping to their vessels, and carrying the gloomy tidings home to Venice. The Republic hastily concluded a five years' truce with its exultant enemy, and having recovered the body of its heroic Doge, honoured his remains with interment in the vaults of the Ducal Chapel (A.D. 1117).*

The Venetian arms were but temporarily tarnished by this defeat. In the East they won renewed lustre at the great sea-fight of Jaffa (A.D. 1122), where the Doge, Dominico Michieli, engaged and destroyed the Saracen fleet. The Archbishop of Tyre describes the action in language which, though probably exaggerated, conveys a vivid idea of its unexampled ferocity. It lasted, he says, from daybreak to sunset. The Moslems fought with sullen courage, and the Venetians only won by boarding their vessels, and engaging hand to hand. The victors stood on their decks ankle-deep in hostile blood; for a

* Daru, "Histoire de Venise," *in loc.*

circuit of two miles the sea was "incarnadined" with the slaughter; and the numerous corpses which were thrown upon the shore, and lay there unburied, poisoned the air with pestilential odours.

This great victory was followed by the siege of Tyre, which, after a five months' resistance, surrendered to the Crusaders. These successes, due in a great measure to the courage of the Venetians, and the capacity of their leader, aroused the jealousy of the Greek emperor. War broke out. The Doge Michieli swept the imperial coast with fire and sword, and extended his ravages over the fair and smiling Archipelago, burning, blighting, and harrying Rhodes and Scio, Samos, Paros, Mitylene, Andros, and Lesbos—those "isles of Greece" which, in the old time, had given birth to heroes, sages, gods, and goddesses—and carrying off their young men and maidens to be sold as slaves. His desolating career was uninterrupted by a single check, and he amply earned the expressive epitaph inscribed upon his monument: *Terror Græcorum jacet hic*—Here lies the terror of the Greeks!

The booty which he brought from the East was of no ordinary kind. Besides great numbers of slaves, it consisted of ten Turkish galleons and their rich freights; of the gold, gems, stuffs, and fruits of Tyre, Rhodes, and the Ionian Isles; and other miscellaneous articles of plunder, among which not the least prized were the embalmed remains of SS. Donatus and Isidore.*

War with Greece was renewed in 1171, provoked by the duplicity and fraud of the Emperor Manuel Comnenus. Alarmed at the vast extent of the Venetian commerce,

* Hazlitt, "History of the Venetian Republic," i. 333.

he sought to deal it a deadly blow by suddenly seizing upon all the merchant vessels then lying in the imperial ports. When the tidings of this unparalleled confiscation reached the City of the Isles, its inhabitants raged with a speechless wrath. From the Doge to the meanest fisherman ran the electric flash of a common sympathy, and a deep longing for vengeance burned in every heart. One entire family, and that the oldest and bravest in Venice, in emulation of the devoted patriotism of the Roman Fabii, volunteered their whole race to the services of the commonwealth, and contributed a hundred warriors for her defence. There was soon no lack of swords, or of hands to wield them; and money was procured by raising contributions from the principal citizens through the agency of a so-called "Chamber of Loans" (*La Camera degl' Imprestiti*), which paid the creditors of the state a fixed annual interest, and eventually, under the name of the Bank of Venice, became the model of all similar establishments.

Scarcely three months had elapsed before the Doge Vitale found himself at the head of one hundred and twenty well-manned and well-equipped vessels. He immediately sailed for Dalmatia, and severely punished those cities which had been encouraged to rebel by the reverses of the Republic. At Scio he was met by the ambassadors of the artful Comnenus. They assured him of the emperor's pacific intentions, and, at their instance, he despatched envoys to Constantinople in quest of satisfactory explanations. The Greek thus obtained time, which was all he wanted. He calculated on the chances of delay, and was not mistaken. The plague broke out at Scio, and soon converted the winter-camp of the Venetians into one vast lazar-house. Death was busy with its thousands and tens of thousands. The mortified Doge re-embarked in seventeen vessels the scanty remainder of his once splendid host, and contrived to make his way back to Venice.* He had gone forth to conquer; he returned in humiliation and shame. A great war could not have wrought a more complete desolation. Not a family in the state but was stricken by the calamity; not a house but echoed with the voice of mourning. Of the hundred gallant scions of the great Giustiniani race, *all* had perished. Like the Fabii, they had devoted themselves a sacrifice on the altar of their country. The parallel was complete; for, as with the Fabii, one boy survived to perpetuate the glorious name, so a forgotten monk, drawn from the oblivion of a cloister, and released from his vow of celibacy, preserved to Venice the stock of one of her noblest families.

A CURIOUS MODE OF ELECTION.

We must here notice an important change in the administration of the state. The choice of a Doge had previously been vested, either ostensibly or virtually, in the suffrages of the whole assembled people. Such a procedure, however, experience had proved to be open to great abuses, and another mode of election was adopted, which, in time, was found scarcely less objectionable. A law was passed transferring the right of election into the hands of a select few. Eleven citizens

* Daru, "Histoire de Venise," *in anno* 1171.

were named for this purpose, and a majority of nine voices out of the eleven was required to render their choice valid. The first Doge nominated upon this novel system was Sebastiano Ziani (A.D. 1173). He was assisted in the discharge of his duties by a *Signory* of six members, a *Collegio* of six-and-twenty, a *Senate* of sixty, and a *Grand Council* of four hundred and eighty. Of these three great divisions of government, the Grand Council seems to have represented the sovereignty, the Senate the legislative or deliberative body, and the Collegio the executive. The Signory were the Doge's intimate and confidential advisers. Thus were his prerogatives gradually confined within the narrowest limits, which each succeeding year tended still further to abridge, until at last he became no more than "the first puppet of the state," the leading figure in show and pageant, deprived of all real authority, and even of that personal influence which the sovereign possesses in a constitutional government. From the rule of an absolute prince, Venice in due time passed under that of a secret and despotic oligarchy.*

THE FAMOUS SIEGE OF ANCONA.

The Republic was at this epoch beset by many difficulties. It had enemies in the East and in Italy. But the new Doge and his counsellors addressed themselves with signal vigour to the task of defeating their projects. Abandoning the traditional Venetian policy, they formed an alliance with the great German emperor, Frederic

* These changes are clearly explained by Mr. Hazlitt.

Barbarossa, and despatched an expedition against Ancona, whose commercial greatness had aroused their jealousy. They blockaded the port, while the imperial forces, under the rapacious Christian, Archbishop-elect of Mentz, invested it by land. It should be acknowledged that the besieged opposed a chivalrous resistance to their formidable foes. Buoncompagno, a contemporary, relates some brilliant proofs of their heroic valour. A widow—widowed, perhaps, during the siege—her name was Stamura—seized a lighted torch, and, under a storm of arrows and darts, advancing towards the beleaguring lines, set fire to a lofty wooden tower—a part of the siege-works—which, rapidly blazing, extended a destructive conflagration through all the military engines of the allies. A young lady of rank, observing a soldier prostrate on the ground from fatigue and want, offered him her breast that he might regain renewed strength for the struggle; but the man, scorning to be surpassed in heroism, sprung to his feet as if fired with fresh life, and returned to the post of duty. One of the Venetian galleys, a ship of colossal bulk, was known by the appropriate name of *Il Mondo*, "the World." A monk of Ancona, whom his sacred vows prevented from serving in the ranks, yet who longed to prove that he was no degenerate son of his country, resolved upon the destruction of this vessel. A skilful swimmer, he gained the prow, carrying an axe between his teeth, and before he was discovered, succeeded in severing the cables which moored her to her anchorage. Then, rapidly diving under water, and rising only at intervals to gain breath, he returned to the shore uninjured by the missiles poured upon him, and was received by his countrymen with shouts of admiration. Meanwhile the unwieldy ship, drifting among its lesser consorts, involved them in its own danger; and though it was saved with the loss of the greater part of its cargo, several other galleys were driven ashore and destroyed.*

NOBLE DEEDS OF NOBLE SPIRITS.

But famine, with all its horrors, prevailed in the beleaguered city, whose brave defenders fed upon seaweed, vermin, and the wild grasses which clung to its walls of stone. They would not yield, however. A woman, heart-broken by the hunger of her two sons, opened a vein in her left arm. The blood that flowed she mixed up with spices and condiments—for these dainties still abounded, though of wholesome food the lack was so pitiful—and fed them with the disguised beverage, thus supporting their young existence at the cost of her own. Against such a spirit of patriotism neither Venice nor Germany could prevail. And at length relief came. A small force of Ferrarese was led to Ancona by a gallant gentleman of Ferrara, named Marchesella. By a circuitous route he contrived to reach the heights which overlook the city, whence he could see it surrounded on every side by the besieging hosts. As soon as the shades of night descended, he spread his little band over as wide a space as possible, and directed each soldier to bind two or three blazing torches to his lance. They then marched down the hill

* Buoncompagno, "Obsidio Anconæ" (in Muratori), p. 21, *et seq.*

at a deliberate pace, waving to and fro their fiery brands. The imperial commander, when aroused by his sentinels, saw with infinite surprise the advancing lights of an immense army. He immediately ordered a retreat, and fled in all haste to Spoleto, while the Ferrarese entered Ancona in triumph; and the next day the Venetians abandoned their seven months' blockade (November 1176).

POPE AND EMPEROR: A HISTORIC SCENE.

They held aloof for the next three years from the contest which the emperor still maintained with the states of Lombardy; but when they perceived that he was gaining a preponderance which threatened them with too powerful a neighbour, they abandoned their alliance, or rather their neutrality, and espoused the cause of the Lombard league. They received Pope Alexander III., the Emperor's most determined foe—who had fled to their city in disguise, and was discovered by the Doge working as a gardener in the convent of La Carità—as an honoured guest, and despatched an embassy to Frederic requiring him to desist from hostilities against the Roman Pontiff, and to acknowledge his spiritual dominion.* The haughty Barbarossa plucked his red beard in wrath, and exclaimed: "Return, and make known to your prince and senate that I, the Roman Emperor, demand from them a fugitive and a foe. Unless

* Sismondi, "Histoire des Républiques Italiennes;" Milman, "History of Latin Christianity;" Von Ranke, "German History in the Reformation Period;" Hallam, "Middle Ages;" Bryce, "The Holy Roman Empire." See also Muratori, "Antiquitates Italiæ," dissertatio xi.

they straightway deliver him up to me in chains and as a captive, I denounce war against them. I declare them the enemies of my empire. No treaty shall avail for their defence, nor God nor man shall shield them from my revenge. I will pursue them, by land and by sea, until I have planted my victorious eagles on the gates of Saint Mark's."

The Republic, undaunted by his menace, and resolved to support the Pontiff, immediately prepared for hostilities; but all its exertions could only provide Ziani with thirty-four ships of war to oppose the sixty-five galleys which Pisa, Genoa, and Ancona had placed at the disposal of Otho, the Emperor's son. A Venetian Doge, however, in those days of the Republic, did not count odds. Ziani attacked the imperial fleet off the Istrian coast, and, after a six hours' fight, gained a complete victory. When one reads of forty-eight galleys captured and two sunk, one seems to be perusing the account of an English naval victory in the good old times before steam and ironclads had come to the succour of inferior maritime powers. The conquerors returned to Lido in triumph. The Pope met Ziani at the Piazzetta; and from thence they proceeded in solemn state to the cathedral, where they offered up a thanksgiving for the victory which had crowned the arms of Venice and the Church. As soon as the last strain died away, Alexander turned to the Doge, and, presenting him with a ring of gold, "Take it, my son," he exclaimed, "as a token of true and perpetual dominion over the sea as your subject; and every year, on this day of the Ascension, shall you and your successors make known to all posterity that the ocean belongs

INTERIOR OF ST. MARK'S.

to Venice by the right of conquest, and that she is subservient to her, as a spouse is to her husband." *

* Dr. Dyer, "History of Modern Europe," i. 42.

UNDER THE ROOF OF ST. MARK'S.

Frederic now experienced the truth of the old adage, that misfortunes visit us, "not as single spies, but in battalions." * The battle on the Istrian coast was followed by a terrible defeat of the imperial forces at Legnano, which so broke the pride of the Emperor that he sued, "with bated breath," for peace (A.D. 1176). It was therefore resolved that a congress should meet at Venice for the settlement of the claims of the Lombard cities and the adjustment of the pontifical sovereignty. Frederic in his despair consented to everything, and, a truce of six years having been agreed upon, expressed his desire to ratify it in person.† He landed on the

* Dean Milman furnishes the following character of the famous emperor, Dante's "good Barbarossa:"—"He was a prince of intrepid valour, consummate prudence, unmeasured ambition, justice which hardened into severity, the ferocity of a barbarian somewhat tempered with a high chivalrous gallantry—above all, with a strength of character which subjugated alike the great temporal and ecclesiastical princes of Germany; and was prepared to assert the imperial rights in Italy to the utmost. Of the constitutional rights of the emperor—of his unlimited supremacy, his absolute independence of, his temporal superiority over, all other powers, even that of the pope—Frederic proclaimed the loftiest notions. He was to the empire what Hildebrand and Innocent were to the popedom. His power was of God alone; to assert that it was bestowed by the successor of St. Peter was a lie, and directly contrary to the doctrine of St. Peter."—MILMAN, "History of Latin Christianity."

† But for the assistance of Venice and the Lombard cities, the Emperor would undoubtedly have triumphed over his formidable antagonist, and given a new direction to the history of Venice. The scene in St. Mark's porch was therefore of the highest importance. "It was the renunciation, by the mightiest prince of his time, of the project to which his life had been devoted; it was the abandonment by the secular power of a contest in which it had twice been vanquished, and which it could not renew under more favourable conditions."—JAMES BRYCE, "The Holy Roman Empire," pp. 88, 89.

Piazzetta of San Marco on the 23rd of July, and on the following day was escorted to the cathedral by the Doge, the senate, the councillors, and the nobles, with all the splendour which Venice could array. The scene within the sacred pile was singularly gorgeous. There sat enthroned the triumphant Pope, clothed in his sumptuous vestments, and bearing on his brow the triple crown; while around him was disposed a glittering crowd of prelates and ambassadors, blazing with jewels, and in all the pomp of rich attire. As the Emperor drew near he uncovered his head, cast aside his purple mantle, and, flinging himself upon the ground, crawled onward to kiss the Holy Father's feet.*

The memories, dark and bitter, of twenty years of wrong and disaster then flashed with a sudden shock upon Alexander's brain. He had been dethroned, proscribed, persecuted, dishonoured; a price set upon his head; the dignity of the Church had been outraged in his person; its authority over its own priesthood had been imperilled; and now, as his enemy knelt before him in the dust, he celebrated the triumph both of the Church and himself. Elate with the consciousness of victory, he planted his foot on the neck of the prostrate Emperor, and repeated the words of David (Psalm xci.): "Thou shalt go upon the lion and the adder; the young lion and the dragon shalt thou tread under thy feet." "It is not to thee, but to St. Peter, that I kneel," murmured the indignant prince. Alexander trod a second time and more firmly upon his neck, exclaiming, "Both to *me* and to St. Peter;" nor did he relax the pressure

* Compare the accounts of Daru and Sismondi.

until the Emperor appeared to acquiesce.* The vaulted roof then echoed with the jubilant strains of the *Te Deum*. On quitting the cathedral the Emperor conducted Alexander to his horse, and held his stirrup while he mounted.† He would have performed the lowliest offices of a lackey, but the Pope wisely spared him any further humiliation.‡

This pacification was finally completed by the Peace of Constance (A.D. 1178), which again raised the Republic to an influential place among European powers. She was hailed as the liberator of Italy and the protector of the Holy See. Her ascendency in the East was restored by the victories which she had won in the West, and the Byzantine court was glad to purchase her alliance by heavy bribes.

* The spot where this ceremony took place is marked by a square stone of red marble.

> "In that temple porch
> The brass is gone, the porphyry remains."—ROGERS.

† Wordsworth has celebrated this event in a sonnet, which may not be known to all my readers:—

> "Black demons hovering o'er his mitred head,
> To Cæsar's successor the Pontiff spake:
> 'Ere I absolve thee, stoop, that on thy neck,
> Levelled with earth, this foot of mine may tread!'
> Then he, who to the altar had been led—
> He, whose strong arm the Orient could not check—
> He, who had held the Soldan at his beck—
> Stooped; of all glory disinherited,
> And even the common dignity of man!
> Amazement strikes the crowd; while many turn
> Their eyes away in sorrow, others burn
> With scorn, invoking a vindictive ban
> From outraged nature; but the sense of most
> In abject sympathy with power is lost."—*Eccles. Sonnets*, xxxviii.

‡ There is little doubt that these circumstances are of a legendary character, and were designed to increase the significancy of an event which in itself was sufficiently significant.

"BLIND OLD DANDOLO."

Passing over the dogeship of Orio Malipieri (A.D. 1178–1192), our rapid survey brings us to the reign of the greatest of Venetian princes, and the most splendid period of Venetian history—that of Enrico Dandolo. It includes the Fourth Crusade, and the conquest of Constantinople by the Western armies—events which Gibbon has narrated with more than his ordinary felicity of style. Our limits preclude us from doing more than glancing at a subject so comprehensive and so replete with lofty interest; but the reader, if his curiosity is excited by our sketch, may refer to the pages of the great English historian.*

Enrico Dandolo was elected Doge in 1192. He was eighty-four years old, and blind, having lost his sight either through a wound received in battle, or through tortures inflicted upon him by the Greek Emperor when he acted as Venetian ambassador at the court of Constantinople. Of "blind old Dandolo," however, we know little before his elevation to the ducal throne. That he was no ordinary man his achievements in his last years sufficiently demonstrate. That he was gifted with eminent talents, and that his prudence and sagacity had procured him the respect of his fellow-citizens, we may infer from his election to so conspicuous a post.

* Compare Gibbon ("Decline and Fall," chap. lx.) with the scarcely less admirable account by Sismondi ("Histoire des Républiques Italiennes," ch. xiv.) The best original authority is Geoffrey de Villehardouin, who served in the expedition.

Though old, he was not infirm, but even exhibited the vigour and fire of a robust manhood.

He soon gave proof of his elasticity of spirit by promptly chastising the Pisans for an insult they had offered to the Republic. He would have carried his vengeance further, but paused at the request of the Pope (Innocent III.), who was bent upon re-arraying Christendom against the infidel rulers of the Holy Land (A.D. 1200). The French nobles embraced the project of another holy war with enthusiasm. An immense army was soon collected ; but to avoid the misfortunes of previous enterprises, it was determined to proceed to Palestine by sea ; and as means of transport could only be furnished by the Venetians—then the most powerful of maritime states—ambassadors were dispatched to Venice in the hope of securing her assistance. Dandolo received them with honour, and they were afterwards admitted to an audience with the Grand Council. Several days were spent in negotiations, which resulted in an agreement that Venice should furnish *palanders*, or flat-bottomed vessels, for the transport of 4500 horses and 9000 esquires, and ships for 4500 knights and 20,000 sergeants or foot-soldiers. This force was to be maintained at the cost of the Republic for nine months; but she was to receive, in disbursement of her expenses, the magnificent sum of 85,000 marks.* Dandolo also undertook to equip 50 galleys at the expense of the Republic, but with the important provision that, so long as the alliance continued, all conquests by sea or land should

* Equal to about £170,000; or, at the present value of money, eight times that amount, or £1,360,000.

be divided equally between the contracting parties. These terms are sufficient to show that Venice was actuated rather by sordid greed and lust of gain than by any sympathy with the objects of the Crusades. They were accepted, however, by the ambassadors, and a general assembly of the people met to confirm them. The stately palace and chapel of St. Mark were filled with eager citizens; and mass having been performed, the Doge requested the ambassadors to proclaim the nature of their mission. "Illustrious Venetians," said Villehardouin, on their behalf, "the greatest and most powerful barons of France have dispatched us to implore the aid of the masters of the sea for the deliverance of the Holy City from the bondage of the infidels. They have enjoined us to fall prostrate at your feet, until you have granted their prayers and undertaken to avenge the wrongs of Christ." The six ambassadors then threw themselves upon their knees; and their noble appearance, the eloquence of their words, and the moving spectacle of their tears, stimulated the enthusiasm of the multitude. With a shout, like the sound of an earthquake, they exclaimed, "We consent! we consent!" The Doge then ascended the pulpit, and addressed to his subjects an animated appeal: "Behold, seigniors, the honour which the Lord hath bestowed upon you, in disposing the bravest warriors upon earth to seek your friendship, before that of all other nations, in so glorious an enterprise as the rescue of our Saviour's sepulchre." *

* Villehardouin, lib. i.; "Chronicle of Andrew Dandolo," in Muratori, tome xii.; and Gibbon, ch. lx.

THE FOURTH CRUSADE.

Early in 1202, under the leadership of Boniface, Marquis of Montferrat, a knight who had already distinguished himself in Paynim warfare, the Crusaders began to assemble at Venice, where they encamped on the island of San Nicolo. Hither came the wealthy Count of Flanders, the powerful Count of Blois, and the most famous nobles of France and Germany. The Venetians had more than fulfilled their part of the treaty; stables were constructed for the horses, barracks provided for the troops; magazines were overfilled with provisions and forage; and so gallantly equipped a fleet rode in the lagoon that Christendom, it was said, had never seen its equal. But the splendour of the scene was obscured by a sudden cloud. Many of the Crusaders had preferred a different route: the Flemings had chosen the long voyage through the Straits and the Mediterranean; some of the French and Italians had set sail from Marseilles and Apulia. On those who had assembled at Venice, therefore, fell all the cost of the expedition, and, notwithstanding the sacrifices of the chiefs, the amount collected fell short of the stipulated sum by 34,000 marks.

The Doge, however, felt how much shame and dishonour would attach to Venice if she abandoned the Crusade on so mean a pretext. He was equally unwilling to lose the chance of gilding his declining years with the surpassing glory of a Christian hero. But fully aware of the selfish policy of his countrymen, he contrived to satisfy their greed while he prevented any failure of the enterprise, by persuading the Crusading leaders to assist him in the reduction of the revolted Dalmatian cities as a compensation for the deferred payment. Zara, the principal offender, lay on their route down the Adriatic, and the only obstacle was the papal injunction that the Crusaders should engage in no hostilities with a Christian power. The Doge, however, refused to recognize the Pope's right to interfere; and the barons comforted their consciences with the belief that, at all events, the Holy Father could not have intended to protect a rebellious city.*

The command of the land forces had been unanimously conferred upon the Marquis of Montferrat, but it was as yet undetermined who should lead the Venetian armada. The Doge himself settled the question. After mass had been celebrated in St. Mark's, he suddenly ascended the tribune, and addressed the people: "Siegniors," he said, "you are sharing with the bravest people upon earth the most glorious enterprise which mortal can undertake. I am a very old man, infirm of health, and in greater need of repose than glory; yet as I know none more capable of guiding and directing you than myself, who am your sovereign, if it be your pleasure that I should take the sign of the cross to watch over your movements, and leave my son in my stead to protect our country, I will cheerfully go, and live and die with you and the pilgrims." The multitude, as if with one voice, exclaimed, "We beseech you, in God's name, to do as you have said, and go with us." Dandolo descended from the tribune, knelt before the high altar, and fixing

* Sismondi, ch. xiv.; Villehardouin (in Ducange), sect. 36, 37, 38.

the cross on his ducal cap, shed tears of holy enthusiasm. His son was appointed regent during his absence, and many of the Venetian nobles followed their sovereign.

THE EXPEDITION SETS SAIL.

The fleet sailed on the 9th of October 1202. It numbered fifty galleys and four hundred and fifty other vessels, all gay with blazoned banners, with the colours of different European nations, with the gleaming shields of the knights, and the glitter of axe and spear. Forty thousand warriors, animated by the love of glory and a fanatic devotion, seemed a host fit to conquer the world. "Of a truth," cries the old chronicler, "it was a noble spectacle." And the Crusaders, overcome with a tumult of emotion, broke out into chant and litany as they glided down the Adriatic.

Their enthusiasm was somewhat damped when they descried the strong defences of Zara. How can we hope to capture such a city, they exclaimed, unless the Lord himself assist us? But their leaders were not men to hesitate. The fleet, moving irresistibly onward, burst the chain or boom stretched across the mouth of the harbour. Knights and sergeants leaped ashore; there was mounting of steeds, and hurrying to and fro, and the clink of spade and pickaxe; the whole host was soon encamped, and Zara, on St. Martin's Day, found itself surrounded by the toils. The inhabitants, unable to resist so formidable a force, on the sixth day surrendered. Their lives were spared, but their rebellion was punished by the demolition of their walls and the pillage of their houses.

The year was now near its close, and the Crusaders determined to make Zara their winter quarters. Its maritime portions were occupied by the Venetians; the allies took possession of the remainder. But bitter feuds soon broke out between the different races that made up the motley host, and Christian blood was shed by men who had linked themselves together in the name of Christ. The Pope launched the thunders of excommunication at the heads of their leaders, and only the Marquis of Montferrat, who was not present at the siege, and Simon de Montfort, who had quitted the camp, escaped the pontifical wrath. The timid were terrified, and the devout scandalized. But the Venetians went on their way unmoved, never having recognized, in public affairs, the right of the Roman Church to interfere.

The season for renewed operations was rapidly approaching, when the Crusaders received a proposition that exercised a considerable influence on the fortunes of their great enterprise.

THE TWO ALEXII.

The throne of the East was at this time occupied by the Emperor Alexius Angelus. He had gained it by deposing his brother, whom he also deprived of sight. This brother, the weak and unworthy Isaac Angelus, had a son, likewise named Alexius, who conceived that he might deliver his father and recover the imperial crown by the assistance of the Crusaders' host. He offered the barons a splendid bribe. He promised, in his own and his father's name, that as soon as they should be seated on the Byzantine throne, they would terminate the long schism which had rent asunder the Greek and Latin Churches, and restore the Greek empire to the lawful supremacy of the Roman see. He undertook to reward the labours and merits of the Crusaders by the immediate payment of two hundred thousand marks of silver. He offered to accompany them in person to Egypt; or, if they preferred it, to equip, at his own cost, ten thousand men for a year's service, and to maintain, during his whole life, five hundred knights as a permanent garrison in the Holy Land. The Venetians, who saw in this new enterprise a far more tempting channel of national aggrandizement than in a crusade against the Moslems, immediately agreed to his terms, and pressed their acceptance upon the allied princes and barons. The Pope and his party were wroth at such a delay of the projects of the Church, but the majority of the Crusaders were dazzled by the magnificence of the Greek prince's promises. The discontented few abandoned the expedition; the French counts and the Venetians hastened their preparations for departure, and the gorgeous armada finally set sail from Zara, in enthusiastic assurance of a speedy victory and boundless wealth.*

At Corfu they made their rendezvous, and gathered up their scattered squadrons. For three weeks they refreshed their men and horses. The young Alexius landed, and was received with the honours due to the future Emperor of Byzantium. Elate and cheerful, the whole force re-embarked on the eve of Pentecost, and resumed their voyage. The day, says Villehardouin, was

* Villehardouin, sect. 62.

bright and auspicious; the winds blew soft and favourable, as we spread our canvas before them. So glorious a sight was assuredly never seen before. Far as our gaze could reach, the sea shone with the white sails of ship and galley. Our hearts throbbed with joy, and we felt that so noble an armament might achieve the conquest of the whole earth.*

Gibbon has paraphrased the old chronicler's narrative with splendid felicity. †

The Crusaders, he says, doubled without accident the perilous Cape of Malea, the southern cape of Peloponnesus or the Morea, made a descent in the islands of Negropont and Andros, and cast anchor at Abydos, on the Asiatic side of the Hellespont. These preludes of conquest were easy and bloodless; the Greeks of the provinces, without patriotism or courage, were crushed by an irresistible force; the presence of the lawful heir might justify their obedience; and it was rewarded by the modesty and discipline of the Latins. As they penetrated through the Hellespont, where

> "Helle's tide
> Rolls darkly heaving to the main,"
>
> (*Byron.*)

the magnitude of their navy was compressed in a narrower channel, and innumerable sails seemed to darken the face of the waters. They again spread their wings abroad in the ample basin of the Propontis (the modern Sea of Marmora), till, three leagues to the west of Constan-

* Villehardouin, sect. 62.

† Gibbon, "Decline and Fall of the Roman Empire," ch. lx (vol. vi. pp. 548, 549)

CONSTANTINOPLE.

tinople, they beheld the capital of the East rising from her seven hills, and dominating over the continents of Europe and Asia. When the Crusaders contemplated the lofty walls and stately towers that fenced it round about—the tall spires and swelling domes of its five hundred palaces gilded by the sun and reflected in the mirror-like waters—its walls crowded with soldiers and spectators, of whose disposition towards them they were wholly ignorant—their hearts sunk, and the stoutest could scarcely repress the feeling that never since the beginning of the world had so great an enterprise been undertaken by such a handful of warriors. But hope and valour soon revived their spirits, and every man, says Villehardouin, looked to the condition of the weapons which he would be called upon to use in the glorious conflict.

LANDING OF THE CRUSADERS.

The fleet cast anchor before Chalcedon, and the chivalric host was disembarked. The third day afterwards both fleet and army moved towards Scutari—a place whose name is now so fatally familiar to English ears—where they halted for five days, and plentifully supplied themselves with forage and provisions. Here the first collision occurred between the Greeks and the invaders. A detachment of eighty lances fell unexpectedly, at some eight miles from the camp, on the tents of the great Duke Stryphorus, guarded by five hundred Greeks. The disparity of numbers did not check the onset of the Crusaders, who were completely successful, and rewarded for their valour by a splendid booty.

The Emperor Alexius was roused from a dream of indolent complacency by the near approach of the Christian army, and fell, as is the manner of such men, at a single bound, from the heights of vain-glorious arrogance to the depths of servile humility. He attempted to conceal his apprehensions under the cloak of boastful speech, and the ambassadors who represented him indulged in eloquent hyperboles. "Lords," he exclaimed, addressing the Christian leaders, "the Emperor Alexius is not ignorant that you are powerful princes and warlike. But he wonders that you, as Christians, thus enter the territories of one who is also a Christian. If you are bound for the Holy Land to deliver the Sepulchre of our Lord, he will supply you with such assistance as you may need. He would wish to avoid inflicting any injury upon you, not because he lacks the power, for were you twenty times more considerable you could not depart without his permission, nor prevent his destroying you, if such were his pleasure."

The Doge and princes made answer through their spokesman, Conon de Bethune :—

"Fair sir, you inform us that your lord wonders greatly that our princes and barons have entered his imperial territories. They are not his; for he holds them unjustly, having sinned against the laws of God and man. They belong to the lawful heir, to the young prince now seated among us, and to his father, the Emperor Isaac, whom an ungrateful brother has deprived of his sceptre, his freedom, and his sight. If your master will confess his guilt, and supplicate his nephew's forgiveness, we will intercede in his behalf, that he may be permitted to live in affluence and security. But be not so rash as to venture a second time into our presence; our reply will be made in arms, in the palace of Constantinople."*

On the tenth day the Crusaders prepared to attempt the passage of the Bosphorus, whose opposite shores were defended by seventy thousand Greeks. They divided their host into six battalions or divisions, commanded by Baldwin, Count of Flanders, who led the van, his brother Henry, the Counts of St. Pol and Blois, Matthew of Montmorency, and the Marquis of Montferrat, who headed the reserve. The transports effected the passage without meeting any molestation. Then arose a noble emulation among the Crusaders, and, to the sound of trump and clarion, the knights, though

* Villehardouin, sect. 130, *et seq.*

clothed in heavy armour, sprang into the sea. Squire, and archer, and man-at-arms were not a whit less eager; and, as they reached the shore, they formed with admirable discipline in separate companies. The emperor and his Greeks never paused to cross lances; they vanished from the scene like snow before the sun, and the rich plunder of the imperial tents fell into the hands of the Latins. The horses were then disembarked; the knights mounted, and the six divisions moved forward in preconcerted order. It was resolved to take advantage of the panic of the Greeks, and make a land and sea attack to open the entrance of the harbour. On the following morning, therefore, the soldiery stormed the important town of Galata, while the Venetian galleys, led by the *Aquila* (or Eagle), and crowding on all sail, bore down upon the huge boom, or chain, stretched across the passage, and drove irresistibly through it. Twenty ships of war, the relics of the Greek navy, were either sunk or taken, and the Crusaders' fleet rode triumphantly at anchor in the port of Constantinople.

ATTACK UPON BYZANTIUM.

The roar of battle now gathered round the walls of the imperial city. After a pause of four days the fleet moved up to the other extremity of the harbour, while the land forces advanced at the same time along the shore, crossed the united channel of the rivers Barbyses and Cydaris ("The Sweet Waters"), and encamped against the front of the capital, "the basis of the triangle which runs about four miles from the port to the Propontis." The Greeks defended themselves with unexpected vigour. They made repeated sallies; and their swift cavalry, sweeping round the adjacent country, cleared it completely of provisions. But if the besieged were active, the besiegers were patient, and calmly bore the torments of fatigue, sleeplessness, and insufficient food. After ten days' toil the preliminary works were completed, and two hundred and fifty engines of war hurled a storm of ponderous stones against the walls. The naval attack meanwhile was skilfully and energetically conducted by the Venetians, "who employed every resource that was known and practised before the invention of gunpowder."

A combined assault was delivered against the city on the morning of the 17th of July (A.D. 1203). A breach having been effected, the Crusaders rushed to the attack; but met with so doughty a resistance, that only fifteen knights and sergeants could gain the summit of the wall, and these were either slain or taken prisoners. More fortunate the Venetians. Their vessels, marshalled in a line which extended more than three bow-shots, approached the towers and the wall which stretched along the shore. The mangonels were planted upon the decks, and the flights of arrows and javelins were thick as hail, yet did the Greeks valiantly defend their posts. The rope-ladders on the ships, suspended to the yard-arms, fell so near the walls that in many places the foes fought together with sword and lance, and the shouts were great enough to shake sea and earth; but the galleys notwithstanding could gain no opportunity of reaching the land. Now, exclaims the old chronicler, now shall you hear tell of the dauntless valour of the Duke of Venice, who, old and blind as he was, stood upon the prow of his galley, with the standard of St. Mark unfurled before him, inciting his people to push on to the shore on peril of his high displeasure. By dint of almost superhuman exertions, they ran the galley ashore, and springing out, bore St. Mark's banner before him on the land. And when the Venetians saw their glorious flag advancing towards the foe, and that their duke's vessel had been the first to touch the ground, they pushed on in emulous discontent; and the men of the palanders, contending with each other who should leap on shore the quickest, soon commenced a furious assault. And lo! the banner of St. Mark was suddenly seen waving from one of the towers, as if planted there by an invisible hand—the Venetian who bore it having probably been cut down immediately—and then the five-and-twenty towers which strengthened the ramparts were presently occupied.

In order to secure their position, the Venetians set fire to the houses between them and the Greeks, thus creating an impassable barrier of flame; and under cover of the confusion that prevailed, they collected their plunder, and began to despatch it in boats to the camp.*

Meanwhile the Emperor Alexius determined on a last effort to preserve his menaced crown, and, gathering his armed myriads, directed a sally from three gates at once upon the six battalions of the Crusaders' army. The soldiers of the Cross immediately closed up their array behind the palisades which they had erected; the archers and crossbowmen forming the first line, the horses the

* Villehardouin, sect. 75–90.

second, and the sergeants or infantry being massed in the rear. But their scanty numbers, compared with the hosts of Byzantium, might be likened to the soldiers of Miltiades in front of the Persian thousands, or that band, "faithful but few," which fought and died with Roland on the memorable field of Roncesvalles. Tidings of their peril, however, were conveyed to Dandolo, and the blind old hero, with a soldier's noble loyalty, relinquished the advantageous position he had so hardly won, and led his men to the assistance of their allies. Stout hearts are worth many a battalion; and though the hosts of Alexius might easily have crushed the Crusaders, they were awed by the firm front and confident bearing of their enemies, and the emperor gave the signal for retreat. The Crusaders warily followed in their track, not knowing but that some ambush might await them, and heartily thanking Heaven for their deliverance from apparently inevitable destruction. God never rescued people, says Villehardouin, from more imminent peril than that which this day threatened the pilgrims, the boldest of whom rejoiced when it was passed.

THE CROWN OF VICTORY.

On the morrow the welcome but unlooked-for intelligence reached the Crusaders that, during the night, the usurper Alexius had collected a treasure of ten thousand pounds of gold, and shamefully abandoning his crown, his wife, and his subjects, had escaped in some small fishing-bark to an obscure harbour in Thrace. As soon as they were apprized of his flight, says Gibbon,* the Greek nobles sought pardon and peace in the dungeon where the blind Isaac expected each hour the visit of the executioner. Again saved and exalted by the vicissitudes of fortune, the captive, in his imperial robes, was replaced on the throne, and surrounded with prostrate slaves, whose real terror and affected joy he was incapable of discerning. At the dawn of day hostilities were suspended, and the Latin chiefs were surprised by a message from the lawful and reigning emperor, who was impatient to embrace his son, and to reward his generous deliverers.

AFTER INCIDENTS.

We must pass very briefly over the remaining incidents of this remarkable expedition, in which success was mainly won by the prudence, skill, and courage of the Venetians and their prince. Alexius and his father were solemnly crowned under the dome of St. Sophia. Large rewards were lavished upon the Crusaders; yet, however willing the emperor was to give, he could not give freely enough to satisfy their greed. To prevent conflicts between two races so discordant and so naturally hostile as the Greeks and Latins, the allies were provided with quarters in the suburb now called Pera; yet frequent opportunities arose for bringing into collision the lofty superiority of the one, and the cunning scornfulness of the other. At first the emperor was unwilling to allow

* Gibbon, "Decline and Fall of the Roman Empire," ch. lx. He founds his narrative upon Nicetas, *in Alexis Commen.*, i. 3, ch. 10.

the departure of those stout soldiers to whom he owed his crown; but as he became more firmly seated on his throne, and the Crusaders more extortionate in their demands, he grew impatient of his painful position. Unhappily for himself, Alexius possessed neither steadfastness of character nor political sagacity. He had not the courage to throw himself wholly upon the patriotism of his subjects, and appeal to their feelings of nationality, nor had he the loyalty to attach himself firmly to the Crusaders, and secure their devotion to his interests. In this perplexity he was doomed to be the victim of a fresh trouble, in a conspiracy organized against him by his kinsman and favourite, a prince of the house of Ducas, surnamed Mourtzouphlus, or Mourzoufle, from the close junction of his black and shaggy eyebrows (A.D. 1204). Profoundly sharing in the hatred of his countrymen against the presumptuous Latins, he had won their confidence and was recognized as their leader. He contrived to allure Alexius into his power; stripped him of his robes, loaded him with chains, and flung him into prison, where he was afterwards murdered. He then seized upon the crown, and prepared to justify his usurpation by vigorous efforts to restore peace and order in the distracted empire. The Crusaders immediately denounced him with acrimony. In the remembrance of the former friendship and generosity of Alexius, and his unhappy death, they forgot his later indifference to their interests. Their wrath was further inflamed by the preaching of the priests, who now, for the first time, approved of the war against Constantinople.

The winter passed in energetic preparations on both

sides for the hostilities which both sides foresaw could not long be avoided. In the spring of 1205 war broke out. But the second siege of the imperial city was more protracted and difficult than the first. Mourzoufle displayed both personal courage as a soldier, and military capacity as a general. He made an attempt to burn the Venetian fleet in the harbour, but it failed through the skill and bravery of the besiegers, and the drifting fire-ships wasted their flames on the sea.* In like manner some desultory attacks hazarded by the Latin soldiers were bravely repulsed. For some weeks the fortune of war decided neither in favour of the Greeks nor the Crusaders; and the latter at length becoming convinced that the land fortifications of Constantinople were impregnable, it was resolved to deliver the final assault from the harbour. The land forces were therefore embarked on board the fleet, which, on the morning of the 9th of April, approached that quarter of the city ravaged by the Venetian fires on a previous occasion. The pilgrims behaved with the valour proper to soldiers of the Cross. With lance and spear they engaged their enemies hand to hand, but the Greeks displayed an unwonted power of resistance, and their overwhelming numbers baffled all the efforts of the besiegers. There was no help for it, but to retreat to the ships, which sheered off from the well-defended walls.

* The Greek emperor also headed a brilliant sortie, but was as brilliantly defeated. He only escaped by abandoning his shield, his war-chariot, and his imperial gonfalon. The Iconia (or "Ancone" of the French chronicler), a sacred standard, enriched with some precious relics and an image (εικων) of the Virgin, was captured on this occasion. It afterwards fell into the hands of Dandolo, and was transmitted to Venice.—*Villehardouin*, sect. 119.

THE "PILGRIM" AND THE "PARADISE."

Yet were not Dandolo and his brethren-in-arms discouraged. A second attack was resolved upon; and it was determined to link the ships together in pairs, that a greater force might be brought to bear upon each tower. For two days the troops rested. On the Monday they once more advanced against the city, and were again received with the most courageous opposition. For hours the terrible battle rolled to and fro in varying eddies. But towards mid-day a strong north wind drove the ships nearer shore, and two, whose names were of auspicious omen—*felici auspicio*—the *Pilgrim* and the *Paradise*, carrying the Bishop of Troyes and Soissons, bore down in linkèd strength on one tower. The ladders were lowered from the yards, and, inflamed by the eloquence of the prelates, and the promise of a hundred marks of silver, the knights leaped upon the battlements. The tower was won. This example incited the pilgrims to unparalleled deeds of valour. Four other towers were scaled, and carried; three gates were burst open; and the French knights, advancing from the shore, rode straight through the city to the imperial pavilion. To the terrified imagination of the Greeks they were preceded by a single warrior, of superhuman dimensions, aspiring to the stature of eighteen yards (ἐννεόργυιος), and wearing on his brow a towering helm, which seemed to menace ruin to all who dared oppose him! Before this phantom the Greeks fled in a panic of fear. The Latins poured into the conquered city, marking their progress by heaps of dead and dying foes. Upon a scene of slaughter and rapine,—woe, grief, joy, exultation, terror—all that carnival of the passions which runs riot on these terrible occasions,—fell the "holy calm of night," and the vanquished were left to brood over their defeat, while the scanty band of the conquerors watched and waited, like Cortez and his handful of warriors amid the defeated hosts of Mexico.*

VICTORY OF THE LATINS.

Mourzoufle, who, if an usurper, was, as the accounts of his enemies abundantly prove, not the less a hero, made a fruitless attempt to inspire his partizans with fresh courage, and then, through the Golden Gate, which had remained unopened for twice one hundred years, escaped into the wild recesses of Thrace. In the morning a suppliant procession, with crosses and images, besought the pity of the conquerors, who mercifully sheathed their swords, and permitted all who would to leave the city. But if they restrained their cruelty, they put no limits upon their greed. From palace, and church, and bazaar, they gathered an incredible amount of spoil; the spices, silks, and exquisite stuffs of the East; gold, and silver, and precious stones;—such wealth as the soldiery of the West had never even conceived in their wildest dreams! No peculation, no individual dishonesty was allowed. All was accumulated in one stock, and afterwards divided according to the rank and merits of the Crusaders. But the meanest soldier received a share which elevated him into opulence for the remainder of his life.

* Villehardouin, sect. 126-131.

SPOILS OF WAR.

The historian cannot record without regret that the precious relics of ancient art excited no cupidity in the minds of those who might have been powerful enough to preserve them. The finest memorials of antiquity, over the meanest of which the modern connoisseur would gloat in an ecstasy of enjoyment, were shattered and destroyed by the bigoted iconoclasm of these Western barbarians —*οἱ τοῦ καλοῦ ἀνέραστοι βαρβαροι*—not less ruthless, and far more guilty, than the Norse spoliators of ancient Rome. The only relic which escaped the general wreck was the famous four horses of gilt bronze, sometimes attributed to the admirable workmanship of Lysippus. These, which, in the course of a changeful career, had passed from Alexandria to Rome, and from Rome to Byzantium, were now removed by Dandolo to Venice, where they have ever since surmounted the central portico of the Cathedral of San Marco.*

"Before St. Mark still glow his steeds of brass,
Their gilded collars glittering in the sun."—BYRON.

The amount of plunder which fell to the lot of the Venetians has been estimated at 500,000 silver marks, representing a total in English money of about £900,000. Allow for the different value of money in the thirteenth and the nineteenth centuries, and the reader will obtain an approximative idea of the splendid booty which rewarded the pilgrims for their sufferings and fatigues.†

* It should be noted, however, that Napoleon Bonaparte carried them to Paris in 1797, but they were restored to Venice after his downfal.

† Villehardouin, sect. 124–126.

THE FIRST LATIN EMPEROR.

Satiate with pillage, the Latins next proceeded to elect a successor to the defeated Mourzoufle, and Baldwin, Count of Flanders, sprung of the royal blood of Charlemagne, was unanimously hailed Emperor of Romania. The wisdom and courage of Dandolo, to whom the capture of the city was mainly owing, then received due recompense. He was permitted to tinge his buskins with the imperial hue of purple; he was styled Despot of Romania, and Lord of One-Fourth and One-Eighth of the Roman Empire, and to his country was allotted a vast and fertile territory, embracing part of the Byzantine coast, and the richest islands of the Archipelago and Adriatic. The aged Doge was crowned with an exceeding weight of glory, and seldom, if ever, has it been given to a man so venerable in years to compass such matchless achievements and earn such deathless renown. But it was fated that the sun which had burst forth with so much splendour, even at the wane of day, should not set in a like magnificence. The empire but recently acquired by the swords of the Latins, was soon menaced with a myriad foes, among whom the most formidable were the Bulgarians, under their chief, Calo Johannes. Encouraged by their support, the Greeks rose in arms against their invaders; the Venetians were driven from Adrianople; and in almost every town the Latin garrison was overpowered or compelled to seek safety in flight. The fabric raised like an exhalation in a few brief months, seemed doomed to vanish even more rapidly than it had risen. Like one of those palaces which, in Eastern fables, are constructed in a single night by the labours of the genii, but which disappear at the approach of a hostile spirit, the Latin Empire of Romania was fated to fall to pieces before the attacks of its contemptible foes, ere it had been organized or thoroughly consolidated.

A DISASTER, AND A RETREAT.

Without waiting to collect his scattered forces, the Emperor Baldwin pressed forward to chastise the advancing Bulgarians. He had with him about one hundred and fifty lances, and their usual train of bowmen and men-at-arms, some seven hundred in all. Dandolo, not less chivalrous, followed with his Venetian soldiery. They soon came up with the enemy, who had adopted the Parthian tactics of enticing their pursuers by a pretended flight, and then turning upon them when disordered, confused, and spent with the chase. Through the rashness of the Count of Blois the emperor was involved in a dangerous skirmish, which the stratagem of the Bulgarians and the hot spirit of the Crusaders converted into a rout. Both the count and the emperor fought like Paladins, but they were overwhelmed by numbers; the count fell on the field, the emperor was taken prisoner, to suffer a long captivity, and afterwards meet with a cruel death. The prudence, courage, and skill of Dandolo and Villehardouin saved the remainder of the Latins from destruction.* At dead of night they silently broke up their camp, and after three days of incessant toil and anxiety, surrounded by a cloud of enemies, and suffering from a

* Villehardouin, sect. 193, *et seq.*

lack of provisions, contrived to lead back their troops to Rodosto. Meanwhile, Calo Johannes had spread his troops over the whole empire, and without the walls of Constantinople the Latins possessed only Rodosto and Selymbria.

DEATH AND CHARACTER OF DANDOLO.

Ceaseless fatigue, and the anxiety induced by these terrible reverses, proved too much for the ninety-eight years and feeble frame of Enrico Dandolo. After a short illness he passed away from the scene of strife, early in June 1205, leaving behind him a glorious memory and the fame of a heroic career. He was scarcely less eminent as a statesman than as a warrior. His mental vigour was only equalled by his physical energies. His was the ready arm and the gallant soul; and his, too, the far-reaching sagacity of the thoughtful politician, a brain fertile in resource, a firm will, and an unconquerable patience. He elevated his country to the height of greatness by a combination of prudence, enterprise, tact, and chivalrous daring, which is rarely met with in the same individual. He was at once its Marcellus and its Fabius, its shield and its sword; he legislated in the council like Epaminondas, and in the field of battle fought like Pelopidas. He seems to have been less open than other eminent sons of Venice to the charges of craft and selfishness. Like most truly great men, he was capable of warm feelings, and touched by the impulse of noble motives; and if, in the clash of conflicting interests, he preferred the claims of his own country to those of any other, without too minutely investigating their comparative justice, it can only be confessed that he was no cosmopolitan, but what, perhaps, is infinitely better, a loyal patriot. He was one of those

> "Whose names are ever on the world's broad tongue,
> Like sound upon the falling of a force;" *

and the story of

> "Blind old Dandolo, Byzantium's conquering foe," †

still serves to point a moral as well as to adorn a tale.

THE THREE INQUISITORS.

During the absence of the Doge at the theatre of war, the administration of Venice had been to some extent remodelled. To investigate the abuses which, from time to time, might creep into the government, a Commission of five members was appointed, entitled *Correttori della promission Ducale,* and they were also charged with the omission, or addition, as occasion required, and the Great Council willed, of those clauses in the Doge's oath which might be necessary for the preservation of the honour and liberties of the commonwealth. A Board of three members, *Inquisitori del Doge defunto,* was likewise created, whose strange position it was to survey the career of the deceased prince, to investigate any charges preferred against his character, and, if these were proved, to exact from his heirs a satisfactory compensation. The Venetians, in this, were unmindful of the sage maxim of antiquity: *De mortuis nil nisi bonum.*

* P. J. Bailey, "Festus."

† Byron, "Childe Harold."

PIERO ZIANI.

Piero Ziani was elected to Dandolo's vacant throne. Under his government the Venetians wisely abandoned the distant conquests, which would have exhausted their resources, disposing of them to such wealthy citizens as were prepared to complete their subjugation at their own cost, and to hold them as fiefs under the Republic.* Thus arose various duchies and principalities, which, in the course of events, were swallowed up in the neighbouring kingdoms. Venice only reserved to herself the Ionian Islands and Candia, and the latter island proved for many years a source of weakness rather than of strength.

FIRST GENOESE WAR.

In the reign of Giacomo Thiepolo (A.D. 1228) a Civil Code was consolidated—one of the earliest systems of domestic legislation introduced into Europe; and the capital received many important architectural embellishments. Then followed a period of comparative peace under Rainiero Zeno (A.D. 1252), which, during the dogeship of Lorenzo Thiepolo, was broken by the outbreak of the first great war with Genoa. The bold and enterprising sons of that powerful state now rivalled Venice on the sea which she had proudly considered her own. They monopolized the rich commerce of the East,† which, descending the channels of the Oxus, the Volga,

* Sismondi, "Histoire des Républiques," ii. 431.

† Gibbon, "Decline and Fall of the Roman Empire," ch. lxiii.

and the Don, was transferred to Genoese vessels in the harbours of the Crimea. These they had forcibly seized and surrounded with strong fortifications. It was evident that the pretensions of the two states would soon bring them into collision. With ever-increasing envy the Venetians watched the growth in power and wealth of their formidable competitors, who regarded the Queen of the Adriatic with at least an equal hatred. "Jealous of the Venetians," says Hallam,* "by whose arms the Latin emperors had been placed, and still maintained, on their throne, the Genoese assisted Palæologus in overturning that usurpation. They obtained in consequence the suburb of Pera, or Galata, over against Constantinople, as an exclusive settlement, where their colony was ruled by a magistrate sent from home, and frequently defied the Greek capital with its armed galleys and intrepid seamen. From this convenient station Genoa extended her commerce into the Black Sea, and established her principal factory at Caffa, in the Crimean peninsula. This commercial monopoly, for such she endeavoured to render it, aggravated the animosity of Venice."

An opportunity soon arose for these secret fires to break into open flame. The arrogance of the Genoese at length out-wearied the long-suffering Emperor of the East, and he applied to the Venetians for assistance, which was readily granted. Hostilities commenced in 1265, and were continued for eight years with varying fortune, but no diminution of ill-feeling. The Genoese were repeatedly beaten, but never conquered. Swept off the seas, they yet contrived to land a force in Candia,

* Hallam, "Europe in the Middle Ages," i. 444.

which destroyed the Venetian colony, and as fast as one fleet was annihilated they fitted out another. In 1269 the European powers forced them to pause in the cruel strife; but even then they refused to accept a peace, and could only be induced to sign a truce for a few years.

Yet, while conducting this sanguinary war, both republics were disturbed by internal commotions. With those of Genoa we need not concern ourselves. In Venice, severe taxation occasioned numerous insurrections, which could only be quelled by bloodshed. In the midst of this disorder the death of Zeno necessitated the election of a new Doge, and the jealousy of the citizens sought to fence it round with fresh precautions.

ELECTION OF THE DOGE.

The new scheme was designed to guard against the various evils connected both with election by open suffrage and election by lot. It was presumed, says Hallam, that among a competent number of persons, though taken promiscuously, good sense and right principles would gain such an ascendency as to prevent any flagrantly improper nomination, if undue influence could be excluded. For this purpose the ballot was rendered exceedingly complicated, that no possible ingenuity or stratagem might ascertain the electoral body before the last moment. A single lottery, if fairly conducted, is certainly sufficient for this end. At Venice as many balls as there were members of the great council present were placed in an urn. Thirty of these were gilt. The holders of gilt balls were reduced by a single ballot to nine. The nine elected forty, whom a further lot reduced to twelve. The twelve chose twenty-five by separate nomination. The twenty-five were reduced by lot to nine, each of whom selected five. Once more these forty-five were reduced to eleven; the eleven elected forty-one; and the forty-one chose the Doge.* The process seems as absurd as it was complex, but in practice worked satisfactorily. It may be reduced to the following formula:—

$$30 = 9 = 40 = 12 = 25 = 9 + 5 = 45 = 11 = 41 = 1.$$

Daru describes it in the following Italian rhymes:—

"Trenta elegge il Conseglio,
Di quei Nove hauno il meglio:
Questi elegon Quaranta,
Ma chi piu in lor si vanta
Son Dodeci, che fauno
Venti cinque: ma stauno
Di questi soli Nove,
Che fan con le lor prove
Quaranta cinque a ponto;
De' quali Undeci in conto
Eleggon Quarant' uno,
Che chuisi tutti in uno,
Con Venti cinque al meno
Voti, fauno il Sereno
Prencipe che coregge
Statuti, ordini e legge." †

An English writer has versified the above in easy doggerel:—

"From the Council's nomination
Thirty meet; Nine keep their station;
Forty next by these are chosen,
Who, by lot, become a dozen.
Five and twenty then combine
To produce another Nine;

* Hallam, "The Middle Ages," i. 459.

† Daru, "Histoire de Venise."

Hence are Five and Forty given,
Who diminished to Eleven,
Are by Forty-one succeeded;
Of whose final votes are needed
Five and twenty, to create
The presiding Magistrate;
The Serene, by whom elected,
Thus, our Statutes are protected." *

The year 1289 was marked by the establishment of the Inquisition at Venice; but its wary rulers took care to prevent any encroachment of the ecclesiastical upon the temporal power; and they so effectually restricted its jurisdiction, that it was never able "to strike its roots deeply into Venetian soil."

A YEAR OF SHAME.

In 1293 war was renewed with Genoa, but the result was this time disastrous to the Venetians. A Venetian fleet, it is true, surprised and burned Pera, ravaged the Crimean coast, and destroyed Caffa; but the Genoese, speedily recovering themselves, rebuilt Pera and surrounded it with impregnable fortifications, while, by despatching a powerful armament into the Adriatic, they struck a blow at the very heart of their enemy. The Genoese were encountered by a superior Venetian force off Curzola; but Lambe Doria, the Genoese admiral, manœuvred with so much skill that he secured a decisive victory. It was indeed complete; sixty-five Venetian ships were burned, and eighteen, with seven thousand prisoners, captured. Among the latter were the

* "Sketches from Venetian History," i. 202.

Venetian admiral, Dandolo, who deprived his captors of an expected triumph by dashing his head against the side of the galley; and Marco Polo, the famous traveller, who had but just returned from the court of Kublai Khan, the Tartar prince, after an absence of forty years in strange and remote countries.

The cup of Venetian disgrace was not yet full. In the following year the Genoese again defeated their antagonists, off Gallipoli, and the haughty Queen of the Adriatic was glad to secure the mediation of Matteo Visconti, Lord of Milan. But as soon as peace was concluded in 1299, Venice secretly began to prepare for a future struggle which should retrieve her lost honour.

CHANGES IN THE VENETIAN GOVERNMENT.

A glance must here be given at the further changes which were effected in the government of the Republic, and which finally vested all authority in the hands of a secret and exclusive oligarchy. Through the influence of the Doge Gradenigo—whom Sansorino characterizes as "a prompt and prudent man, of unconquerable determination and great eloquence"*—a decree was passed which, in effect, limited the composition of the great Council to the families then represented in it, and successfully prevented the introduction of any popular element. This is historically known as "The closing of the Council" (*La Serrata del mazor Conscio*)—A.D. 1297—and marks the date from whence the second period of Venetian history may justly be computed. The first

* Sansorino, "Venezia Descritta," p. 564, &c.

period was the government of an elective monarchy; the second, the government of the nobles. It lasted for five hundred years, during which Venice reaped the fruits of her former energies, consumed them, and—expired.* In 1319 the existing Council was declared permanent and hereditary, and whoever could prove his ancestral right was permitted, at the age of five and twenty, to put forward his claim for enrolment in the Golden Book of the Nobility (*Il Libro d'Oro*).

THE PAPAL INTERDICT.

These innovations were not effected without some resistance on the part of the people, but each insurrection was mercilessly repressed. The popular discontent was further aggravated by the distress which had been yearly increasing since 1307, when Pope Clement V. laid all the terrors of the interdict on the Republic, in punishment of the Venetian occupation of Ferrara, a territory which he claimed for the Roman See. Humbled abroad and weak at home, the Republic, indeed, seemed on the verge of ruin; and even among the nobles there were not wanting men who thought that a change of government was the only panacea for the national ills. The conspiracy of Thiepolo, in 1310, was the most formidable which had hitherto threatened the state. It was, however, detected by the sagacity of the Doge, and suppressed by his vigour. The conspirators were punished with merciless vengeance; and to guard against the repetition of a similar attempt, a civil inquisitorial tribunal,

* Ruskin, "Stones of Venice," i. 3. Compare Daru and Sismondi.

armed with terrible powers, with entire freedom from all responsibility and appeal, with exclusive authority over every individual in the state—the famous and infamous "Council of Ten" (*I Dieci*)—was established. It effectually crushed out the last sparks of popular liberty; it usurped the authority of the great Council, and, in time, deposed or put to death the head of the state at pleasure; it established in Venice a reign of terror, and becàme an inquisition from whose watchful eye and avenging arm no individual could escape: yet it secured such efficiency, promptitude, and energy in the executive, that the long stability of the Republic, as a judicious writer remarks, was probably owing to this, the most remarkable, the most formidable, and the most execrable part of her government.

III.

The Second Period.

> A dying glory smiles
> O'er the far times, when many a subject land
> Looked to the winged Lion's marble piles,
> Where Venice sate in state, throned on her hundred isles.
>
> BYRON.

A MEDIÆVAL LEGEND.

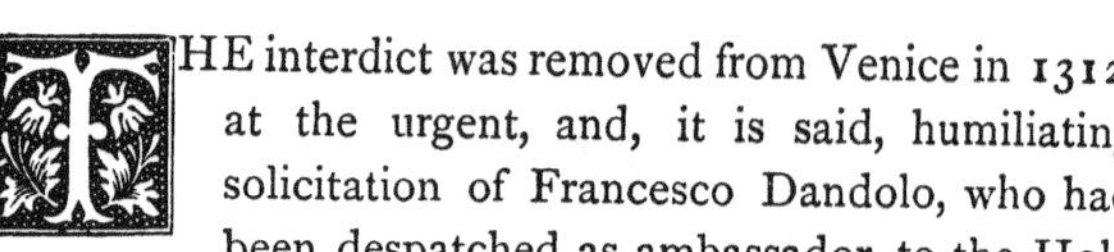

THE interdict was removed from Venice in 1312, at the urgent, and, it is said, humiliating solicitation of Francesco Dandolo, who had been despatched as ambassador to the Holy See, and who, in 1327, was rewarded for his services by elevation to the ducal throne. It was during his rule that Venice aided the Carrara in overthrowing the tyranny of Mastino della Scala, and restored them to their awful patrimony in Padua. She gained as the price of her assistance the districts of Treviso and Bassano, and it is singular that this not dishonourable achievement was destined to embroil the Republic in a protracted and dangerous war, and to revolutionize completely her foreign policy.

The reign of the Doge Gradenigo (A.D. 1339) was disturbed by a series of insurrections in Candia, which, however, present no features of interest for the general reader. Of more importance, perhaps, because singularly illustrative of the character and temper of the age, is the following incident, which the historian Sanuto relates with solemn gravity:—*

The waters had risen in Venice to an extraordinary height, and the flood was still increasing, when, one stormy night, an aged fisherman moored his bark for safety to the bank of the Canal di San Marco. Hardly had he done so when a stranger arrived, and requested to be ferried across to San Giorgio Maggiore, and conquered the fisherman's hesitation by the promise of a splendid fee. The passage was safely effected. The stranger landed, and, after an absence of a few minutes, returned, and with him a companion. The fisherman was ordered to row them to San Nicolo di Lido. His timidity was again conquered by a heavy bribe. A third stranger joined the boat at San Nicolo, and the mysterious voyage was then continued to the Two Castles of Lido. Just as they entered the strait, a galley was seen skimming the tempest-torn Adriatic; a galley freighted with devils, who hurried onward, yelling and waving their arms aloft, to bury Venice in the deep. The strangers rose, made the sign of the cross, and bade the demons begone. Immediately the waters sunk; the storm subsided; and the devil-burdened galley vanished into nothingness. The fisherman ferried back his strange passengers to their respective landing-places, and de-

* Sanuto, *apud* Muratori, "Antiquitates," xxii. 607, *et seq.*

manded his fee from the person who had first engaged him. "Go," said he; "go to the Doge and the Procuratori, and make known to them that but for our interposition Venice would have perished in the waters. I am St. Mark; my two comrades are St. George and St. Nicholas. Desire the magistrates to pay you." "How," quoth the wary boatman, "how can I expect the prince to believe my unconfirmed story! He will think it a delusion of my fancy." "Take, then, this ring," and the evangelist pulled one from his finger, "and bid them look for it in my treasury, whence it will be found missing."

The fisherman, on the morrow, executed the saint's behest. To the surprise of the Doge the ring was discovered to be missing, and its temporary custodian was therefore rewarded with an annual pension. Moreover, a solemn procession and thanksgiving were appointed in annual commemoration of the rescue of Venice from inundation by the three saints.

In 1343, during the sovereignty of Andreas Dandolo,* Zara once more revolted against the Venetian yoke. A force of twenty-seven thousand men was despatched to compel its surrender. The siege lasted for eighteen months, but Louis of Anjou, the Hungarian king, who had advanced to its relief, having been totally defeated by Marino Faliero, the Venetian commander, the unfortunate city abandoned all hope of independence, and capitulated.

* "A man early great among the great of Venice; and early lost. She chose him for her king in his thirty-sixth year; he died ten years later, leaving behind him that history to which we owe half of what we know of her former fortunes." —Ruskin, "Stones of Venice," ii. 69.

THE GREAT PLAGUE.

The year 1348 was the year of the Great Plague. Through all Europe swept the Destroying Angel, striking down youth and age, man, woman, and child, with a horrid and speedy death. It crossed the snowy barriers of the Alps; ravaged the wilds of Russia; penetrated even the ice-bound recesses of Iceland; while the land of the orange and the myrtle everywhere resounded with the voice of mourning. Florence lost a hundred thousand of her citizens; Naples, sixty thousand; Genoa, forty thousand; and Venice lamented more than half her population. The streets of the great Italian cities, once gay with the hum of business, were silent as the tomb, save when the solemn chant of the Miserere rose upon the air. In the blooming country-side the husbandman had suspended his labour; the cottages were shut up and closed; the plough stood still; the dame no longer plied her distaff; the vines hung on the trellis unheeded,—in the presence of the viewless but ubiquitous Terror men shrunk from the ordinary pursuits of life, and those who sought not the shrine and the sanctuary, endeavoured to drown their uneasy thoughts and panic fears in the intoxication of the wine-cup. Italy, in 1348, was one vast charnel, and for generations that fatal year was never mentioned but with an emotion of dread.

SECOND GENOESE WAR.

Heaven's scourge was succeeded by one of man's own making. In 1349 the smothered fires of hate again broke out between Venice and Genoa, and, exhausted as they were by the ravages of the plague, each drew the sword with frenzied eagerness. The first success was on the side of the Venetians, who defeated the Genoese fleet in the Bay of Caristo, in the island of Negropont. Both powers then addressed themselves to further warlike preparations, and Venice concluded an alliance with the King of Arragon. In February 1352 the allied fleets passed the Dardanelles, and, under the command of Nicolo Pisani, approached the Bosphorus. They numbered seventy-five galleys; the Genoese, under Doria, no more than four-and-sixty, but these were of larger size. Eight Greek ships, moreover, suddenly deserted the Venetian admiral, reducing his armament to an equality with his enemy. It was evening, and a terrible storm arose as the two fleets came into collision, but the battle raged with incessant fury through all the dark and tempestuous night. It recalls, in many respects, those sanguinary engagements between the Dutch and English, which distinguished the wars of the Protectorate and Charles the Second's reign. Ship fought with ship, man contended sword in hand with man. The hurricane, the rapid currents, the hidden rocks, increased the horrors of the fight, and when morning dawned upon the scene, it was doubtful to which of the combatants the victory might be ascribed. If the allies had lost four-and-twenty galleys, the Genoese had to mourn the destruction of nineteen of their larger vessels. On both sides the slaughter was about equal. The Venetian fleet, however, was too disabled to renew the combat, and Pisani retreated, unpursued.

In the spring of 1353, the Genoese, bent upon the humiliation of their rival, despatched a squadron to ravage the Adriatic coast. The insult was speedily punished. The Venetian admiral came up with Grimaldi's weakened fleet in the Bay of Cagliari, enticed him by a skilful stratagem to offer battle, and then crushed him with his vast superiority of force. Thirty ships were captured, and nearly five thousand prisoners taken. Great would have been the glory of Venice on this memorable day, had she not polluted her laurels with the blood of her captives.—(August 29).

The balance of war now inclined to the other side. Putting forth all their strength, like a lion in the toils, the Genoese once more equipped a formidable armada, which penetrated into the Adriatic, and insulted the very shores of Venice. Pisani was recalled for their protection, but before his ships could enter the gulf, the Genoese had nimbly quitted it, and carried fire and sword to other quarters.

MARINO FALIERO—OMENS.

In 1354 Marino Faliero, the victor of Zara, was elected Doge. His reign opened with a calamity, as it closed in crime and dishonour. The Genoese, under the heroic Doria—always a name of renown in Genoese annals—encountered Pisani and his fleet off Sapienza (November 3rd). The latter were moored in two lines in the harbour, and seemed to present an impregnable front; but the Genoese, like the British fleet at the Nile, unexpectedly doubled on their enemy, by passing between him and the shore, and attacking him on his unprepared side. The inner line defeated, the Genoese surrounded the outer squadron, and compelled Pisani, with thirty ships and nearly 6000 prisoners, to surrender. Venice was thus left unprotected; she could not arm a single galley; and had the Genoese pushed on to the attack without delay, she might have ceased to reign as a sovereign state. Doria, however, did not press his advantage, and a truce for four months was concluded between the conquerors and the conquered.

Before the truce could be extended into a peace, or fresh hostilities commenced, and while Venice, bleeding at every pore, was straining her resources to the uttermost to guard herself against foreign foes, she was brought to the verge of ruin by the treason of her most honoured citizens.*

We have said that the reign of Marino Faliero began in disaster. It was ushered in by many of those circumstances which after-events convert into omens. On the day of his public entrance into Venice, the Lagoon was shrouded in so thick a mist as to render impossible or dangerous the passage of the gilded *Bucentaur*, and the new Doge was constrained to approach his capital in an obscure gondola. The spot selected for his landing was also of evil augury. The boatmen, misled by the fog, instead of disembarking their princely and noble passengers at the *Riva della Paglia*, touched at the Piazzetta, where, between the Two Columns, all public executions

* For the best accounts of Faliero's conspiracy, see the histories, already quoted, of Daru and Sismondi.

took place. To these incidents Byron, in his well-known tragedy, makes the Doge himself allude,—

> "Thou canst not have forgot, what all remember,
> That on my day of landing here as Doge,
> On my return from Rome, a mist of such
> Unwonted density went on before
> The Bucentaur, like the columnar cloud
> Which ushered Israel out of Egypt, till
> The pilot was misled, and disembarked us
> Between the pillars of St. Mark's, where 'tis
> The custom of the state to put to death
> Its criminals, instead of touching at
> The Riva della Paglia, as the wont is,—
> So that all Venice shuddered at the omen." *

CHARACTER OF THE DOGE.

It should be remembered by the reader that the Marino Faliero of poetry is not the Marino Faliero of history, and that the conspiracy which has shrouded his name in eternal infamy, originated not, as the poet would have us believe, in the exquisite sensitiveness of an honourable mind, but in the workings of a moody, choleric, and ambitious spirit. Faliero, a successful soldier and a powerful noble, found himself, as Doge, but the chief actor in a theatrical show, and chafed with all the irritability of a proud mind against the innumerable restrictions which limited his authority. He longed for a firmer grasp and a wider rule. It is possible that he sympathized with his discontented subjects, whom a disastrous war had deeply wounded, and who groaned beneath an intolerable burden of taxation. To these motives was added another, more immediately personal.

* Byron, "Marino Faliero," act v., s. 2.

Faliero, at an advanced age, had wedded a young and beautiful woman of unblemished fame. Their disparity of years was calculated to excite the ridicule of the wits. At all events, it was felt by the Doge himself. At one of his public banquets, a young cavalier, named Michele Steno, incurred his prince's displeasure by his familiarity with one of the ladies in attendance on the Dogaressa. The hot youth revenged himself by affixing to the ducal chair some ribald words, which wounded Marino Faliero in his tenderest susceptibilities :—

> "Marin Falier, the husband of the fair wife; others kiss her, but he keeps her." *

The offender was soon discovered, and summoned before the Forty, who taking into consideration his youth, his levity, and other circumstances of an extenuating character, contented themselves with sentencing him to two months' imprisonment, and then to one year's banishment from Venice.

Here it would have been wise for the Doge to have suffered the scandal to drop. His wrath, however, mastered his prudence. He protested that the Council had dealt over-mercifully with treason out of disrespect to the ducal dignity. Steno, he said, ought to have been condemned to be hanged by the neck, or at least, to be banished for life.

CONSPIRACY OF FALIERO.

"Now," says the old chronicler, quaintly,† "it was fated that my Lord Duke Marino was to have his head

* Sanuto, *apud* Muratori.

† We adopt the excellent translation given in the notes to Byron's tragedy.

cut off." In those days, you see, historians did not busy themselves about laws and principles, motives and reasons; they traced everything to destiny. "And as it is necessary, when any effect is to be brought about, that the cause of such effect must happen, it therefore came to pass that, on the very day after sentence had been pronounced on Sir Michele Steno, being the first day of Lent, a gentleman of the house of Barburo, a choleric gentleman, went to the arsenal, and required certain things of the masters of the galleys. This he did in the presence of the admiral of the arsenal"—Bertuccio Israello, a man as proud and passionate as the Doge himself—"and he, hearing the request, answered, 'No; it cannot be done.' High words arose between the gentleman and the admiral, and the gentleman struck him with his fist just above the eye; and as he happened to have a ring on his finger, the ring cut the admiral and drew blood. The admiral, all bruised and bloody, ran straight to the duke to complain, and with the intent of praying him to inflict some heavy punishment upon the gentleman of Cà Barburo. 'What wouldst thou have me to do for thee?' answered the duke; 'think upon the shameful gibe which hath been written concerning me, and think on the manner in which they have punished that ribald Michele Steno who wrote it; and see how the Council of Forty respect our person.' Upon this the admiral answered, 'My Lord Duke, if you wish to make yourself a prince, and to cut all those cuckoldy gentlemen to pieces, I have the heart, if you do but help me, to make you prince of all this state; and then you may punish them all.' Hearing this, the duke said,

'How can such a matter be brought about?' and so they discoursed thereon."

To assist them in their schemes, the two conspirators summoned Bertucci Faliero, a nephew of the Doge, and Filippo Calendaro, a naval captain of eminence and authority. It was agreed to intrust the secret to six other associates, most of them men of plebeian origin. The details of the revolution were then arranged. It was concerted that sixteen or seventeen leaders should be stationed in various parts of the city, each being at the head of forty men, armed and prepared; but the followers were not to know their destination. On the appointed day they were to make affrays amongst themselves here and there, in order that the duke might have a pretence for tolling the bells of San Marco—which bells were never rung but by order of the Doge—

"The last poor privilege they leave their prince!"—

and at the sound of the bells, these different parties were to concentrate upon San Marco, through the streets leading to the Piazza. And when the nobles and leading citizens should come into the Piazza to know the cause of the riot, then the conspirators were to cut them in pieces; and this cruel work being finished, my Lord Marino Faliero, the Duke, was to be proclaimed the Lord of Venice. Things having been thus settled, they agreed to fulfil their intent on Wednesday, the 15th day of April, in the year 1355. So covertly did they plot, that no one ever dreamed of their machinations.

The day approached when the mine was to be sprung which would shatter the government and constitution of

COURT OF THE DOGE'S PALACE.

Venice into hopeless ruin. Nor was the danger averted by the insight or suspicions of her rulers. Even the Council of Ten was lulled into security. It was the private remorse of one of the conspirators which, as in the case of our own Gunpowder Plot, saved the state. Beltrano was much attached to a nobleman named Lioni, marked, like others of his class, for slaughter. The evening before the fatal day, he betook himself to his patron's house, and solicited him to remain at home on the morrow. The patrician's suspicions were excited by the request, and by the ambiguous reasons which Beltrano urged for compliance with it. Ordering his servants to detain the conspirator, Lioni sought the counsel of his friends, Giovanni Gradenigo, afterwards Doge, and Marco Cornaro, who, returning with him to his house, subjected Beltrano to a severe examination, and finally wrung from his fears a full account of the conspiracy.

There was no time for hesitation. The three nobles immediately called together the Ten, the Forty, and the principal magistrates, who were doubtlessly appalled to find themselves hovering on the very verge of destruction. Swiftly assembling the guards and secret police, they seized upon the ringleaders at their own houses, set a strong watch at the palace gates, forbade the keeper of the bell-tower to toll the bell on any pretext, and adopted such other precautions as were demanded by the gravity of the crisis.

There was no difficulty to be apprehended in dealing with the meaner conspirators; for them the law provided rack and gibbet; but treason on the part of the prince towards the state of which he was the head, the framers of the Venetian constitution had never suspected as possible. The Ten, however, associated with themselves twenty of the leading men of the commonwealth, and summoned the Doge before them. Faliero was at that very time consorting in his palace with people of great estate, gentlemen, and other good men, none of whom knew yet how the fact stood. Though surprised by the sudden overthrow of his ambitious hopes, he preserved unshaken the firmness of his mind and his haughty spirit. He denied nothing; he extenuated nothing. He heard his sentence unmoved, and neither implored nor expected mercy.

DEATH OF THE CONSPIRATORS.

The other ringleaders were hanged, some singly, some in couples, between the red pillars of the Piazzetta; Calendaro and Bertuccio with gags in their mouths. The duke's sentence was delivered on the 16th of April, and ordered him to be beheaded on the landing-place of the stone staircase, the Giant's Stair, where the Doges take their oath when they first enter the palace. On the following day, the 17th of April, the palace gates being closed, Faliero had his head cut off about the hour of noon; and the cap of estate was taken from the duke's head before he came down the staircase. When the execution was over, it is said that one of the Council of Ten went to the columns of the palace over against the place of St. Mark, and that he showed the bloody sword unto the people, crying out with a loud voice, "The terrible doom hath fallen upon the traitor!" and the doors were opened, and the people all rushed in to see the corpse of the duke who had been beheaded.

Faliero's remains were conveyed by torchlight in a

EXECUTION OF MARINO FALIERO.

gondola to the Church of San Giovanni e Paoli, where they were buried without the usual rites. In the outer wall the stone coffin is still embedded, though the inscription which it formerly bore, "*Hic jacet Dominus Marinus Faletro Dux*," is no longer legible. His lands and goods were confiscated to the state, with the exception of two thousand ducats, of which he was allowed to dispose; and his portrait was not admitted among those of his brother Doges which adorned the Hall of the Great

Council, but in the frame which it should have occupied was suspended a black veil, inscribed with the tragic legend,—

> "Hic est locus Marini Faletro decapitati pro criminibus."
> [This is the place of Marino Faliero, beheaded for his crimes.]

The chronicler, Sanuto, informs us that the following epitaph was proposed to be engraven on his tomb:—

> "Dux Venetum, jacet heic, patriam qui perdere tentans,
> Sceptra, decus, censum perdidit, atque caput."

Imitated:—

> Here lies interred that Doge of Venice, who
> His country basely seeking to betray,
> Lost fame and power, lost wealth, lost life, lost all,
> On the same fatal day!

YEARS OF STRIFE AND CHANGE.

Over the next thirty years our historical survey must pass lightly. Giovanni Gradenigo succeeded Marino Faliero on the ducal throne. Both in his reign, and in that of his successor, Giovanni Dolfino,* Venice was involved in a disastrous war, which compelled her eventually to abandon her pretensions on the Dalmatian coast of the Adriatic. In 1361, while Lorenzo Celsi was

* He was elected Doge while, as provveditori, he was conducting the defence of Treviso against the forces of the King of Hungary. The Venetians sent a message to the besiegers that their newly-elected prince might be suffered to pass their lines; but the request was denied, the Hungarians rejoicing that they held the Doge of Venice prisoner in Treviso. Dolfino, however, with two hundred picked horsemen, cut his way through the enemy by night, and reached Malghera in safety, where he was met by the Senate. His dogeship was brief and unfortunate. The surrender of Dalmatia broke his heart, his eyesight failed him, and he died of the plague four years after his accession to a throne he had not coveted.

Doge, the Republic received as a bequest the precious library collected by the poet Petrarch, which, enlarged by later additions, now ornaments the principal saloon of the ducal palace. The years 1364 and 1365 were disturbed by the insurrection of the Candiotes; an insurrection crushed by the Venetians with merciless severity. The island was almost depopulated, and some of its most fertile districts were converted into a desert.

In 1367, Andrea Contarini, a scion of one of the noblest Venetian families, was raised to the ducal throne, though not without his own most strenuous opposition. There was little indeed in the pageantry of the dogeship to compensate for the slavery both of the man and the prince which it involved, and Contarini's cultivated mind and refined tastes were best adapted to adorn and be happy in a private career.

At the outset of his reign he was called upon to deal with the intrigues of Francesco da Carrara, the Lord of Padua. The arms of Venice were successful, and compelled him to sue for peace, which he obtained on terms that did but inflame his hatred. He was required to pay a heavy tribute, to demolish his forts, to surrender certain towns as a guarantee of his good faith, and to take an oath of fidelity to the Republic on his knees. Brooding over his wrongs, the subtle prince spared no pains to form such alliances as should enable him to avenge them. At first his failures were many and his disappointments severe. But an unexpected and most powerful friend suddenly came forward when and where he least expected such help.

The East had once more become the scene of rivalry

between Genoa and Venice, each power endeavouring to monopolize for itself the commerce of the Black Sea and the Mediterranean. A Venetian adventurer, named Carlo Zeno, a man of extraordinary daring, firm resolution, and unexampled energy, had been induced to undertake the perilous enterprise of restoring Calo Johannes to the throne of Constantinople, from which he had been deposed by the Emperor Andronicus. The latter discovering the plot before it was ripe for execution, Zeno hastily effected his escape on board a small boat to the squadron commanded by his father-in-law Giustiniani. The two set sail for the island of Tenedos, which the deposed prince had made over to Venice, were warmly welcomed, and planted on its shores the banner of St. Mark. Then they crowded on all sail for the Adriatic, and contrived to obtain the sanction of their government to what was, in fact, a violent breach of the law of nations. Reinforcements were despatched to the garrison of Tenedos, and Carlo Zeno appointed to their command.

Genoa looked upon this transaction with jealous rage, and eagerly joined the Greek emperor in avenging it. But the sultan having espoused the cause of Calo Johannes, Andronicus found himself unable to oppose so powerful an enemy, and abdicated the throne which had proved to him so uneasy a seat. The war between the two Italian republics was then transferred to regions nearer home. Both foresaw the importance and the perilous character of the struggle into which their passions — and nations are as easily guided by their passions as individuals—had plunged them, and endeavoured to strengthen themselves by alliance with other powers. Venice was joined by Lusignan, King of Cyprus; Visconti, Lord of Milan; and the Marquis di Carréto, who ruled over Castel-Franco, Noli, and Albenga. A formidable league, however, was formed against her; for her wealth had excited the envy of some, and her pride the hatred of many. Its principal members, besides Genoa, were Francesco Carrara, Signor of Padua; the Duke of Austria; the Queen of Naples; and the King of Hungary. Against such a preponderance of force did the Queen of the Adriatic enter upon the famous War of Chiozzia.*

THE WAR OF CHIOZZIA.

During the winter of 1378 a Genoese squadron harassed the Dalmatian coast with fire and sword, intercepted Venetian commerce, and kept the capital in a panic of alarm. The Venetian fleet, commanded by Pisani, a seaman of skill, courage, and resolution, having been weakened by the ravages of an epidemic disease, its complement was made up by a hasty conscription of landsmen. Under such circumstances, Pisani felt he could not cope with the well-equipped ships of the Genoese, manned by the best and hardiest seamen of the world; but the impatience of the Venetian government prevailed over his calmer judgment. He was ordered to attack, and he obeyed the order. Off Pola he bore down upon the enemy with such vehemence that

* See Muratori, *ut antè*, vol. xvii. For contemporary chroniclers, Stella and Gataro; Sismondi, "Histoire des Républiques," vii., pp. 205–232, &c.

the Genoese admiral's ship was taken and himself slain; but he could not maintain the fury of his onset, and discipline and tactics prevailed over headlong courage. The defeat was total. The Venetians lost 15 galleys, and 1900 men were taken prisoners. Pisani, rescuing the remains of his shattered fleet, returned to Venice. His foresight and his courage should have gained him his government's approval, even in the hour of disaster; but the oligarchy were jealous of his fame, and of the esteem and love with which the populace regarded him. They repaid his services by flinging him into prison.

Meanwhile the Genoese fleet, strengthened by repeated reinforcements, rode in triumph before the long natural ramparts which separate the Lagoon from the Adriatic (A.D. 1379). Six navigable channels intersect the long narrow islands that form this barrier, besides that broader outlet of Brendolo, opposite Chiozzia, into which the waters of the Adige and the Brenta discharge themselves. The direct communication between Chiozzia and Venice consists of a canal, which traverses the entire length of the Lagoon in a course of about five-and-twenty miles.

Notwithstanding the difficulties of the enterprise, Pietro Doria, the Genoese admiral, determined upon striking a blow at Venice herself. He coasted along Malamocco, burned the chief village on the island of Pelestrina, which forms a bulwark to the port of Chiozzia, forced the passage, and, anchoring off Chiozzia, took possession of its eastern suburb. Had he at once attacked the town itself, there is no reason to doubt but that it would have fallen an easy prey to his arms. But arrogance and ostentation were the leading vices of Doria's character, and, satisfied with his success, he re-embarked his men, and sailed down the gulf to display the spoils of his prowess.

Venice now endeavoured to prepare for the perils which threatened her. She equipped fifteen galleys, but could man only six of them, from the indignation with which the people regarded Pisani's imprisonment. Strong defences were raised in the port of Lido; cannon—but recently introduced into warfare*—were mounted on either side of the channel; hulks were moored across it, so as to intercept the advance of an enemy; while Chiozzia was hastily fortified, and its garrison increased by a reinforcement of one thousand men.

Meanwhile, Genoa had added to Doria's fleet of forty-eight ships of war several hundred sail of lighter vessels, provision-ships, and transports, and had despatched instructions that he should storm the Venetian capital, and bring home in chains as many of her nobles as he could secure. Joined by one hundred light barks from Padua, he commenced operations against Chiozzia early in August, the land forces being commanded by Francesco Carrara in person. The allies were animated with enthusiasm; the love of glory, the lust of vengeance, the greed of plunder, stimulated their exertions; while, on their part, the Venetians fought with the despair of patriots, who knew that the fortunes of their fatherland were involved in their success or failure.

* It may interest the reader to be told that, according to recent researches made by Mr. H. T. Riley, the earliest passage known as referring to the use of cannon in England occurs in an inventory of munitions of war provided by the City of London in 1339.

They opposed a steadfast resistance to the murderous attacks of their enemies; but the gallantry of their defence could not prevail against overwhelming numbers. On the 16th of August the final attack was delivered, and Chiozzia fell. In that brief ten days' siege more than 6000 Venetians perished, and 3500 prisoners were taken, of whom the noblest were cruelly put to the sword. The town was handed over, in accordance with the terms of the alliance, to the Carrara.

VENICE IN PERIL.

Chiozzia fell at sunset; the sad tidings reached Venice at midnight, and her populace, pouring into the public places, filled the air with groans and cries of despair. Whither should they flee? To whom, in that hour of darkness, could they look for help? The bell tolled solemnly from the moonlit tower of St. Mark's, and the braver spirits, at its awful summons, buckled on their armour. But most, in weeping crowds, thronged the aisles of the different churches, or muttered out their sins at the confessional, or derived what hope and comfort they could from participation in the Eucharist. It seemed to all as if the last hour of Venice, of the beautiful City of the Isles, of the proud Queen of the Adriatic, had at length arrived. They reminded one another of her past glories, of her bygone heroes, of Ordelafo and Dandolo, of victories won on many a well-fought field.

And now, perhaps, the haughty Genoese were already hurrying on to her destruction; as vultures gather about a corpse, so might their innumerable sails be hovering on the misty Lagoon. But once more Venice was to be saved; rather by the caution of her enemies than the sagacity and heroism of her sons. Carrara urged the admiral to cross the Lagoon and strike at the capital, while its citizens were powerless with terror; but Doria, it may be, was awed by the lustre of her long career of glory, and believing that she could more easily be reduced by famine, proceeded to establish his forces securely in the commanding position which their valour had acquired.

The universal cry at Venice was for peace. The Doge, Contarini, in the midst of the blackness and desolation preserved the calmness of a great ruler, but he could not refuse to see that future safety could only be secured by present submission. He despatched ambassadors to Carrara and Doria, who were empowered to make any concessions short of an absolute sacrifice of the liberty of their country. The terms were such as to satisfy even the hatred and ambition of the Lord of Padua, and he strongly advised the Genoese admiral to accept them. But the latter felt that his country's desire of vengeance would only be satisfied by the destruction of her ancient rival. The ambassadors had brought with them seven Genoese prisoners, ransomless, as a peace-offering. "Take back your captives," exclaimed the haughty Doria, "for within a few days I will release both them and their companions from your dungeons! By God above, ye signors of Venice, ye shall have no peace, either from us or from the Lord of Padua, till we have first put a curb into the mouths of those wild horses that stand upon the Place of St. Mark. Place but the reins once in our hands, and we shall know how to bridle them for the future!"

PISANI THE SEA-KING.

Despair restored the old energies of the state. All her artisans were summoned to the construction of a fleet which should, at all events, delay the enemy's approach. And the value of a great man being always felt in the hour of danger, every eye was now turned to the heroic Pisani, who languished in a prison because he had deserved well of his country. He was unanimously called to superintend the defensive measures which the emergency required. The government notified to their victim that he was free, and invited him to take his seat, on the following day, in the Great Council. Pisani displayed as much moderation in his triumph as he had shown patience in adversity. He spent the night in prayer. The next morning he attended mass, and partook of the Holy Supper, as a pledge that he had put aside all memory of the wrongs he had endured. Then he repaired to the Council Chamber, and listened with dignified composure to the harangue of the Doge. In reply, he expressed his entire devotion to the service of his country, and called upon all her children to sink their feuds and differences in the presence of a common danger. "Would to God," he concluded, "I could devote to the sacred enterprise with which you intrust me, and which I undertake with all my soul and spirit, a vigour and an intellect equal to my desires and affections ! But *these*, at least, shall not be wanting to Venice." As he descended into the Piazza, the excited multitude thronged around him with eager outbursts of applause. "Pisani ! viva Pisani !" they cried aloud. "My friends," said the modest patriot, "the rallying shout of a true son of Venice should rather be, *Viva San Marco!*"

TO ARMS ! TO ARMS !

The appointment of Pisani as admiral swept away the discontent of the populace, and every order of the state seemed inspired with fresh energy. The defences at Lido were strengthened under his direction ; the canals were fortified, or occupied by large vessels armed with artillery ; the unskilled landsmen who had volunteered for naval service were regularly drilled ; and thirty-four galleys equipped as the nucleus of a fleet.

The Genoese had not been wholly idle while Venice was so promptly arming. They had occupied the island of San Erasmo, which, with that of Chiozzia, commanded the mouth of the harbour, and had made some attempts to enter the strait ; but in these skirmishes the advantage was rather with the Venetians, and tended to raise their spirits. The balance against them, however, was terribly heavy. Every access to the continent was blocked up by the forces of Carrara ; and the King of Hungary had taken possession of almost all the Venetian towns in Istria and along the Dalmatian coast. It needed a patriot's heart in Venice to cherish a patriot's hope. Great states, however, are not killed by sudden blows. They perish of the decay of many years, or fall after a protracted struggle, like the Troy of the Homeric Iliad. Venice was not doomed to any such premature extinction as her enemies meditated. Besides her hastily-equipped fleet in the Lagoon, she had a squadron cruising in the Levant, under that daring adventurer Carlo Zeno; and no exertions had been spared to make known to him the tidings of his country's danger. It was hoped that his squadron would return in time to strengthen the contemplated attack upon the Genoese forces.

The enthusiasm of the people, however, would not permit the Doge and Pisani to mature their well-laid schemes, and they resolved to assume the offensive without further delay. Their enemies, reposing too securely in the consciousness of their strength, and ignorant of the vast exertions of the Venetians, and of the result of these exertions, had partly dismantled their fleet in the harbour of Chiozzia. Taking advantage of this supineness, Pisani and Contarini, on the evening of the 23rd of December, amid the wildest shouts of enthusiasm and the swell of martial music, embarked on board their galleys, descended the channel of Lido, and finally took up their position *off* the entrance of the Strait of Chiozzia. Great was the consternation of the Genoese when they found themselves thus formidably menaced. There are, however, two channels of approach to Chiozzia—one of which the Venetians had thus sealed up with their fleet; the other, that of Brendolo, was still open, as was also the canal leading to Venice. Pisani determined to close these by sinking vessels across them; and then, patiently watching his foe from without the Lagoon, to wait for that surrender which famine would render inevitable. In the first part of his design, after some severe fighting, he succeeded; but to maintain the blockade proved a task of extreme difficulty. The weather was bitterly cold; storms were frequent; to guard against the attempts of the Genoese to raise the sunken vessels demanded incessant watchfulness; harassed, hungry, and worn, the seamen could no longer repress their discontent. Pisani appeased them with a promise that he would raise the blockade if the fleet of Zeno, which would render him sufficiently powerful to make a direct attack upon the enemy, did not arrive by the 1st of January 1380. Again the existence of Venice hung upon a thread. If the blockade were raised, whither should the fleet retire? Not to Venice, which, already suffering from scarcity, could afford no relief to twenty thousand seamen. Moreover the Genoese, stimulated by success and embittered by recent events, would not fail to attack the capital immediately. Columbus not more eagerly looked for signs of land, when the failure seemed imminent of his holy enterprise; Charlemagne, beset by Paynims, listened not more anxiously for the sound of Roland's horn; than Pisani watched, as the New Year's first morning dawned over the seas, for the coming vessels of Carlo Zeno.

ARRIVAL OF ZENO.

They came; or here we might close the record of Venetian history. They came—fourteen stout galleys, manned by veteran seamen—and were received with a tumult of exultation which brought hysterical tears to the eyes of many. They came; and Venice was saved. Even if the Genoese broke the blockade, she could now meet them on the seas with a force equal, if not superior, to their own.

The Venetian admiral pressed the investment of his enemies with great vigour. Constant engagements took place between the hostile forces, the Genoese fighting with desperate valour to regain, if they could, the advantages they had so supinely lost. But fortune refused to smile upon them. A brilliant attack delivered by Zeno, on the 19th of February, drove them from Brendolo, with a loss of nearly four thousand men, besides immense spoil in armour and artillery. Thus pent up within the walls of Chiozzia, the Genoese were reduced to the direst extremities by hunger. A fruitless attempt was made to relieve them, on the 6th of June, by a Genoese fleet under Maruffo; but he was effectually baffled by Pisani's superior skill. On the 15th, a desperate sortie was made by the wan, spectre-like battalions of Chiozzia. They were cut down by the Venetians like ripe corn by the reapers. There was no more to be done, and on the 22nd of June Chiozzia surrendered, with all that remained of the splendid armament which had so nearly achieved the destruction of Venice.*

PEACE CONCLUDED.

The war lingered on for nearly another year, but both states were too exhausted to attempt any great effort. The

* The great admiral, Pisani, died early in the following year, and Venice bitterly mourned the loss of her ablest seaman.

mediation of the Duke of Savoy was, therefore, gladly welcomed. By the Peace of Turin (August 8, 1381), Venice lost Tenedos, which passed to the Genoese, and the province of Trevisano, which fell to her great enemy, the Carrara. By these losses, however, she was really a gainer; as to hold these possessions had weakened her forces in times of trouble. Upon a hasty view, says Hallam,* the result of this war appears more unfavourable to Venice; yet, in fact, it was the epoch of the decline of Genoa, which would seem to have overstrained her energies in one last desperate effort to crush her ancient rival.

A WEB OF INTRIGUE.

A few months after the signature of peace, the Doge Contarini died, spent with fatigue and with the burden of his gray hairs. To him succeeded Morosini (A.D. 1382), who, four months after, perished of the plague, together with 20,000 of his countrymen. Morosini, it should be observed, had carried off the ducal bonnet in competition with the great seaman Carlo Zeno. He was seventy-four years old when elected; and, according to Sansorino, a most learned and prudent man, who effected several reforms. "It was generally believed," says Sabellico, "that had his reign been prolonged, he would have increased the dignity of the state by many noble laws and institutions; but by so much as his reign was full of hope, so was it brief in duration." Elected on the 10th of June, he died on the 15th of October. The reign of the Doge

* Hallam, "The Middle Ages," i. 449.

Veniero was marked by a renewal of hostilities with the Carrara, in which Venice found herself allied with Della Scala, the powerful Prince of Verona, while the Carrara was supported by the dark and subtle Galeazzo, one of the ablest of the Viscontis, Dukes of Milan. The latter seized upon both Vicenza and Verona, apparently in the interests of his ally, but then concluded a secret treaty with the Venetian Republic, and directed his arms against the unfortunate Carrara. Unable to excite the patriotic sympathies of his own subjects, the Lord of Padua abdicated in favour of his son, Francesco Novello; but the change in no wise brightened the prospects of his dynasty. The allies advanced rapidly upon Padua, whose traitorous citizens refused to arm against them, and both princes fell into the hands of their enemies. Venice and the Visconti then divided the spoil; the former recovering both Corfu and Trevisano.

But the Republic soon found that a dangerous neighbour was seated at her gates, in the person of the Milanese Duke, whose ambition was controlled by no sense of justice or honour. He aspired to bring all Italy under the rule of his sceptre, and worked for this end with singular steadfastness of purpose. One by one he was absorbing the meaner states; and Venice had unwittingly played his game by assisting in the ruin of Verona and Padua. She now had reason to fear that herself might be the next victim. Suddenly changing her policy, she found means to communicate with the young Carrara, and announced her willingness to assist him in recovering the throne from which she had just deposed him! He contrived to effect his escape from the clutches of his enemy. Florence and Bologna espoused his cause, and the Paduans, weary of the despotism of Visconti, received him with open arms.* Before the end of August 1391 he was firmly re-established on his ancient throne; and in the following spring repaired to Venice, to express his gratitude for the favours he had received, and his hope that thenceforth peace would prevail between him and the Republic. The only cloud that darkened his sunny horizon was his father's death, which occurred in 1393, and closed a career of singular infelicity.

The eyes of the Venetian Government were next turned towards the East, where the rapid progress of the Moslems had begun to excite their serious alarm. Bajazet, the fourth Ottoman sultan, had stripped the Greek emperor of all his territories except Constantinople, and exacted from him an annual tribute. To defend their own commercial interests, rather than to prop up a decadent empire, Venice, Hungary, and Genoa formed, in 1396, a league against the aggressive government of the Turks, which was approved, and to some extent supported, by France and England. The Venetian fleet was completely successful in the ensuing campaign, and the Cross waved triumphant on every sea; but the military expedition, which numbered upwards of 100,000 men, was crushed in the fatal battle of Nicopolis (September 28, 1396), owing to the temerity and ignorant imprudence of the French.

The long dogeship of Veniero closed in peace (A.D. 1399). It had been marked by unusual abundance and

* Gataro, *apud* Muratori, vol. xvii. 570, *et seq.*

prosperity at home, and the capital had received some of its most splendid architectural embellishments. The Campanile di San Marco was completed; the Piazza adjoining the Rialto was paved with marble; and the southern side of the Piazza di San Marco fashioned into its present glorious ensemble.

NOTABLE EVENTS.

In the reign of Michaele Steno several noteworthy events occurred. The Emperor Robert visited Venice, where he was entertained with numerous gorgeous spectacles (A.D. 1401); Visconti terminated his stormy career under, as was believed, the "baleful shadow" of a blood-red comet (September 3, 1402); hostilities broke out between the Genoese and the Venetians, whose fleet, under the illustrious Carlo Zeno, won a signal victory off Sapienza (October 6); and the Republic perpetrated the most criminal act of perfidy in its history by suddenly declaring war against Carrara, invading and capturing Padua, and obtaining possession, under promises of generous treatment, of the ill-fated prince and his two sons (A.D. 1404–5). We glance rapidly over these events, for the tale of fraud, and unscrupulous ambition, and cruel treachery, is a sickening one. The Carraras were flung into prison, and, after a brief interval of hesitation on the part of the Doge and his counsellors, were foully murdered (February 17–18, 1406). Of their unhappy race, two survivors, for the present, escaped the bloody vengeance of Venice: for the younger sons of Francesco had eluded her grasp. Of these, Ubertino died a natural death at Florence in 1407, and the fate of Marsilio we shall have hereafter to record. For so cruel and treacherous a murder the warmest apologists of Venice can find no apology. The Carraras were sovereign princes, over whom the Republic possessed no jurisdiction; nor had they committed any crime against the state. The Council of Ten could only excuse the deed on the nefarious plea of the national interest: a dead man, they said, makes no war (*Uom morto non fa guerra*)! *

In the year 1418, at the ripe age of eighty-four, after a long and glorious career, distinguished by the highest patriotism, courage, generosity, and fidelity, died Carlo Zeno, one of the worthiest sons of Venice.

WAR AND PEACE.

Our limits compel us to pass over the long wars with Milan, alternating as they did between success and disaster, and terminating in the establishment of Francesco Sforza on the ducal throne of that famous city. They were marked by many romantic incidents, and by some great battles. Marsilio da Carrara was tempted to make a dash at his patrimonial inheritance of Padua, but on his way thither was arrested by the agents of the Council of Ten, and carried a prisoner to Venice, where he met with the same doom as his brothers and father. The Venetian army was defeated in a great battle by the famous Milanese general, but the Republic eventually

* Sanuto, *apud* Muratori, xxii.

became a considerable gainer by the war, and added to her territories Bergamo and Brescia. Peace was concluded at Lodi in the spring of 1454.

STORY OF THE TWO FOSCARI.

These events occurred during the dogeship of Francesco Foscari, which was also distinguished by the visit of the emperor Frederick III. to Venice in 1453, and the capture of Constantinople, in the same year, by the Turkish sultan, Mahomet II. The Queen of the Adriatic, however, showed no inclination to join or to lead a crusade against the Infidels; but, on the contrary, was the first European power that concluded a treaty with them, in which, we may add, she consulted only her own interests, and made no provision for the rights of other nations.

The reign of Francesco Foscari lasted thirty-five years; thirty-five years of warfare, but also of constantly increasing prosperity. He had deserved well of his country, and now, bent with the weight of a stormy career, he tottered on the threshold of the grave. It was not fated that he should pass away in peace. As early as 1433 he had besought the Senate to accept his abdication, but had been refused. Nine years afterwards he repeated the request, and the Senate, not content with a second rejection, but desirous to prevent on the part of his successors any similar action, which tended to throw too strong a light on the miseries of the ducal throne, insisted that he should take a solemn oath to retain his crown of thorns for life. The marriage of his only surviving son,

Giacopo, in 1450, to the heiress of "the illustrious" race of Contarini, threw a gleam of sunshine on his darkling path. It was celebrated with a pomp and a splendour in which all Venice shared :—

> "To convey her home,
> The Bucentaur went forth ; and thrice the sun
> Shone on the chivalry, that, front to front,
> And blaze on blaze reflecting, met and ranged,
> To tourney in St. Mark's."—ROGERS.

Four years afterwards the young noble was denounced to the Ten as having received presents from foreign potentates, contrary to the suspicious laws of Venice. He was probably innocent. Nevertheless, he was put to the rack in the presence of his own father ; his sufferings extorted an incoherent confession ; and it then became the terrible duty of Foscari to sentence him to banishment from the land he loved so well. On his way to Napoli di Romania, he was delayed by illness at Trieste. The Doge availed himself of the opportunity to plead for some indulgence to his son, and so far succeeded that Giacopo was permitted to reside at Treviso, where his wife shared and brightened his exile.

It happened, however, that in the winter of 1455, Hermolao Donato, one of the Ten, was assassinated in the streets of Venice. So great a crime demanded a victim, and, partly because no other could be found, partly from some insignificant circumstances which the Ten considered suspicious, Giacopo was arrested as the murderer, brought to Venice, and again tortured in his father's presence. He was made to undergo the cruellest agonies, but persisted in declaring his innocence. Mental and physical misery overthrew his reason; but, as soon as it was restored, the unhappy youth was exiled to Candia; and there, too, he was ordered to remain, even after Nicolo Erizzo had confessed, on his death-bed, that Donato had fallen by his dagger! *

SORROWS OF GIACOPO FOSCARI.

Banished from his country, from his wife, from his children, from his parents, Giacopo was consumed by a burning fever. Life grew an intolerable burden, and in the summer of 1456 he determined on a desperate expedient to secure his return to Venice, even if he returned as a malefactor, and perished there as a criminal. He addressed a letter to the Duke of Milan, soliciting his interference with the Senate. This letter he left open in a place where he knew it would be seen by the spies who surrounded him. His expectations were fulfilled. He was summoned to Venice to answer for the crime of having solicited foreign intercession with the Venetian Government.

Brought before the Doge and the Council, Giacopo at once acknowledged that his offence had been committed solely to ensure his removal to his native city. The vindictive oligarchs would accept no such touching and simple explanation of his foolish action. They professed to believe that some dark deed, some subtle project, lay concealed beneath the mask of a pretended simplicity. Once more he was racked, and *thirty times* were his agonized limbs stretched upon the fatal cord. He was

* Daru, "Histoire de Venise," tome ii.

borne to his father's apartments bleeding, torn, dislocated, hovering between life and death. His sentence of exile was then renewed, with the addition that the first year should be passed in prison. The only grace accorded him was permission to see his family before their final separation.

> " Then all clung round him, weeping bitterly;
> Weeping the more, because they wept in vain.
> Unnerved, and now unsettled in his mind
> From long and exquisite pain, he sobs and cries,
> Kissing the old man's cheek: 'Help me, my father!
> Let me, I pray thee, live once more among ye:
> Let me go home.'—'My son,' returned the Doge,
> 'Obey. Thy country wills it.'"—ROGERS.

Giacopo reached his Candian prison, where compassionate death, in a few weeks, released him from his unmerited sufferings.

DEPOSITION AND DEATH OF THE DOGE.

For his unhappy father the cup of bitterness was not yet full. He was compelled to play his part as the puppet of a gilded pageant, and to smile on the men whose ingenious cruelty had broken his heart and slain his son. One of the foremost in all these base transactions was a chief of the Ten, Giacopo Loredano, who, conceiving his family to have suffered at the hands of the Doge, though his belief rested on the most trivial suspicions, had bound himself to vengeance by a deadly vow. Having stricken down the lion's whelp, he now aimed at the lion. He moved his associates that Foscari should be deposed from the dogeship, on the ground of his great age and neglect of duty. The Ten shrunk at first from the strange contradiction of compelling an abdication which they had refused to accept when twice volunteered by the Doge. Loredano's influence, however, prevailed, and the Ten requested Foscari to resign the ducal sceptre. The old man replied, that having sworn at the request of the Great Council never to abdicate, he could not violate his oath. The Ten were not to be baffled. Usurping the prerogative of the Great Council, they discharged him from his oath, summarily declared his office vacant, pensioned him with 2000 ducats yearly, and ordered him to quit the ducal palace in three days. Loredano gratified his vengeance by presenting the decree with his own hand. Foscari, not recognizing him, inquired who he was. "I am a son of Marco Memmo," was the answer. "Ah! your father," said the old prince, with a sigh,—"your father was my friend."

> "And now he goes. 'It is the hour and past.
> I have no business here.'—'But wilt thou not
> Avoid the gazing crowd? That way is private.'
> 'No! as I entered, so will I retire.'
> And, leaning on his staff, he left the House,
> His residence for five-and-thirty years,
> By the same stairs up which he came in state:
> Those where the Giants stand, guarding the ascent,
> Monstrous, terrific. At the foot he stopt,
> And, on his staff still leaning, turned and said,
> 'By mine own merits did I come. I go,
> Driven by the malice of mine enemies!'"

The poet is historically accurate. The aged Doge refused to quit the palace by any private exit, but openly descended the Giants' Stairs. He was beloved by the common people, both for his past achievements and his great sufferings. He received their sympathy; but the Council forbade all open expression of it by a peremptory decree: Death for the man that durst mention the deposed prince's name!

THE LEDGER OF VENGEANCE CLOSED.

Five days afterwards Pascale Malipieri was elected Doge. The bell that announced his accession from the campanile of San Marco tolled at the same time Foscari's death-knell. He endeavoured to suppress his agitation when the sounds fell upon his ear, but in the intensity of his mental struggles broke a blood-vessel, and expired at the age of eighty-four. Then Loredano took down one of his ledgers,—for, like most of the Venetian nobles, he was engaged in commerce,—and turned, it is said, to one blank leaf. On the opposite page, among his list of debtors, he had written:—

"Francesco Foscari: for the death of my father and my uncle."

He now took his pen and coldly recorded the discharge of the debt:—"*He has paid me.*"

> "When Foscari's noble heart at length gave way,
> He took the volume from the shelf again
> Calmly, and with his pen filled up the blank,
> Inscribing, 'He has paid me.'"—ROGERS.*

To the reign of Foscari must be ascribed the establishment of the Three Inquisitors of State; two of whom

* See the story of Foscari as told by Sanuto, in the 22nd volume of Muratori; by Sismondi, in his History, vol. x., 41–46; and Daru, in his elaborate work, tome ii.

were selected by the Ten from their own body, and one from the Doge's council; and to whose hands was intrusted almost the whole executive authority of the Republic. The dungeons of Venice were placed at their disposal; the lives and liberties of its citizens, from the Doge to the meanest gondolier, depended upon their will; they controlled the governors, commanders, and ambassadors of the commonwealth; their procedures were entirely secret; they owned themselves responsible to none but the body that annually elected them; they organized and directed an army of spies, at home and abroad, in the council chamber and the palace; they bribed, they tortured, they defamed, and they slew. Never were the liberties of a state more unreservedly sacrificed to secure its material aggrandizement; never was a dark and sanguinary despotism obeyed with a more implicit submission.

LIFE IN VENICE.

Here we may pause to glance at the wealth, power, and social life of Venice in the fifteenth and at the commencement of the sixteenth centuries, preparatory to a rapid survey of her decline and fall.

The Republic at this epoch ruled over an extensive territory. In Italy its possessions included the rich plain which stretches from the Julian Alps to the Adige and the Mincio, as well as the fertile provinces of Brescia, Bergamo, and Crema. The lion of St. Mark placed one paw on the opulent island of Cyprus, and another on that of Candia: while Dalmatia, Istria, and part of

Albania; Argos, the island of Corfu, and Napoli di Romania; Eubœa, and the romantic peninsula of the Morea in Greece, with many of the fairest isles that stud the "blue Ægean Sea," owned the sway of the Venetian government.

As a commercial power, Venice was foremost among the nations of Christendom. She had planted her factories in Egypt, in the Levant, on the shores of the Black Sea. Her ships were the chief carriers of European merchandise. She was the channel through which the spoils of the East flowed into the treasuries of the West. More wealthy than Tyre, she drew to herself the products of every nation. England and Spain sent their wool, Lombardy its flax, for her looms to weave into cloth and linen. Her exquisite manufactures of glass were coveted by all the princes and nobles of Europe, whose wives and daughters decked their locks in her mirrors, and clothed their persons in her glowing silks. Sanuto tells us that she yearly exported goods to the value of 10,000,000 ducats, on which the profits amounted to 4,000,000, showing how large was the rate per cent. obtained by these successful merchants. Their houses were valued at 7,000,000, which yielded an annual rental of 500,000 ducats. The commercial navy of the Republic numbered 3000 ships, carrying 17,000 able seamen; and 300 more ships, with 45 galleys, manned by 19,000 sailors, composed her war-armada. In her busy dockyards 16,000 carpenters were always at work. Her mint coined annually 1,000,000 ducats of gold, 200,000 pieces of silver, and 80,000 solidi. The spices and fruits of Egypt and Syria were paid for at the rate of 50,000 ducats per annum, and the wools of England cost 100,000. The

Venetian merchants sent weekly to the Florentines 7000 ducats in exchange for Catalonian wool, grain, silk, gold and silver, thread, wax, sugar, and violins. Its printing-presses diffused their finely-printed sheets all over Europe, and nobly helped in the great work of the Renaissance. But why multiply these details? Venice, at the time we speak of, was the bank, treasury, and storehouse of Europe; its merchants were princes; its keels furrowed every sea; like Midas in the old fable, all it touched turned to gold. An atmosphere of splendour seemed to surround it, and travellers who visited the fairy City of the Isles gazed in astonishment on the rare luxuries that everywhere dazzled the vision. Like the Arabian in the Oriental tale, they could see nothing but gold, and silver, and gems, apparently amassed by the toils of genii, and not to be touched by the profane hands of barbarians!

The canals were thronged with richly decked gondolas, whose boatmen made the air musical with their measured chants, and whose occupants were radiant in silks and velvets of many colours. The quays glowed with the rich dresses of the burghers, and the fantastic attire of their wives and daughters. Worthy of such brave beings were the houses which they inhabited, many of them being of white Istrian marble, decked out with porphyry and serpentine, and even commoner buildings being built of stone, and very high and stately. The interiors were fitted up with splendid furniture, with rich hangings and tapestry, with glass and mirrors, and with what the Venetian prized still more, the glorious productions of a Titian, a Bellini, and a Tintoretto. The public edifices and the churches exhibited a like magnificence, and the

Byzantine character of their architecture lent them a peculiar air of quaintness. Neither then nor now has Venice seemed to the stranger like a European city; it has always worn an Oriental aspect, though the quick subtle life of the West has throbbed hotly and fiercely under its fantastic foreign mask.

THE VENETIAN GOVERNMENT EXAMINED.

The observer who considers its oligarchical government from a constitutional point of view, never fails to inveigh against its cruel despotic spirit. It is certain that the people had no voice in it; it is not so certain that they felt its harshness, or desired any change in its administration. The Venetian rulers, however, were wise in their generation. They never weighted their subjects with an intolerable taxation; and the revenue, moderately raised, was always economically spent. The government, remarks Sismondi,* cost the people nothing. The people themselves looked with pride upon the employment of their money in the public works. The provinces of the *terra firma* were carefully secured from the exactions of the soldier, and, as far as might be, from the invasion of the enemy. From the period of its foundation, the majesty of Venice had never been profaned by the foe; hostile feet had never trodden its Rialto; foreign princes had never sat in authority in its halls. From the noble to the peasant all were animated by a burning love for their inviolate isles, and all were ready, if the need arose, to give their lives for St. Mark.

* Sismondi, "Histoire des Républiques."

MICHELET ON VENICE.

Of the Venetian government a great French historian has written in defence. What was Venice? he asks.* A city, an empire, he replies; an unique creation of art, which maintained itself by great skill; an Oriental government which we must judge by the infinite difficulties that surrounded it—being at once so small and yet so great, and compelled to keep together an assemblage of twenty different races. This wonderful task was only achieved by an administration no less strong than sagacious, by action as discreet as prompt, which did not scruple at cruelty or force. Nevertheless, when we have penetrated the mystery of terror, we find that the shadows which enveloped its government and gave it strength have been calumniated. The gloom has frightened us, but we see little blood. The state prisons of Venice were not, indeed, of sufficient magnitude to accommodate many prisoners. How shall we compare its Piombi and dungeons with the Bastilles, Spielbergs, and Cronstadts, with which the kings have covered Europe?

All the thinkers of the time — Comines, Machiavel, and Boethius, the latter at heart and in mind an ancient republican—assert that the Venetian was the best of the sixteenth century governments.

There were three things at Venice grand and unique: a grave and economical government—no court, no organized system of pillage, no court favourites; a government which fostered its subjects, opening up new channels for their commerce and their free industry; and, finally, a

* Michelet, "Histoire de France: La Renaissance," pp. 321–323.

government immovable by Roman intrigues, and liberal in the promotion of thought and intellectual enterprise, extending an asylum to bold thinkers as readily as Holland itself. Where was the printing-press free? Where was raised the voice of man in the European public system? In two cities—Venice and Bâle. Erasmus, the Voltaire of the epoch, shared his life between them. From the sacred printing-presses of the Aldi and the Frobens has issued the light of the world. The great revolution which Gutenberg inaugurated came to a height only at Venice, about 1500, when Aldus abandoned the massive *folio* of the pedants for the ubiquitous *octavo*, the father of handy books and rapid pamphlets—innumerable legions of invisible spirits, which did their work in the night, and created under the very eyes of the tyrants the circulation of liberty.

The gloomy streets of Venice, the narrow passages of its canals, the black, hearse-like gondolas which threaded them—behold in these the holy nest of the halcyons, which, in the bosom of the seas, nourished free thought. And who can see without emotion that Piazza of St. Mark, where countless pigeons, mingling with the promenaders, bear witness to Italian tenderness? In this piazza it was—this rendezvous of the human race, this gathering-place of all nations—that Asia spoke to Europe by the voice of Marco Polo; that Humanity, in the mind-bound ages, before the invention of printing, communicated with itself; that the globe had then its brain, its *sensorium*, its first self-consciousness.

THE DISCROWNED QUEEN.

Hitherto we have been dazzled by the glories of the Queen of the Adriatic—by her wealth, her power, her heroism, her successes. In the great blaze of the meridian sun we have scarcely noticed its spots. But henceforth the lustre gradually dies out of the picture. We seem to follow a conqueror to his grave. It is as if some jubilant and triumphant strain of music painfully closed in a protracted dirge.

All Athens hated Aristides because he was just. All Europe hated Venice because of her good fortune. The Pope had a special cause of enmity in her steadfast defiance of the authority of the Church. In pursuance of his daring designs of aggrandizing St. Peter's chair, Pope Julius II. resolved to crush her power, and found little difficulty in securing the co-operation of the Emperor and the Kings of France and Spain. At the outset he approached Venice with a caressing hand and a gentle voice, and entreated her, as a true daughter of the Church, to restore those portions of the Romagna and Rimini which, he said, justly belonged to the Holy See. Venice replied that she had recently won them by the sword from Cæsar Borgia, and by the sword would keep them. Immediately Julius clothed himself in apostolic dignity, and denounced Venice as rebellious and ungrateful, heretical and accursed (A.D. 1508). Then was formed the famous League of Cambray, which banded the four greatest European powers against the doomed Republic. Louis of France took the field in hot haste. With

12,000 horse and 20,000 foot he crossed the Adda, and encountered the Venetians, under Pittigliano and D'Alviano, at Agnadello (May 14). The former general, with half the force, was too cravenly cautious, and perhaps at too great a distance, to render the gallant D'Alviano any help; and, after a desperate struggle, the victory remained with the French. Six thousand Venetians lay dead upon the field, having fallen in grim order as they had fought. Onward pushed the triumphant Louis. Caravaggio, Peschiera, Cremona, successively fell into his hands, and the echoes of his cannon startled the marble colonnades of Venice. But the merchant-princes of the Republic bated not one iota of heart or hope. Every citizen flew to arms; the city was placed in a position to withstand a siege; a fleet of fifty galleys was rapidly equipped; private wealth was poured into the empty treasury; the garrisons in Greece and Illyria were recalled to the defence of their country; and from morn to night, and night to morn, the capital resounded with the din of preparation. The Venetian rulers also took thought how they might eke out the lion's skin with the fox's. If they could not conquer they might divide their enemies. To deal with perfidious France was fruitless, and would be degrading; but to the Pope they might apply with success, for if he hated a free Venice, he hated France and Germany much more. He was an ambitious priest, but he was also an Italian, and he saw and felt that Venice was the brain and heart of Italy.*

* This rapid summary is founded on Guicciardini (lib. viii., vol. 2); Brantome's "Vie de Louis XII.;" and Michelet's "Histoire de la Renaissance."

THE TABLES TURNED.

The Republic offered him the Romagna, and asked for absolution. To Maximilian, the German Emperor, who was so poor as to be surnamed "the Penniless," she proffered the acceptable donation of 50,000 ducats. Meanwhile, the Pope was pleased to forgive the suppliant Republic, and astonished the world by a sublime edict, which released it from the censures of the Church and the allies from the engagements of the Treaty of Cambray (A.D. 1510). He then united his forces with those of Venice, which saw itself rescued from ruin at the very moment that hope seemed impossible. Having pacified the King of Spain by the investiture of Naples, the redoubtable Pontiff* led his army against the French, and besieged Mirandola. Strange turn of Fortune's wheel!—singular change of scene! First, the League of Cambray unites Germany, France, Spain, and the Holy See against Venice: now, the Holy League unites the Pope, Spain, and Venice against France! (A.D. 1511.) The banner of the *fleur-de-lis*, however, asserted its old

* Michelet has sketched the portrait of Julius with great vigour:—"A hard and violent Genoese, changeable as the winds of his native state, engaged the attention of all Europe by his rough outbreaks and military prowess. Men laughed at a Father of the Faithful who preached nothing but death, blood, and ruin—whose benedictions were cannonades. He was an old man, seemingly about eighty, wrinkled, bent, avaricious, but only for the needs of war. He was choleric, especially after drink, though he never drank to excess. He never neglected the interests of his family, but really loved only the grandeur of the Holy See, its temporal greatness, the aggrandizement of the patrimony of St. Peter. For this purpose he dared everything. Men saw him at Mirandola push the assault; a bullet traversed his tent, and killed two men: not the less he directed the approaches, lodging under fire in the midst of trembling cardinals, and would fain have entered the breach."—*La Renaissance*, p. 333.

renown, and the chivalrous Bayard inspired his countrymen with emulous patriotism. At Brescia and at Ravenna,—where the illustrious Gaston de Foix terminated so prematurely his career of glory,—the arms of France were victorious; but her weakened army could not afford the cost of these victories, and, dispirited but not dishonoured, its generals led it back across the snowy Alps. Maximilian then abandoned his old ally, and accepted the Venetian ducats. All Northern Italy shook off the French yoke, and Venice found herself relieved from fear of her enemies. The formidable league, which had portended utter annihilation, apparently left her dominions unimpaired, with the exception of the Romagna, ceded to the Papal Church (A.D. 1513).

CAUSES OF VENETIAN DECLINE.

Yet from this time Venice ceased to be a European power, and her decline was as rapid as her growth had been surprising. Twice more, indeed, she vindicated her ancient military prestige: at Marignano, where, in alliance with the French, her troops inflicted a crushing defeat on the Swiss and Spaniards (September 15, 1515); and again at Lepanto, where her fleet (October 7, 1570), in conjunction with the Spaniards, repulsed — almost annihilated — the Turkish armada, and checked the Moslem in his advance upon Christendom. This last was a great service to Europe, and worthily closes what may be termed the European annals of Venice.

THE STRUGGLE WITH THE POPE.

Yet in her after-history there occurs one memorable passage, which shows her possessed of her ancient spirit, and capable of living up to her old renown. We refer to her struggle with Pope Paul V.,—a struggle on the part of the civil power to prevent the predominance of the ecclesiastical; a struggle for the privileges of civil liberty and the supremacy of civil law. And in this great and all-important struggle, whose benefits all Europe is now enjoying, it has justly been said that the part played by the Venetian Government was one to merit the admiration and gratitude of mankind.*

The reaction which had taken place after the Lutheran Reformation had enabled Rome to recover a considerable share of her former power and influence, and to rivet her chains more firmly over the larger portion of the European continent. This reaction was partly due to the reform effected in the Roman Church itself; a reform which had purified the morals of her priesthood, and restored the strict observance of at least an external piety; and partly to the foundation of the remarkable brotherhood of the Jesuits, whose zeal, implicit obedience, and unscrupulous ability were steadily directed to one great end—the universal establishment of the authority of Rome. These causes were largely operating in favour of the ancient Church,—which, moreover, appealed to the minds and hearts of men by the traditional claims of a venerable antiquity and the splendour of a ceremonial worship, no less than by her lofty

* T. A. Trollope, "Paul the Pope and Paul the Friar," *passim.*

assertion of infallibility, and her supposed possession of exclusive privileges—when Paul IV. was elevated to the Papacy. Originally bred as a lawyer, he was a man of limited judgment, narrow views, and a very imperfect comprehension of the spirit and tendencies of his age. Instead of patiently watching the course of events, and allowing the Catholic reaction to spread in secret, or promoting it by judiciously lending the influence of the Church in support of those European sovereigns whom fear or necessity might induce to pay for it by large concessions, he sought to establish by one grand effort the supreme authority of the Pontiff, and to sweep away all the restrictions with which the more independent European Governments had hemmed in the ecclesiastical power.

It was in Italy that he first began this dangerous scheme of aggrandizement; and it was here that he met with a check as unexpected as it was fatal. Availing himself of the dogmas laid down and confirmed by the General Council of Trent—a parliament of priests and ecclesiastics, which had held a series of sittings, from 1545 to 1563, for the decision and settlement of the articles of Christian faith—he began the war at Naples. Here an ecclesiastical notary, who had refused to give notice of a marriage to a civil court, as the law required, had been sentenced to the galleys. Paul demanded his release, and when it was refused, hurled an excommunication at the viceroy, who thereupon gave way. Elated with his victory, he next insisted at Malta, and afterwards in Savoy and Parma, on the right of presentation to certain benefices, and in each case he triumphed. On other points of government he was victorious at Lucca and Genoa ; and it seemed as if he was really destined to attain his desired object, and completely establish the supremacy of the ecclesiastical power.

He now resolved to enter the lists against Venice ; a Government which had ever been peculiarly jealous of its own rights, and had cautiously guarded against the admission of ecclesiastics—an order of men owning allegiance to a foreign sovereign—to any degree of power and influence in the state ; a Government which had always, and resolutely, opposed the pretensions of the Papacy, and consequently had never been held by the Roman court in any particular favour or esteem. Various troublesome and irritating questions had, within the last two years, arisen between the two powers ; and in conducting them, Venice had been materially assisted by the opinion and advice of one of her most remarkable sons, Frà Paolo Sarpi—a monk and yet a patriot, a liberal thinker and yet a member of the Romish Church, an ecclesiastic and yet a bold opponent of the extravagant claims of the ecclesiastical power. He was a man of original genius, and shrewd, clear intellect, who had thought out his religious belief for himself, and seems to have devised an *ideal* church, to be created by purifying the Romish Church from her accrescent corruptions. How impossible this was, and is—how logical Rome is, and has ever been, in her claims, her deductions, and her very errors—how intimately her teaching and her practice are bound up together—was no more perceived by many clear and powerful minds in Frà Paolo's day than it is at present. He remained, therefore, in the

Romish communion, while steadfastly denouncing the ambition and resisting the encroachments of its Head, and, though a Servite monk, was the life and soul of the struggle waged by his country with the ecclesiastical power.

It happened that at this time the Venetian Government had thrown into prison two priests who had been guilty of the most infamous crimes—a certain Count Brandolino, abbot of Nervesa, and a certain Canon Saraceni, of Vicenza. These acts of justice were denounced by the Papal court as encroachments of the civil power on the recognized ecclesiastical immunities; and Paul V., appealing to the decisions of the Tridentine Council, declared he would not suffer any jurisdiction to be assumed by any civil authority over any ecclesiastical person whatsoever. He also demanded that the two priests should be surrendered to the officers of the Church.

But the Pope had a further ground of hostility against Venice. The Republic, alarmed at the number of monastic establishments existing in their territories, and at their increasing absorption of new property in land or houses, had passed laws forbidding the introduction of any new religious order, or the foundation of any church, monastery, or almshouse, without express license from the Government.

"The motives," says Mr. Trollope,* "on which the Venetian Government had originally based these laws, and at various subsequent dates confirmed and renewed them, and on which it now defended them against the opposition of the Pope, were, as set forth in their replies to the court of Rome, the loss which the state suffered by the

* T. A. Trollope, "Paul the Pope and Paul the Friar," p. 163.

exemption from taxation of so large a portion of the property of the nation, the impossibility of obtaining from the necessarily overtaxed remainder the amount of money needed by the administration for the protection of the country, and especially, as it was urged, for rendering that service to Christendom in general which Venice had ever hitherto afforded by making herself a strong and efficient bulwark against the infidel."

To these pleas, however, and to the arguments in defence of the right of every government to supreme authority over all offenders, whether civil or ecclesiastical, Pope Paul refused to listen. He asserted that as "head of the Church" he was above all men and supreme over all law, divinely intrusted with boundless and irresponsible authority, able to make and unmake kings, and supreme ruler of the earth. Counselled by Sarpi, the Republic denied and resisted these extravagant pretensions, and under the stately rule of the Doge Leonardo Donato—described by Sarpi himself as a "senator esteemed beyond all question the most eminent of the patrician body for the purity of his life, which had been stainless from its youth upwards, for experience in affairs of state, for accuracy of scholarship, wide literary acquirements, and the practice of all noble virtues"—it bore itself throughout the arduous struggle with becoming dignity and moderation. It appealed for sympathy and support to civilized Europe, through the potent pen of the terrible friar, and, meanwhile, refused to surrender its two criminals or to abrogate its laws. In an interview with the Papal Nuncio at Venice, the Doge said, loftily—and in the spirit of those proud English nobles who in the old time declared, "Nolumus leges Angliæ mutari"—"I will not omit to say, most reverend lord, that as I am ready, even at my advanced age, to grasp once more the sword in defence of the Church, even as my ancestors have so often done, so, on the other hand, am I prepared to do the same for the maintenance of our liberties and the honour of the Republic."

To this noble speech the bigoted Pope replied with the thunders of excommunication. In spite of counsel and warning from faithful friends of the Holy See, he drew from the ecclesiastical armoury a weapon which had once been of good use, but was wholly unfit for combat in the seventeenth century. On the 17th of April 1606 was published the fatal document, by which (unless within seven and twenty days full satisfaction had been made) the Doge, the Senate, and the Republic of Venice, were, by the authority of God, of St. Peter and St. Paul, and of Paul V., declared excommunicate, and the city and dominions of Venice placed under interdict; "so that no mass could be celebrated, no sacrament administered, no bell sounded, in all the accursed land."

The game which Paul V. played was a perilous one, and he soon discovered that he had underrated the courage and ability of his adversaries. Instead of being awed into submission by this stroke of Papal vengeance, they were roused to bolder action. Leaving Sarpi with ever-busy pen to state their case to the world, and their ambassadors to exercise the acts of diplomacy in securing the support of the European governments, the Venetian Senate met the move of the Pontiff by a resolute counter-move. They issued a proclamation commanding the clergy to continue divine service without regard to the interdict, against which they entered a formal protest, and they made provision to guard against its introduction into their territory. Against recalcitrant priests, who refused to obey this proclamation, they adopted severe penal measures; and when the three orders of the Jesuits, Capuchins, and Theatines persisted in fidelity to the Holy See, they expelled them from Venice. They found themselves supported in their defiance of Rome by France and the smaller European states, as well as by England, whose ambassador, the famous Sir Henry Wotton, was frank and energetic in his denunciation of the Papal tyranny, and encouraged them in their gallant resistance.

Thus stood the quarrel. Month after month passed by, and the Republic showed no sign of yielding, while every day the Papal position grew more untenable. The most dreaded weapon of the Church was shown to have lost its potency; its edge was irrecoverably blunted. Meanwhile a crowd of hornets buzzed about the unlucky Pope, and inflicted a succession of terrible stings. Sarpi's pen was incessant and powerful; and he was supported by a legion of writers in all countries and languages, who discovered the numerous crevices in the Papal armour, and proved to an amused world the fallibility of the would-be infallible. Paul V. found himself forced to retreat, and in the agony of his mortification resorted to the good offices of Henry IV. of France, who from the first had endeavoured to effect a reconciliation between the two opponents, and now, at the Pope's instance, despatched his kinsman, Cardinal de Joyeuse, to Italy as a mediator.

He was received by the Doge with all honour on the 17th of February 1607.

It is unnecessary to dwell upon the details of the negotiations that ensued. They were conducted with great ability on both sides; but it soon became apparent that Venice had not the slightest intention of yielding any of the important points in dispute, and that if peace were to be concluded, the Pope must abandon his exorbitant pretensions. Some minor concessions the Republic made, but they carefully guarded against any abandonment of the rights of the civil power; they insisted on the removal of the Interdict; and before all, they sternly refused to permit the return of the Jesuits. Beaten and baffled, Rome gave way. The wound she had received in the struggle was severe. "Never again could the great weapon of the Interdict be brought out for the coercion of disobedient nations. The most powerful engine in Rome's arsenal was broken and ruined irreparably. Like an old cannon, spiked, and known to be harmless by everybody, it might still be displayed on the insecure battlements of the Papal fortress, in the hope that some might still be ignorant enough to be terrified by the look of it at a distance." But thenceforth she was compelled to lower her tone and abate her pretensions. The courage and prudence of the Republic had won a victory for which all Europe has reason to be grateful.

In this victory Frà Paolo had no small share. He had helped to bear the brunt of the battle, and so a portion of the glory was rightly his. The Senate heaped honours upon him, and rewarded him with well-earned praise and well-deserved confidence. Here, then, was a victim on whom the baffled Pope could wreak his vengeance, and to get him within his power, he was "invited" to Rome to defend and justify his rebellious conduct. But Frà Paolo was too prudent to be so easily entrapped, and declined the invitation urged upon his acceptance. He quietly continued to divide his time between the duties of his office at the ducal palace, and the learned leisure of his cell in the Servite Convent.

Then Rome resolved upon stronger measures for the punishment of her powerful adversary—an adversary all the more to be dreaded because he lived in the bosom of the Church itself. From various quarters he received hints of impending danger; but nothing, says Mr. Trollope, could induce Sarpi to believe, low as he esteemed the morality of the Roman Court, that the holy father could descend to the level of a common assassin. He, however, attended so far to the counsel of his friends as to cause himself to be accompanied by three friars, in his daily walk from his convent to the Ducal Palace, and back again in the evening. But it so happened that in the dusk of the 5th of October 1607, his companions having been unexpectedly detained, the friar started homewards with no other attendants than his servant, Fra Mamio, a lay brother of the convent, and the patrician Malipero, an infirm and aged man. Suddenly a band of ruffians sprang upon them, one of whom seized the old patrician, another the lay brother, while a third dealt a shower of poniard stabs on the person of the friar. Of these, only three wounded him—two in the neck, and one which passed into the head behind the ear, and came out at the root of the nose on the same side of the face. The dagger remained firmly fixed in the bones of the face, and Sarpi fell to the ground as if dead.* Some women, who had seen the deed from a neighbouring window, raised an alarm, and people hurried to the spot. The assassins then liberated their two captives, and firing their pieces in the air to create excitement and occasion confusion, succeeded in escaping; while Sarpi, who was found to be still breathing, was immediately carried to his cell in the convent close at hand.

The indignation which this atrocious crime aroused in Venice was extraordinary. Neither the Papal Nuncio nor his family durst leave their house for several days, and the populace would assuredly have burnt it to the ground had not troops been dispatched to protect it. Crowds surrounded the Servite Convent, anxious for tidings of the sufferer. The Council of Ten adopted various measures for his future protection, and the government summoned the most famous physicians in Italy to watch over his condition. It was ascertained that the leader of the assassins was one Ridolfo Poma; four thousand ducats were offered for his capture, and two thousand ducats for any of his companions. They escaped, however, to Rome, and were secretly sheltered by the Papal Government. Meanwhile, an outcry of disgust and indignation was raised from one end of Europe to the other against the Roman Court, which soon found that by the act designed to gratify its vengeance it had dealt yet another blow at its influence over the minds of men.

* T. A. Trollope, "Paul the Pope and Paul the Friar," pp. 364, 365.

It is satisfactory to state that Frà Paolo recovered, and enjoyed many years of laborious life in the service of his country and the world.*

Though, in this great struggle with the Church, the Venetian Republic had displayed a spirit and an energy worthy of its palmiest days, yet not the less surely had the hour of its decadence come. Our limits forbid any attempt to set forth its successive stages.

The discovery of the New World by Columbus, of the passage to India round the Cape of Good Hope by Vasco di Gama, were two great causes of its downfal, by diverting commerce into new channels. But not only did Venice decline, other powers rose. It was the rapid growth of Holland, France, Spain, and England, as maritime nations, that sealed her destiny. The greatest commercial power will always have the greatest navy; and as the western empires absorbed the world's commerce, so they gradually gathered immense fleets, which effectually deprived Venice of all pretensions to the sovereignty of the seas. One by one she lost her fairest colonies; her fame and influence sunk; and with the old imperial power died away the old imperial spirit. Something of her decay was due to the inherent vices of her form of government; much to the luxurious indolence that took possession of her citizens. It may be said of them, that they absolutely wallowed in foul and loathsome lusts. After the peace of Passarowitz, in 1718, which limited

* For a fuller account of this remarkable historical episode the reader may consult Bianchi Giovani's "Biografia di Frà Paolo Sarpi" (2 vols., Zurich, 1836); "Westminster Review," vol. xxxi.; Ranke's "History of the Popes;" and T. A. Trollope's "Paul the Pope and Paul the Friar" (London, 1861).

her dominions to portions of Lombardy, Friuli, and Istria, parts of Dalmatia, and Albania, and the Ionian Islands, with a population of about 2,500,000 souls,—after the peace of Passarowitz, and during the brief remainder of her independent existence, Venice sought distinction as a general mart for pleasure. She became the Capua of modern Europe, "the loose and wanton" realm,—

> ". . . Her court where naked Venus keeps,
> And Cupids ride the Lion of the deeps.".

Long prosperity and prodigious opulence, says Mr. Howells, had done their worst; and the patricians and the lowest classes of the people, their creatures and dependents, were thoroughly corrupt; while the men of professions began to assume that station which they now hold, and in the schools the children of the bourgeoisie surpassed those of the nobles in quickness and learning. Beneath this certainly respectable middle class were the idle, dissolute people, amused with a succession of public shows and brutal sports; and above them were the patricians, who spent themselves in the invention of new pleasures, and the enjoyment of the old ones. The picture which Venetian writers paint of the last days of the Republic is one of the most shameless ignorance, the most polished corruption, and the most unblushing baseness.

Its last Doge was Luigi Manini. It was he who surrendered the capital to Napoleon Bonaparte in 1797, and signed the death-warrant of a state which had lived too long for its own fame. By the treaty of Campo Formio, Istria, Dalmatia, Venice and the Dogado were transferred to Austria; and by Austria the Venetian territories were held with a hand of iron, never disguised by the silken glove,* until the Prussian war of 1866 opened up a means of relief from their bitter thraldom. By the treaty of Prague, between the King of Prussia and the Emperor of Austria, they were allowed to determine their future fate by the now popular method of a vote by universal suffrage. Almost to one man, the loyal Venetians, who had longed for years to breathe the fresh air of liberty, decreed their annexation to the kingdom of

* The Venetians made a bold effort in 1848–9 to recover their independence. Austria at the time was distracted by the revolution which had broken out in Hungary and Vienna, and the Italian provinces seized the opportunity to throw off a detested yoke. In Venice a republic was proclaimed, and Daniel Manin, a man cast by nature in the old heroic mould, was elected, first its president, and afterwards dictator. Hopes were entertained of succour from the Piedmontese and Lombards; but Austria pouring a large army into the Milanese under the veteran Radetzky, the Sardinian army was annihilated on the field of Novara. The good offices of England and France were solicited, but neither government was at that time prepared to disturb what was called "the balance of power in Europe." Thus abandoned to their own resources, the Venetians continued the struggle with a courage and a resolution worthy of the best days of the Republic. The garrison was composed almost wholly of volunteers; but they fought with incredible valour, and endured with sublime patience the most terrible sufferings. To provide the government with funds, the citizens poured into the treasury all their little hoards, their plate, their personal ornaments, and their jewels; and the most delicate ladies attended on the sick and wounded with tender solicitude. Venice would have been saved if patriotism and enthusiasm could have supplied the place of battalions and artillery, provisions and stores. But the struggle was too unequal. Towards the end of August, the supply of bread in the city was utterly exhausted, and the horrors of famine were enhanced by those of pestilence. Out of a population scarcely exceeding 200,000, two hundred died daily of cholera alone. The Venetians persevered to the last, and finally extorted from the Austrians honourable terms of capitulation, which were formally accepted by besiegers and besieged on the 24th of August 1849. Daniel Manin, the leader of the chivalrous struggle, immediately quitted Venice with his wife and daughter, and retired to Paris, where he earned a livelihood by giving lessons in Italian, until, widowed and childless, broken-hearted and exhausted, he died of disease of the heart, September 22, 1857, in his fifty-fourth year.

Italy (641,758 votes against 69); and welcomed Victor Emmanuel into their liberated capital with banners and triumphal music, and such shouts as men only give when released from a cruel and hateful slavery. May a day of brightness, sunshine, and prosperity now dawn upon the old historic City of the Isles! Englishmen, forgetful of her faults, mindful of her grand achievements, remembering her Dandolos, Pisanis, and Zenos, will echo the prayer of all loyal Italians,—*Esto Perpetua!*

> "Once did she hold the gorgeous East in fee;
> And was the safeguard of the West: the worth
> Of Venice did not fall below her birth,
> Venice, the eldest child of Liberty.
> She was a maiden city, bright and free,
> No guile seduced, no force could violate;
> And, when she took unto herself a mate,
> She must espouse the everlasting Sea.
> And what if she had seen those glories fade,
> Those titles vanish, and that strength decay;
> Yet shall some tribute of regret be paid
> When her long life hath reached its final day:
> Men are we, and must grieve when even the shade
> Of that which once was great is passed away."
>
> WORDSWORTH.

In conclusion, let us express our gratification that the material prosperity of Venice is reviving under the auspices of the Italian Government. Her trade, which had been gradually declining, has undergone a remarkable resuscitation; her port is crowded with ships; railways on the mainland connect her with the heart and life of Italy; new buildings are springing up on a colossal scale; and her citizens seem to have thrown off the lethargy which so long oppressed them. Her manufactures of glass, jewellery, gold and silver stuffs, laces, silks, velvets, and the like, are slowly but surely increasing; and a recent visitor (Mr. A. H. Layard), whose authority is beyond dispute, bears the frankest testimony to the new vigour and energy which animate

THE QUEEN OF THE ADRIATIC.

BRIDGE OF THE RIALTO.

Part Second.

THE FINE ARTS, LITERATURE, MANNERS AND CUSTOMS OF VENICE.

———o———

The whole world without art and dress
Would be one great wilderness.

BUTLER.

I.

The Fine Arts in Venice.

For after-ages shall retrack thy beams,
And put aside the crowd of busy ones,
And worship ye alone—the master-minds,
The thinkers, the explorers, the creators!

ROBERT BROWNING.

F Venice owes much of her past greatness to her warriors and statesmen, she owes most of her present renown to her sculptors and painters. Barren victories and political triumphs are soon forgotten by the world, or remembered only by the student of history; but the masterpieces of the artist challenge the admiration of ages, and for ever preserve the fame of the State that gave them birth. Thousands who have never heard of Zeno or Morosini have gazed with delight on the work of Sansovino, or stood enraptured before the glowing canvas of Titian. These "things of beauty" the world never willingly lets die, and generation after generation repeats the grateful praise due to their creators.

Sculpture in Venice flourished chiefly in connection

with architecture. It formed no particular school, and was distinguished by no national characteristics. It gave to posterity none of those glorious statues which represent the ideal of strength or beauty formed by a sensitive and refined people, but was mainly employed in the decoration of the superb edifices raised in obedience to the demands of wealth, luxury, or ambition. In this way it wrought laboriously and successfully. There is much to admire, and more to study, in the sculptured ornament of the stones of Venice. No connoisseur can fail to detect the excellencies of the tomb of the Doge Vitale Falieri (belonging to the close of the eleventh century) in the cathedral of St. Mark; or that of the Dogaressa Felicia, wife of Vitale Michieli (of the twelfth); or the surpassing beauty of the monuments of Morosini and Gradenigo. Scarcely less note-worthy are the statues of the Twelve Apostles ranged upon the balustrade of the choir of St. Mark, executed about 1394 by Giacobello and Pietro Paolo; the ancient image of the Virgin, a bas-relief, dating from 1345, which is now placed above the principal entrance of the Academy of the Fine Arts; the finely-wrought bas-reliefs on the tomb of the Doge Andrea Dandolo, belonging to the same period, in the baptistery of St. Mark; and the rich bronze gates of the Ducal Church, cast in 1300 by Maestro Bertuccio, a goldsmith of Venice, and distinguished by their unrivalled beauty.

But the most remarkable and original works of the sculpture of this epoch are the capitals that crown the pillars of the Doge's Palace, supposed to have been designed and wrought by Filippo Calendario. It is astonishing what a wealth of fancy and poetic feeling have been lavished upon these. Our youthful readers will perhaps be surprised that we can speak in such warm terms of productions so apparently trivial. The capital of a column! What is it? A hundredweight of stone, embellished with a wreath, or mayhap a figure or two, or a sheaf of foliage. No; it is, or it may be, something more. It may be a proof of the care with which Genius elaborates the smallest detail. It may illustrate the truth that the good workman thinks nothing unworthy of his best labour, and will finish off a corbel with as much thoughtful completeness as the span of some noble arch, or the breadth of some magnificent façade. The young too often forget that perfect work is the result of conscientious attention to the minutest details.

These capitals are composed of exquisite tufts of leaves, amid which, like Ariel lurking under the blossom that hangs on the bough, or fairies in a lily's cup, certain symbolical figures are engaged: such as Chastity, Injustice, Avarice, Temperance, Alacrity,—all full of life and movement, and treated with great delicacy by the sculptor's chisel. They are instinct, moreover, with a deep meaning. Far from being the sudden inspiration of a fertile fancy, they would seem to have been the result of prolonged meditation, and, as personifications of the virtues and vices, intended to awake religious thoughts in the mind of the spectator.

Let us take an example or two.

On one side of the ninth capital is the figure of *Faith*. She has her left hand on her breast, and the cross in her right, inscribed, "Fides optima in Deo."

We may compare it with Spenser's description of Fidelia:—

> "She was arrayèd all in lily white,
> And in her right hand bore a cup of gold,
> With wine and water filled up to the height,
> In which a serpent did himself enfold,
> That horror made to all that did behold;
> But she no whit did change her constant mood:
> And in her other hand she fast did hold
> A booke, that was both signed and sealed with blood;
> Wherein dark things were writ, hard to be understood."

On the second side, Fortitude is presented as Samson tearing open a lion's jaw. On the third, Temperance bears a pitcher of water and a cup. On the fourth, Humility, with her head veiled, carries a lamb in her lap. The fifth side is devoted to Charity; a woman with her lap full of loaves, giving one to a child, who stretches his arm out for it across a broad gap in the leafage of the capital.

Justice, crowned, and with her sword, appears on the sixth side. On the seventh, Prudence: "a man with a hook and a pair of compasses, wearing the noble cap, hanging down towards the shoulder, and bound in a fillet round the brow, as occurs so frequently during the fourteenth century in Italy in the portraits of men occupied in any civil capacity."

On the eighth side, Hope is personified as a woman, full of devotional expression, holding up her folded palms as in prayer, and looking to a hand outstretched towards her from the midst of sunbeams.*

The reader will now understand with what patience,

* Ruskin, "Stones of Venice," ii. 336–341.

labour, and thoughtful care the sculptor of the Ducal Palace did his work.

Towards the end of the fifteenth century, what is called the Tuscan School of Sculpture, renewed and reinvigorated by Donatello, passed from Pisa to Florence, and thence extended its influence over all Italy. Andreas Ricci of Padua, who, from the excellence of his works in bronze, has been called the Venetian Lysippus, accomplished much in the sumptuous decoration of palaces and churches.

Among the most important monuments of this period we may name, in the first place, the tomb of the Doge Nicolas Trono, in the church of the Frari, raised and ornamented by Antonio Bregno, who was also the architect of the grand façade of the court of the Ducal Palace and of the Giants' Staircase. In the grandeur of its proportions it becomes an edifice in itself; and is copiously enriched with statues and bas-reliefs. The statues, nineteen in number, and larger than life, are especially remarkable for their richly-flowing draperies, equal in grace of outline to the finest Greek works. Lorenzo Bregno, brother or son of the preceding, also distinguished himself as a sculptor: the statue of Benedetto Pesaro, in the church of the Frari; the three life-size figures on the altar of St. Christina, in the church of S. Mater Domini; and the statue of the condottière, or soldier of fortune, Naldi de Brisighella, at SS. Giovanni-e-Paolo, are from his chisel.

The school founded by the Lombardis was also distinguished for its sculpture work, and before all for its ornamental sculpture. And here we should observe that before the days of Donatello and Michael Angelo, high-art sculpture, understood in the Greek sense—that is, as statuary—held but a subordinate rank in the practice of the artists of the Middle Ages and the Renaissance. The majority of the works of the chisel, from the twelfth to the sixteenth century, are simply auxiliaries of architecture. The bas-reliefs so universally employed in the tombs and churches were only accessories of a decorative character, and the system adopted in their composition and arrangement was derived from that in vogue for paintings and mosaics. The statues, generally of small dimensions, and most frequently enclosed in niches, were but one of the numerous parts of the great whole, and their peculiar effect was subordinated to the general effect of the monument on which they figured.

Sculptures belonging to the school of the Lombardis are very numerous at Venice, and nearly all, as we have just said, are connected with architectural compositions. We shall mention only two monuments wherein the distinctive spirit of this school is revealed in a singularly felicitous and characteristic manner: the Zeno chapel, in St. Mark, and the tomb of the Doge Vendramin, in the church of SS. Giovanni-e-Paolo.*

The Cardinal Giovanni Baptista Zeno left considerable legacies, by his will, to various churches and to the Republic. The grateful senate decreed that his memory should be honoured by a sepulchral monument in one of the chapels attached to the Ducal Palace. At first, the work was entrusted to Antonio Lombardi and Alessandro Leopardi. The latter, for some unknown reason, was

* Leon Galibert, "Histoire de Venise," p. 291.

replaced by Zuana Alberghetto and Pietro Zuan della Campana, under the direction of Pietro Lombardi the elder. The tomb, placed in the middle of the chapel, is a simple quadrangular sarcophagus of bronze, on which reposes the cardinal's effigy, in all the pomp of sacerdotal robes: the four sides are adorned with isolated figures, three on each side, supporting the cornice in the manner of caryatides—the whole being of admirable workmanship. The altar, likewise of bronze, with its statues and its carvings, is a marvel of elegance, airy lightness, and perfect taste.

The Vendramin tomb was formerly placed in the church of the Servites (or Servi), one of the largest in Venice; demolished under the revolutionary government, it has since been reconstructed according to the original design, and erected in the church of SS. Giovanni-e-Paolo. Like most of the funereal monuments of this epoch, which were generally built up against a wall, it consists of a simple façade of two Composite orders, placed one above another, resting on a substructure of pilasters, which, in its turn, was elevated on a stylobate or platform of some feet in height. Between the two central columns stands the funereal urn, occupying the entire width of the intercolumniation. All the open portions are enriched with sculptures, and loaded with bas-reliefs; the chisel is everywhere conspicuous. Statues ranged around the sarcophagus, in lateral niches, on pedestals at the angles of the monument, complete the decoration. To Alessandro Leopardi should be ascribed the largest share in the invention and execution of this mausoleum, on which, however, many other artists laboured, and notably Tullio

Lombardi, creator of the statues of Adam and Eve. We say, "creator," for these statues seem to live and breathe: the life of genius has in them

> "So distinctly wrought,
> That one might almost say their bodies thought!"

This is, in truth, the masterpiece of the Venetian sculpture at its happiest moment, and, in conjunction with the palazzo Vendramin, the most exquisite product of the school of the Lombardis. It is a singular fortune for the Doge Vendramin, the descendant of a banker who had paid in ducats for the honour of having his name inscribed in the *Libro d' Oro*, that the two finest monuments of Venetian sculpture and architecture should have been executed for him or his kin, and bear his name!

We should have liked to say something of Bartolomeo Buono, of Guglielmo Bergamasco, and Antonio Dentone, but the exigency of our limited space precludes us from more than this brief reference. We pass on to the sixteenth century, which was eminently rich in illustrious artists.

Foremost among these we place Jacopo Sansovino,* who, from the number and importance of his works, holds the same distinguished relation to Venice as Michael Angelo to Florence, Palladio to Vicenza, and Sanmicheli to Verona. He was not less successful as a sculptor than as an architect; and more than any other master contributed to determine that evidently

* Jacopo Sansovino was born at Florence in January 1479: he died in his ninety-second year, on the 2nd of November 1570.

Florentine taste which, after the time of Michael Angelo, predominated in Venetian sculpture, and throughout all Italy. His own works, and those of his immediate scholars, such as Tiziano Minio, and Desiderio, author of the baptismal fonts of St. Mark, are in the most characteristic Florentine style. Venice is full of his statues and bas-reliefs in bronze and marble. The two colossal statues which adorn the Giants' Staircase, executed by him at the age of seventy-five, are the best known, though not the finest, owing to their too direct imitation of Michael Angelo. Greater originality, elegance, and freedom of touch are visible in the statuette of St. John of the baptismal fonts of the Frari church, in the seated statue of Marco da Ravenna on the gate of the church of S. Justin, in the figure of Apollo and other statues placed in the intercolumniations of the Loggia del Campanile. He especially displayed his genius in his Madonnas—a favourite subject with the Italian artists *—which he treated with poetic sensibility and tender feeling: we may refer, in proof of our remarks, to the Madonna in the Loggia, to another on the altar of the little church in the rear of the Ducal Palace, and to a third on the inner gate of the Arsenal. His great work, however, is the bronze gate of the sacristy of St. Mark, which cost him, it is said, twenty years of patient labour, and which he appropriately inscribed *Opus Jacobi Sansovini*, as if he would have said, "*The* work of Jacopo Sansovini." It is a happy imitation of Lorenzo Ghiberti's unrivalled gates of the baptistery at Florence, which Sansovino, we doubt not, had frequently sketched in his art-apprenticeship: the

* See Mrs. Jameson's "Sacred and Legendary Art: Legends of the Madonna."

two principal panels represent the Resurrection and the Entombment. In the small niches excavated along the rim or border are placed the Evangelists; and the six small busts projecting at the four corners, and on either side of the leaf, are portraits of the artist himself and of some of his friends. Among the latter, we recognize the grave brow of Titian and the audacious physiognomy of Arétino.*

From the school of Sansovino issued a number of able sculptors, several of whom have acquired a worthy position in art, and whose works we meet in Venice at every step. Among these illustrious heirs of the Florentine master, Danase Cattaneo, of Carrara,† combined the talents, not often found united, of architect and man of letters, sculptor and poet. In the statuary work of the Doge Loredano's tomb, in one of the chapels of St. Giovanni-e-Paolo, some symptoms are visible, however, of that meretricious taste for the picturesque which infected the sculpture of the next century. Cattaneo had an important share in the ornamentation of the Bibliotheca Vecchia, rich and varied as it is; and the graceful figures which embellish the arcades are nearly all from his hand. His ablest pupil was Girolamo Campagna of Verona, whose handiwork may be seen in various Venetian churches.

Of Sansovino's scholars another illustrious name is Alessandro Vittoria, born at Trent, but educated and bred at Venice. He excelled his master, and all the sculptors of his time, in the nobility of his style and the

* Galibert, "Histoire de Venise," pp. 291–293.

† He was born at Carrara about 1500; the year of his death is uncertain.

grace of his compositions; in addition to his marbles and bronzes, he executed models for a multitude of works in stucco, and also practised wood-carving. The stuccos with which he adorned the staircases of the Ducal Palace, have, by general consent, come to be regarded as classic models of exquisite taste in design and fertility of invention. The two beautiful caryatides at the entrance of the Bibliotheca Vecchia, the charming figure of St. Sebastian in the church of San Salvatore, the group of the Pietà in the same church, the fine statue of St. Jerome in that of the Frari, and numerous other works which cannot here obtain enumeration, testify to the fecundity and talent of this brilliant artist, who holds among the sculptors of Venice the same position as Titian among its painters.

To the same period belonged Guilio del Moro, a native of Verona, and a pupil of Campagna; Nicolo de' Conti, and Alphonso Alberghetti of Ferrara; Giovanni Maria Mosca, of Padua, who flourished about 1532; and Tiziano Aspetti, of Padua, famous for his works in bronze.

During the seventeenth and eighteenth centuries, sculpture shared in the general decline of the arts; a decline which was universal throughout the European nations, but whose causes it is not our present business to investigate. However, neither talents, nor taste, nor the luxury of art, were wanting at this period. Numerous edifices continued to be erected at Venice, and a new and last generation of sculptors and painters was summoned to decorate them. But the history of art, as of political institutions and state-craft, loses, when we arrive at these epochs of languor and decadence, all interest, and all the charm of curiosity. It is only through an effort of patience and justice that the historian consents to pursue his task, even while abridging it.

The two finest works of sculpture executed at Venice in the seventeenth century, are the tombs of the Doges Bertuccio and Sylvestro Valier, in the church of SS. Giovanni-e-Paolo, by Tirali, and that of Pesaro, in the church of the Frari, by Longhena, so prodigiously rich in projections, mouldings, and architectural and sculptural contortions. The colossal statues of the Valier monument are by Pietro Baratta; those of the Pesaro mausoleum by a German named Marchio Barthelo.*

As for the eighteenth century, the church of the Jesuits, built by a certain Fantoretto, with its statue-cumbered façade, a masterpiece of that absurdly picturesque taste generally characterized by the epithet *rococo*, is a fair résumé of the art of that epoch. The most renowned contemporary artists were engaged upon its embellishment. Among its sculptors, some of whom were very able, let us particularize Guiseppe Toretti, chief of the artist-family of that name; Bonazza, who, with his three sons or brothers, executed the numerous bas-reliefs in the Rosary Chapel of SS. Giovanni-e-Paolo; Cabianca, the brothers Gropelli, Ziminiani, Bernardoni, Baratta, Tusia, Calderoni, Cattalo, and Cattasio. To puerilities like these were reduced in the latter half of the eighteenth century the descendants of Leopardi and Vittoria; and nearly the same condition of things prevailed in the rest of Italy and throughout Europe.

* Galibert, "Histoire de Venise," pp. 293–295.

Who, then, could have foreseen that, before the close of the same century, sculpture would have experienced a revolution, would have undergone a kind of second renaissance! It was still less probable that the mainspring of the movement would be found at Venice, and prove to be a Venetian artist. Such, however, was the case, for the revival was due to Canova.

Antonio Canova was born at Passagno, in the province of Treviso, on the 1st of November 1757. He was the son of a village stone-cutter, who dying while yet Antonio was yet an infant, he was placed with his grandfather Pasnio, also a stone-cutter, but a man of superior intelligence and moral character.

While still a child, Canova learned the rudiments of drawing, and devoted every leisure moment to the modelling of small clay images, enjoying, as a relaxation, his grandfather's recital of old songs, ballads, and traditional stories. In his thirteenth year, his industry and conspicuous ability attracted the notice of a Venetian gentleman, Giovanni Faliero, who placed him in the studio of Guiseppe Toretti, an artist of eminence, to be instructed in the sculptor's art. He removed with him to Venice, where he derived a noble inspiration from the study of the glorious masterpieces by which he was surrounded. His advancement was so rapid, that on the death of Toretti his grandfather was induced to sell a piece of land and raise the necessary funds for providing the young sculptor with a second master, Toretti's nephew, Ferrari.

Among Canova's earliest works were two baskets of fruit, made for the staircase of his patron, Faliero, for whom also he executed his first group of figures, "Orpheus and Eurydice." His next group, a decided advance in artistic feeling and execution, was "Dædalus and Icarus." About this time he settled himself in a studio on the Saint Maurice Canal, where he worked until his departure for Rome in 1780, under the patronage of the Venetian ambassador, Count Zulian. He resided in the Eternal City for a period of twenty years, and there accomplished that great series of works which has made his name immortal in the history of art. In 1798 and 1799 he made an extensive tour in Germany, returning to Rome in 1802, when he was appointed by Pius VII. Inspector-general of the Fine Arts throughout the Pontifical dominions. In the same year he visited Paris, and again in 1810, at the express command of Napoleon, of whom, and of the Empress Marie Louise, he executed two admirable busts. He repaired to London in 1815, and examined the famous memorials of antiquity known as the Elgin Marbles. Honours continued to be poured upon him; he was created Marchese d' Ischia, granted an annual pension of 3600 scudi (about £630), and had his name inscribed in the Golden Book of the Capitol. A life of singular industry and almost unclouded prosperity terminated at Venice, on the 12th of October 1822. His funeral was celebrated with great pomp in the cathedral of St. Mark; his body interred in the church which he had erected at his birth-place, Passagno.

Canova was a man of genius. He was not equal to the greatest of the great Greek sculptors, but he excelled those of the second rank, and his statues are distinguished by an extraordinary amount of grace and refinement.

They may sometimes be feeble, but they are never exaggerated, and few have ever equalled him in rendering the soft delicate outlines of the female figure.

Canova's fertility was remarkable. He has left behind him sixty statues, of which seven are colossal, twelve groups, fourteen cenotaphs, eight grand mortuary monuments, fifty-four busts, twenty-six bas-reliefs, and a great number of unfinished compositions.* Of these Venice possesses but a few. In the arsenal is the monument raised in honour of the noble Venetian admiral, Angelo Erno; a rostral column surmounted by the hero's bust, which a genius crowns, while a fame records his name. In the palazzo Pisani is his group of "Dædalus and Icarus;" and in the house Comello, a bas-relief representing Socrates taking farewell of his friends.

We must now direct the reader's attention to the rise and progress in Venice of the sister-art of PAINTING.

Those characteristics which as a whole impress a specific distinction on Venetian painting, though easily recognized, are not so easily analyzed and defined. With the classification of works of art the same difficulty exists as with the classification of the products of nature. We readily distinguish them by a sort of rapid intuition, which does not usually betray even the least skilful eyes; but as soon as we set to work to determine in detail the features which unite or separate them, we frequently find ourselves embarrassed. Critics have nevertheless agreed that the primary and peculiar distinction of the Venetian school is its superiority in colouring, and the Venetian

* Quatremère de Quincy, "Canova et Ses Œuvres."

masters are chiefly signalized as colourists. Taken in all its bearings, this characterization is sufficiently just, and explains well enough the impression produced by the Venetian pictures compared with that derived from others—as, for instance, the Roman or Florentine.

What strikes us most powerfully in the works of the Venetian school is the rich glowing decoration of colours immediately fascinating and subduing the eyes. An almost necessary condition of this magical effect and brilliant coruscation is, that the area wherein it is displayed should be vast, and peopled with objects capable of receiving and reflecting it with the utmost possible splendour and variety.

Hence the tendency of all colourists, and especially of Venetian, to devote a large part of their compositions to the scene and its accessories, somewhat at the expense of the moral and ideal influence of the subject: involving a strange luxury of arcades, porticoes, colonnades, staircases, balconies; a rich profusion of silks, draperies, hangings, and of all things in fact which will lead themselves to bold contrasts of light and shade, and furnish a motive for radiant illusions of perspective. Sir Joshua Reynolds happily characterized the mode of composition and execution peculiar to the Venetians as the *decorative style;* which, from his pen, was not exactly an eulogium. It is certain that, with the most marvellous talents of execution, the masters of this school never attained to the loftier regions of the art, never conceived any sublime ideal of form and expression; none of them, in any of their works, rose on wings of fire to that sublime sphere where Raphael, Michael Angelo, and Guido matured their powers. Even Titian fails in the more elevated departments of his art, as that art was conceived and realized by the Greeks and by the modern schools of Rome and Florence. But what matters it? the ideal of human beauty, the ideal of the religious sentiment, the ideal of intellectual and moral life had been revealed by these schools; and another ideal remained to be manifested, that of the sensible and material world. The Venetians seized upon this unexplored region, and realized all its splendour and all its beauty. By so doing they did all that remained to be done in the pictorial art, and completed its manifestations.*

Painting at Venice, as elsewhere, had its beginnings in the imitative work of the miniaturists, and especially of the mosaic-makers, more numerous there than in the other Italian cities. The mechanism of the mosaic was learned by the Italians from the Byzantines, and the only pictures embellishing the ancient churches of Venice are mosaics. As a decorative system, it flourished long, and the greatest masters deigned to compose sketches for the *mosaicists.* The figure of St. Mark, for instance, above the central door of the Ducal Church, was executed in 1545 by the brothers Zuccati, from a drawing by Titian.

Painting, properly so-called, made its débût in Venice at the commencement of the fourteenth century. Giotto, who was at Padua in 1306, at Verona in 1316, and in both cities executed considerable works, had his imitators and his pupils, but his style never exercised any great influence at Venice. From this epoch we find in the lagoons works of an entirely different style, executed by

* Galibert, "Histoire de Venise," pp. 278, 279.

native artists. These first confused traces of a local art appear on a grand scale in the fifteenth century, in succession to, and through the examples of, a school of painters of the Isle of Murano, then already celebrated for its works in crystal. The chief of this artist-race was named Quercio. Next to him are ranked one Bernardino, and a certain Andrea, whose "Sebastian Surrounded by Saints," was formerly preserved in the church of S. Pietro Martyri, at Murano. In the school of the latter were formed the numerous painters of the Vivarini family, who for more than a century filled Venice with their productions.

The later and most celebrated representatives of this ancient school were Giovanni and Gentile Bellini. The former was born at Venice in 1422, and died in 1512. The latter, his brother, born 1421, died 1501, was probably named after his father Jacopo's master, Gentile of Fabbriano. Jacopo was also a painter, and it is related as a fine trait of his noble nature, that instead of feeling jealous of his sons, he exulted in their outstripping him. He said it was like the Tuscans for the son to beat the father, and he hoped in Heaven's name that Giovanni would surpass him, and Gentile, the elder, surpass both.

Zun and Zentile, as they were called in the Venetian patois, were brothers in art as by nature, working together, and encouraging and advising each other. While they were engaged in covering the Serrar di Gran Consiglio (or Hall of the Great Council) with glowing representations of the victories of the Republic over Frederick Barbarossa, the Grand Turk Mahomet II. despatched a messenger to request the loan of Giovanni, whose genius he had heard of, and some of whose works he had seen. The Doge was unwilling to spare so illustrious an artist as Giovanni, but substituted his elder brother, who accordingly repaired to Constantinople, and painted the sultan and the sultan's mother. After executing other pictures, he completed a painting of John the Baptist's Head in a Charger. It was shown to the sultan, who critically remarked, from the depths of his own experience, that the artist had left the saint's neck too long, for when decapitated, the muscles always contracted, and drew back into the trunk. "See now!" he cried, and with a sweep of his gem-flashing scimitar, smote off an attendant's head. Gentile owned he was in error; but took care to remove himself without delay from the presence of a critic who illustrated his criticisms in so forcible a manner. He returned to Venice, where he spent many years in the practice of his art.

Of Giovanni Bellini, the palaces and churches of Venice possess several admirable specimens, which are not unjustly exhibited as precious relics. Among these may be named, the Virgin and four Saints in the church of S. Zacharias; Christ and his Disciples at Emmaus in the church of San Salvatore; and the *chef-d'œuvre* in the church of San Pietro at Murano. The Doge Barbarigo presented to the Virgin, who is seated on a throne, by the Apostle Mark.

These great masters were followed by a succession of worthy pupils and imitators, but it was not until the beginning of the sixteenth century that the grandest names of the Venetian school illuminated the history of the art. First of these was Giorgio Barbarelli, better known as *Giorgione* (or the great George), from his tall stature, his surprising physical strength, and his fierce disposition, which gave him somewhat of a Bravo-air. He was born at Castelfranco in 1478, and died at Venice in 1511, aged only thirty-three. It is said of him that he broke through the trammels which had confined his art up to the time of the Bellini, and introduced a boldness of handling, a freedom of outline, and a daring use of lights and shades on which no one had previously ventured. He was the first to practice that admirable fusion of tints which forms so great a part of the beauty of the Venetian colouring. Of his oil pictures the principal are—Christ bearing his Cross, in the church of S. Roch at Venice; his picture of S. Ambrose, in the school of Sarti; and in the church of San Marco, of that saint subduing the Tempest.

One of his ablest and most successful scholars was Fra Sebastian del Piombo, or Sebastiano Veneziáno, born at Venice in 1485. He first gained celebrity as a portrait-painter, but afterwards essayed historical and sacred subjects, in which he displayed great accuracy of drawing, and a surprising command of rich and harmonious colouring. He died in 1547.

A student of Giorgione's style, though not one of his actual pupils, was Jacopo Palma, surnamed Il Vecchio, the elder, born at Sermatta about 1510. One of his finest works may be seen in the church of S. Maria Mater Domini—a representation of the Last Supper. He died about 1558, but the date both of his birth and death is problematical.

A more direct imitator of Giorgione was Paris Bordone,

born at Trevigi in 1513. He was sprung of a noble family, but displaying an enthusiastic love of art, gave himself up to its pursuit with an ardour and a perseverance which secured him a more illustrious title of nobility than that which he owed to his ancestors. He died at Venice in 1588. His principal work at Venice is the picture known as the Ring of St. Mark; in which a fisherman presents to the Doge, seated on a raised dais, and surrounded by his peers, a bag which the patron-saint of the Queen of the Adriatic had sent him as a sign of his protection during the high tide of February 25, 1340, which had threatened Venice with ruin. It is a vast composition, magnificent in colour, full of life and energy, with numerous figures, ingeniously grouped, and remarkable for their animated expression.

Here we may observe, with M. Galibert, that the Venetian painters, far more frequently than those of other schools, have selected their themes from their national history and contemporaneous events; a circumstance easily explained, independently of more general causes, by the constant anxiety of the heads of the Republic to stimulate and maintain the patriotic pride of its citizens, and foster their attachment to its institutions, by the memory of glorious deeds, great triumphs, and illustrious heroes. Hence it became the painter's mission to present to the people the living images of the national power and renown. Three-fourths of the innumerable pictures in the Ducal Palace, executed by order of the Government, are no more than so many pages of Venetian history, splendidly illuminated by Bellini, Paolo Veronese, Tintoretto, the elder and younger Palma, the Bassanos,

Zuccaro,* Liberi, Giulio del Moro, Aliense (or Vassilacchi), Vicentino, and other famous masters of the sixteenth century.

Next to Bordone, the most distinguished of the painters formed in the school of Giorgione was Giovanni Antonio Lécinio Regillio, better known as Il Pordenone, from the name of his birth-place, a small town in Friuli, where he was born in 1484. He was the avowed rival and enemy of Titian, and to excite himself in the artistic struggle which he gallantly but hopelessly maintained, he always worked in his studio with his sword at his side. He painted largely in fresco, but his oil pictures are rare. Of his fresco-work some fine remains may be seen in the churches of San Giovanni-de-Rialto and San Stefano. He died at Mantua in 1540, not without suspicion of poison.

We now come to Titian himself, the greatest name of the Venetian school, and one of the five or six "powerful individualities" in whom is personified the genius of painting.†

Tiziano Vecelli, descended from a noble family of Friuli, was born at the Castle of Lodore in 1477. Having evinced an early bias for the art, he was sent, when ten years old, to Venice, and placed under the protection of his uncle. He received his first instruction from Sebas-

* Zuccaro belonged to the Roman school. Born in 1543; died in 1609. Pietro Liberi, of Padua, was born in 1605, died in 1687. Giulio del Moro, of Verona, was the brother of Giovanni, and best known as a sculptor. Aliense (or Vassilacchi) was born at Milo in 1556; studied under Paolo Veronese, and was very popular at Venice, where he died in 1629. Andrea Vicentino, a pupil of Palma, was born at Venice in 1539; died in 1614.

† Bryan, "Dictionary of Painters and Engravers," *sub nom.*

tiano Zuccati, and afterwards studied under Gentile and Giovanni Bellini. At the outset of his career he imitated Nature with the servility of a copyist, but the pictures of Giorgione awoke the originality of his own genius, and at the age of eighteen he displayed his peculiar powers in a portrait of the head of the Barbarigo family. This was the commencement of his long and glorious career. As his splendid abilities matured, his renown increased, and kings, emperors, and popes contended for the works which left his easel. He visited Bologne at the invitation of Charles V.; Mantua at the request of its duke, Frederigo Gonzaga; Rome, in obedience to the command of the Pontiff; Madrid, at the repeated entreaty of the Spanish sovereign.* Old age did not weaken his powers; and he may be said to have died brush in hand. He lived within one year of the century, perishing of the plague in 1576.†

It is unnecessary to analyze the merits of this famous master. As a colourist he has never been surpassed: there is a glow and a radiance upon his pictures which one sees in the productions of no other artist. His design is pure, his composition spirited; his portraits are remarkable for their nobility of expression and strong individuality of character: and if he lacks the graceful tenderness of Raphael and the sublimity of Michael Angelo, it can only be said that had their peculiar powers been united to his, the combination would have transcended the limits of human nature.

He was an indefatigable worker, and nearly five hun-

* His visit to Spain is doubted by some authorities.

† Galibert, "Histoire de Venise," p. 304.

dred of his productions are known to be extant. At Venice one meets them everywhere. The finest are— The Martyrdom of S. Lawrence, in the church of the Jesuits; The Magdalene, in the palazzo Barbarigo; in the church of the Frari, The Family Pesaro kneeling before the Virgin, surrounded by saints; at S. Roch, The Annunciation; at the Academy of the Fine Arts, The Assumption, and The Presentation of the Infant Virgin at the Temple.

Titian had a crowd of pupils and imitators, among whom the only one who rose nearly to an equality with his master, and who, in fact, became in his turn the founder of a new school, was Jacopo Robusti, surnamed Il Tintoretto, from the trade of his father, a dyer at Venice. Tintoretto was born in 1512; he died in 1594. He painted with great rapidity, and the impetuosity and fire of his disposition communicated themselves to his compositions. He would have attained perfection had he possessed the power of bridling his imagination, and somewhat more of "the passionate patience of genius." As it is, he will always be distinguished by his freedom of drawing, his grandeur of design, and beauty of colour. At the Academy of the Fine Arts may be seen his St. Mark releasing a Slave; at S. Roch, his Crucifixion; the beautiful Marriage at Cana is the treasure preserved in the sacristy of the church of the Salute.

While in Giorgione, Titian, and Tintoretto, the Venetian school realized the loftiest type it was permitted to attain of style and execution, and while developing a strong tendency towards what may be called the materialism of art, it nevertheless aspired to a certain ideal of thought, design, and expression; there rose by its side a school which gave a decided predominance to the exclusively picturesque and sensuous element. The most powerful, the most ingenious, the most brilliant, and most fertile spirit of this transformation, was Paolo Cagliari, best known by the name of Paolo Veronese.

He was the son of a sculptor named Gabriele Cagliari, but his inclination leading him decidedly to painting, he was placed under the tuition of Antonio Badile, his maternal uncle, at that time a painter of distinction at Verona. His genius displayed itself while he was still so young, that Ridolfi observed of him, that in the spring of life he produced most excellent fruit. Removing to Venice, he studied there the works of Titian and Tintoretto. His first productions in the great Adriatic city were the frescoes in the church of San Sebastiano. The Senate having engaged some of the principal artists of the time to decorate the palace of the Conservators, offered a gold medal and chain to the artist whose work should be preferred, and these were won by Veronese. His masterpieces, however, are considered to be the four colossal compositions executed for the churches of S. Georgio Maggiore, S. Sebastiano, SS. Giovanni-e-Paolo, and the refectory of the Padri Servi—the Marriage at Cana (now in the Louvre at Paris), the Feast of Simon, the Saviour at Table with his Disciples, and a different version of the same subject (presented by the Republic to Louis XIV. in 1665). Paolo died in 1588.

The school of Veronese includes some eminent names; as his brother, Benedetto Cagliari; his sons, Carlo and Gabriele; and Baptista Zelotti, of Verona.

An entirely different style was introduced by the Bassanos—so named from their native town—and the masters who followed them. It was a style depending for its excellence on the lively and faithful imitation of nature, and the accurate representation of domestic scenes and objects. In these respects it resembled the Dutch and Flemish schools, but it was distinguished by a more graceful and tender feeling than they display.

The head of the Bassano family was Francesco da Ponte, the elder; born in 1475, died in 1530. The chief in artistic merit, Giacomo da Ponte, his son, born at Bassano in 1510. He began his career by executing grand historical and sacred subjects, after the manner of Titian and Tintoretto, but soon abandoned a flight of invention uncongenial to his inclinations, and devoted himself to the representation of home-scenes, landscapes, animals, and rural life. His colouring is harmonious and agreeable; his power of expression remarkable in its faithfulness and simplicity. He died in 1592.

Towards the close of the sixteenth century Venetian art exhibited unmistakable signs of decadence, from which it never recovered, but year after year sank into a more miserable condition. From the numerous names which have passed into a well-deserved oblivion, we shall rescue only the following:—Palma il Giovine, born at Venice in 1544, died in 1628; Francesco Padouanino, born at Padua in 1552, died in 1617; Alessandro Turchi, called L'Orbetto,* born at Verona in 1582, died at Rome in

* So named because, when a boy, he gained his living by acting as guide to a blind beggar. In this condition he was noticed by Brusasorio, who took him under his protection and tuition. He soon surpassed his instructor.

1648; Giovanni Batista Piazzetta, born at Venice in 1682, died in 1754; Giovanni Batista Tiepolo, born at Venice in 1697, died at Madrid in 1770; and Antonio Canal, or Canaletti, born at Venice in 1697, died in 1768.

The latter artist was the son of a scene-painter, and was himself employed for some years in executing theatrical decorations. After studying at Rome the glorious remains of antiquity, he applied himself to landscape painting, and produced a vast number of Venetian views, remarkable for their admirable perspective and aerial effects. His industry was without let or hindrance; and his works are therefore found in every European gallery, and few good collections in England are without one or more specimens of his bright and graceful style.

This nineteenth century as yet has given no great painter to Venice, and indeed throughout Italy the art seems dead—throughout that land of fame which has emblazoned its annals with the glory of a Raphael, a Caracci, a Michael Angelo, and a Coreggio!

II.

Science and Letters in Venice.

> The one or two immortal lights
> Rise slowly up into the sky,
> To shine there everlastingly,
> Like stars over the bounding hill.
>
> MATTHEW ARNOLD.

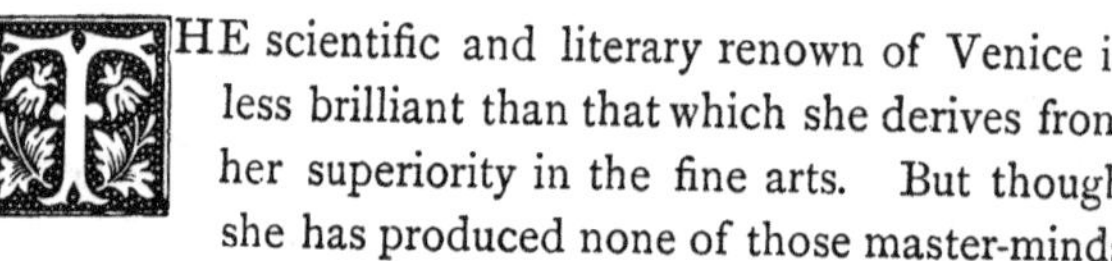HE scientific and literary renown of Venice is less brilliant than that which she derives from her superiority in the fine arts. But though she has produced none of those master-minds who invested mediæval Italy with such surpassing splendour, the precocity of her literary development was as remarkable as her influence on the progress of civilization is undeniable. In the zenith of her power her rulers neither neglected her intellectual culture nor her material resources; and she was at once the great commercial, political, and intellectual centre of civilized Europe, favouring the union and expansion of those sublime ideas which the human mind so laboriously begets.

This mental movement showed itself soon after the capture of Constantinople, when the growth of their commerce in the islands of the Archipelago rendered the Greek language familiar to the inhabitants of Venice, and, consequently, the Greek literature a favourite subject of study with her scholars. Moreover, Greek priests, philosophers, and professors established themselves at Venice, secure in her tranquillity and sharing in her prosperity; and the Latin priests, in discussing their opinions and refuting their dogmas, were led to initiate themselves into their philosophy. The first fruits of this great revolution was the foundation of a library and of several public schools. Its more important results were the establishment of an indigenous literature, and the general diffusion of a knowledge of the classic writers.

Scarcely had the thirteenth century passed away before Venice could boast of a historian really worthy of the name; a historian who could comprehend and relate, with a noble elevation of thought and language, all that affected the great interests of his country—we refer to the Doge Andrea Dandolo. This illustrious prince devoted his leisure to recording the principal events of the nine centuries of the Republic's life; and his work attests the intellectual superiority of the Venetian aristocracy over the majority of contemporary politicians. Long before the appearance of this noble record, from which modern writers have largely borrowed, another patrician had undertaken, at his own cost, a labour of a different kind, far more perilous but not less useful. Marco Polo had spent six-and-twenty years in exploring the Asiatic continent; first of Europeans, he penetrated into the Celestial Empire; into India, across the Ganges, and into the great Indian Archipelago—regions previously unknown to Europe, and concealed in the deep shadows of ignorance, superstition, and fable. What he saw, he described with simplicity and exactness. Later research has but confirmed his accuracy, and in so doing justified his fame. He was the creator, says Malte-Brun, of the modern geography of Asia; he was the Humboldt of the thirteenth century; and his travels will always remain—*monumentum aere perennius*—an imperishable monument to his genius, truthfulness, and courage.

His example inspired a host of imitators, who, directing their adventurous steps towards Egypt, ascended the Nile as far as the First Cataract, and made their way into Nubia and Abyssinia. How much they accomplished for the development of geographical science may be learned from the maps and treatises of Marino Sanuto (1320–1325).

Shut up within her lagoons, and all her resources continually employed in war or commerce, in the augmentation of her territory or the increase of her wealth, Venice, at the epoch of which we are speaking, had found neither the leisure nor the daring to attempt any conquests in the realms of Poetry. Moreover, at this time, all Italy hung spell-bound on the utterances of her triad of great poets — Dante, Petrarch, Boccaccio. Their music so filled the ears of the world that no lesser strains could hope to gain a hearing. It was as if a shepherd's pipe had essayed to compete with the instrument of Cecilia, which, when it joins the tuneful choir,—

"The immortal powers incline their ear;
Borne on the swelling notes our souls aspire,
While solemn airs improve the sacred fire,
And angels lean from heaven to hear."

When the Venetian muse at last broke forth in song, it was not in the language of its native land that it found a voice. Christine of Paris was the daughter of Tomaso Pisano, an astronomer of Venice; but she lived for the greater part of her life at the court of Charles V. of France, and her poems were written in France. She was the most accomplished literary lady of her age, and altogether, as Hallam says, a very remarkable person.* It is sad to reflect that her fate was the too common fate of genius—she died in extreme poverty.

In the fifteenth century, literature and science in Venice attained a remarkable development. A people addicted to commercial and maritime enterprise necessarily made the knowledge of the globe their favourite study. They fluttered their banners in every sea, and if we may credit their annalists, not only anticipated the Portuguese in the Indian Archipelago, but preceded Columbus in his discovery of the New World. They also claim the invention of the mariner's compass. Without delaying ourselves by these exaggerations, we may admit that the Venetian charts published in the fifteenth century show a tolerably exact knowledge of the regions comprised between the Strait of Gibraltar, the Equator, the Continent, and the islands of Cape Verde and the Canaries; that, in 1426, Jacopo Ziroldo indicated several points situated beyond Cape Bojador, which the ancients regarded as the extremity of the world; that in 1436 Andrea del Bianco laid down Scandinavia on the map with surprising accuracy; that Josaphat Barbaro devoted twenty-five years (from 1436 to 1471) to the exploration

* Hallam, "Introduction to the Literature of Europe," i. 98.

of Tartary, Kamtschatka, Persia, and Russia; that in 1455 Ca dà Mosto traversed the Atlantic to within eleven degrees and a half of the Equinoctial; that Paolo Trevisano, in 1483, described Ethiopia and the course of the mysterious Nile; and that the Cabots, in 1496, employed by England, discovered Labrador, and acquired an imperfect knowledge of some communication existing between the Atlantic and Hudson's Bay.*

Here we must refer to the remarkable works of two celebrated men. It was in 1550 that Ramusio, a Venetian who had filled several offices of credit, issued the first volume of his well-known collection of travels; the second appeared in 1559, and the third in 1565. It includes many voyages in Africa, the East Indies, and Indian Archipelago; Magellan's circumnavigation of the globe; travels through northern Europe and Asia; and the conquests of Cortes and Pizarro. Altogether, it was well calculated to fire the imagination of men, and cherish the spirit of enterprise which then animated the breasts of the heroic.

Fra Mauro, a monk of the order of the Camalduli, and of the monastery of S. Michel-de-Murano, near Venice, produced a singularly comprehensive map of the world (1457–1459), now preserved in the library of St. Mark. In Africa it extends to Cape Verde and the Gulf of Guinea on the west, and Darfur and Madagascar on the east; in Asia it lays down the boundaries of China according to the discoveries of Marco Polo. Both by what he did correctly and by what he did incorrectly,

* Galibert, "Histoire de Venise."—See also Cooley's "History of Maritime Discovery."

Fra Mauro encouraged the progress of discovery. By marking several islands, under the names of St. Brundan, Antille, and Berzil, as within a short distance of the Azores, he directed the energy of the navigators in that westward course which eventually led to the shores of America.

In connection with the study of geography, that of astronomy attracted many ingenious minds, and was greatly favoured by the Venetian Government.

While Tycho Brahe was rearing, at his own cost, his celebrated observatory on a solitary island of the Baltic, the Republic despatched astronomers to Egypt to examine attentively the celestial system of Ptolemæus, and to refute its errors. The illustrious Fracastor, meanwhile, attempted a new combination of lenses, and invented the homocentric calculations, by whose aid he demonstrated the planetary system. Marco-Antonio de Dominis, Archbishop of Spalatro, by his treatise on the rainbow, facilitated Newton's inquiries into the polarization of light. Magini, though somewhat superstitious, published a new and ingenious theory of the planets, after Copernicus; and, finally, the "starry Galileo" was attracted to and retained at the university of Padua by the munificence of the Venetian senate, which, the better to honour that lofty genius, wished to assist at his first experiments with the telescope and pendulum. In the other branches of mathematical science we meet with some names of foremost merit. Nicolas Tarteglia, who proposed a method of solving cubic equations; Dorotheas Alimari; Francisco Bianchini; and the geometrician Cognoli.

Returning to the scholars of the fifteenth century, we

feel an emotion of regret at the exigencies which preclude us from doing more than mention the laborious Guarino de Verona, to whose zeal we owe the preservation of many precious Greek classics; Nicolas Pernotti; Barbaro and Romulus Arnasco; Geronimo Alessandro; Ramnusio, the celebrated Arabic scholar; and Malermi, who made the first version of the Bible from the Hebrew text. When the invention of printing revolutionized the world of letters, and opened the flood-gates of universal knowledge, nowhere was the new art more eagerly welcomed than at Venice. As early as 1469, Giovanni di Spira and Nicolas Jansen were honoured with the titles of Printers to the Most Serene Republic: and it was here, from the famous press of the Manutii (Manuzio), that the first book printed in Greek letters was issued. Aldus conceived the noble idea of familiarizing the public with the treasures of Greek literature, and for this purpose surrounded himself with the most illustrious scholars of his time,—Cardinal Bembo, Marino Sanuto, Erasmus, Baptista Egnazio, and others,—with whose zealous help he was able to produce editions of Aristotle, Euripides, and Theocritus. Following in his footsteps, the Venetian printers became famous for the elegance of their types, the correctness of their texts, and the beauty of their paper.

One of the literary heroes of the period was the monk Paolo Sarpi, who, as we have already seen, distinguished himself by the bitterness of his hostility to the temporal power of the Roman pontiffs.

Pietro Sarpi (for Paolo was simply his monastic name*)

* See Mr. T. A. Trollope's "Paul the Pope and Paul the Friar."

was born at Venice in 1552, was educated by his maternal uncle, at the age of fourteen became a novice in the order of the Servites, at twenty took his monastic vows, and at twenty-two was made a priest. His moral austerity was not less conspicuous than his intellectual capacity. He spoke seldom, was partial to solitude, and, up to his thirtieth year, eschewed both wine and flesh. He devoted himself wholly to literary and scientific pursuits; and in mental science propounded a theory of knowledge not unlike, and scarcely less inferior to, that of Locke's. Bringing his scientific acquirements to bear upon theological acquirements, he early acquired a conviction of the falsity of certain leading Romish dogmas, and nourished a spirit of independent criticism which brought down upon him the suspicions of his superiors. In the dispute which arose between Venice and Paul V. respecting the supposed immunities of ecclesiastics from civil jurisdiction, he espoused the cause of the Republic, and stood forward as the able, determined, and energetic opponent of the temporal power of the Papacy. He became, therefore, the object of its unscrupulous hatred, and we have described the relentlessness with which it pursued him. His principal work—published at Geneva—the "History of the Council of Trent," bitterly satirized the Papal pretensions, and was an effective instrument in the hands of Protestantism. "It exhibits," says Mr. Hallam,* "the general excellencies of his manner—freedom from redundancy; a clear, full, agreeable style; a choice of what is most pertinent and interesting in his materials. Much has been dis-

* Hallam, "Literary History of Europe," ii. 398, 399.

puted about the religious tenets of Father Paul; it appears to me quite out of doubt, both by the tenor of his history, and still more unequivocally, if possible, by some of his letters, that he was entirely hostile to the Church, in the usual sense, as well as to the court of Rome, sympathizing in affection and concurring generally in opinion with the Reformed denomination. But as he continued in the exercise of his functions as a Servite monk, and has always passed at Venice more for a saint than a heretic, some writers have not scrupled to make use of his authority, and to extenuate his heterodoxy. There can be no question but that he inflicted a severe wound on the spiritual power."

Father Paul died in 1623. His "History" was translated into English by Dr. Johnson. Bossuet says of him:* "Under a monk's robe, he hid a Calvinist's heart. He toiled in silence to discredit the mass which he celebrated daily; and laboured to effect the complete separation of the Venetian Republic, not only from the Roman court, but also from the Roman Church."

We are unable to trace in these pages the foundation of the various universities, public schools, and academies, which promoted culture and kept alive the lamp of knowledge in the Venetian territories; or of the great libraries fostered by the wise care of the Venetian Government, and of which St. Mark's was indisputably the richest. But a few words must be given to that practical application of scientific truths which has so vast an influence on the welfare and material prosperity of a country. That Venice was famous for its ship-building,

* The great French preacher, however, was not an impartial critic.

none will wonder. She was also remarkable for the immense hydraulic works which she executed, and which vastly increased the power and utility of the waters of her rivers—the Brenta, the Po, the Bacchiglione, the Mentone, the Reno, and the Reneo. Her engineers guided them into new channels; or enlarged or economized the old at will. They invented flood-gates, sluices, and weirs; and conducted irrigation on a large scale and with admirable ingenuity. Benedict Castelli, of Brescia, determined the measurement of running waters; Bartolomeo Ferracina introduced many valuable improvements in the construction of hydraulic machines; Collconi designed gun-carriages, San Michele di Verona angular bastions, and Bernardino Zandrini embankments against the invasion of the sea.

Nor has Venice been wanting in illustrious representatives in the natural and medical sciences. As, for example, Patrizio de Cherso, who indicated the sexes of plants; Sarpi, an ingenious theorist on the circulation of the blood; Fracastor, who was both physicist, physician, astronomer, and poet, and who effected some extraordinary cures; Fallopius, whose anatomical researches will ever perpetuate his name; his successor, Jerome Fabricius (or Aquapendente), who occupied the chair of anatomy at Venice for forty years; and the learned and modest Morgagni, who discovered the various functions of the respiratory organs. He was a man of singularly devout mind, and it is told of him that, one day, in the course of a dissection, he dropped his scalpel in an outburst of reverent admiration, and exclaimed: "Ah, if I did but love God as well as I know him!" He died in 1771.

History, says M. Galibert,* presents itself at Venice under two very distinct aspects: on the one side are ranged the official historiographers, generally elegant writers, more sedulous as to form than substance, eulogists of all the acts of the Republic and defenders of its government to the last extremity; on the other, the few independent writers who have ventured to treat honestly of the annals of their country. Let us first glance at the former class.

Sabellicus (Marc Antonio Coccio) was born about the middle of the fifteenth century, at Vescovaro. He was for several years secretary to the illustrious Cardinal Bessarion, and through his influence obtained the appointment of historiographer and professor of the belles-lettres. He displayed more ability in the latter post than in the former; his history, which is written in Latin, and brought down to the year 1484, being more remarkable for elegance of style than for a correct appreciation of facts or a profound insight into character. From preface to colophon it is a continual panegyric!

The continuator of this eulogistic writer was Andreas Navagero, a Latinist of great taste and fine scholarship, a warm admirer of Pindar, but so bitter an enemy of Martial that he burned a copy of his poems every year. He executed his task with eager zeal, but before his death (in 1529) his fastidiousness found so much fault with the completed work that he condemned it to the same fate as the epigrams of Martial.

The learned Bembo was commissioned to repair the loss, and his work is a masterpiece of pure and forcible

* Galibert, "Histoire de Venise," p. 329.

Latinity. He carried the history of the Republic down to the death of Pope Julius II. in 1513. He out-Heroded his predecessors in the warmth of his colouring. Every personage he deals with is elevated into a hero; every event he records assumes a truly colossal character. Moreover, from his affectation of employing only classical terms, he frequently plunges into the grossest absurdities of expression; as when he speaks of the Pope as elected by the favour of the immortal gods (*deorum immortalium beneficiis*), of the Virgin Mary as a goddess (*dea Loretana*), and converts the Christian *fides*, or faith, into the Pagan *persuasio.*

On the death of Bembo in 1547, Paul Paruta took up the unfinished tale at the election of Pope Leo X., surnamed the Magnificent. The twelve books he has left behind him are written, in conformity with the then established but ridiculous custom, in Latin, and comprise the stirring annals of the years 1513 to 1552. The war of Cyprus he relates with dramatic spirit; and he introduces many valuable dissertations on the civil administration of the Republic, an important subject, too much neglected by the historians of all nations. Paruta held many important offices of state, was honoured with several embassies, and died procurator of St. Mark in 1598. De Thou, the French historian, praises him for his tact and eloquence as a diplomatist, and as a writer he merits commendation for the vigour and perspicuity of his style.

We shall pass over without notice the names of Andreas Morosini, who continued the chronicles of Venice to 1615; Baptista Nani, to 1644; Michaele Foscari, to 1690;

and Pietro Gurzini, to 1713. They were far inferior to their predecessors in talent and erudition. Nicolas Dona undertook the task of fusing all these separate works into one complete whole. His compilation is carried down to the middle of the eighteenth century, but its publication was never permitted; probably because deemed dangerous by the Senate. It might have been unsafe to set before the degraded Venetians a vivid picture of the past glories of their country. After Dona's death, in 1765, no one was willing to accept a commission which the circumstances of the time rendered extremely delicate, and the post remained vacant for nine years, until Francisco Dona was compelled to accept his father's mantle. It was the melancholy fate of this last historiographer of Venice to see the banner of St. Mark trodden under foot by foreign invaders, the Senate dispersed, and the national institutions overthrown. Yet he remained silent; neither a tear nor a regret had he for so terrible a catastrophe! Niebuhr might well assert that the Venetians, at the fall of their Republic, had no other courage than that of resignation!

We turn now to the independent historians. To the chronicle of Dandolo we have already referred. A century later, Coriolano Cippia related with much graphic energy the grand struggle between the Turks and Venetians in 1470. Next came Bernardo Giustiniani, who threw a flood of light on the early history of the Republic; and Gaspardo Contarini, who, in 1510, undertook to explain the action of the complex machinery of Venetian administration. In 1522, Andreas Mocenigo published two histories which are still held in deserved repute; one relative to the wars of Turkey, the other to the famous League of Cambray. Works of high merit we also owe to Pietro Giustiniani, Jacopo Diedo, Carlo Marini, and especially to Vittore Sandi, the latter not less remarkable for the purity of his style than for the impartiality of his tone, and the wide range of his views.

But few Venetian authors have treated of the history of other countries. Those who have done so, however, are praiseworthy for their honesty and freedom from prejudice. We may name Paolo Sarpi, and his "History of the Council of Trent;" Giovanni Michele Bruto, and his "History of Florence,"—a work whose trenchant exposures so alarmed the Medicis, that they endeavoured to buy up and destroy every copy; Pietro Maffei, of Bergamo, who wrote a "History of the East Indies;" and Paolo Emili, of Verona, and Davila, who sketched the "Annals of France."*

The Venetian ambassadors were generally men of insight, shrewd judgment, and acute discrimination. The memoirs which they supplied to their Government of the events transpiring in the courts to which they were accredited, and of the princes, nobles, warriors, and statesmen, in whose society they mingled, were mostly replete with sagacious observation and admirable description. Some of these valuable contemporaneous histories have recently been examined by French and English scholars, with the result of obtaining much novel and important information in reference to points of policy and the course of affairs.

In the domain of poetry Venice has made no great

* Galibert, "Histoire de Venise," p. 331.

conquests, and she has produced no names worthy of being ranked with a Dante, a Shakspeare, a Milton, or a Goethe. Her earlier bards fettered themselves with the chains of a dead language, and sang in Latin. They therefore never appealed to the national heart, and failed to derive any inspiration from the national genius. Of such writers as Giovanni Cotta, of Verona; Basilio Zanchi, of Bergamo; Petro Valerio Bolzani; Andreas Navagiero; and even of Bembo, it may justly be said that their muse is but a resuscitated corpse; their verse is as lifeless as the language in which it is embodied. They wrote only for scholars, and only by scholars are their names now remembered. Julius Cæsar Scaliger is better known as a critic and a grammarian than as the author of an "Ars Poetica;" but to Fracaster may justly be conceded the merit of having imitated Virgil with wonderful felicity, as well in the harmony of his style as in the grace and fidelity of his descriptions.

Two learned ladies should be included in this poetic Pleiad: Veronica Gambura, of Brescia, who died at Correggio, in 1550; and Cassandra Fedeli, surnamed *Decus Italiæ*, the "Boast of Italy," equally distinguished as musician, poet, and scholar, who died at Vicenza, in 1567, aged one hundred and two.

The first Venetian poet who tuned his lyre to native strains was Nicolas Agostini. He flourished early in the sixteenth century, and proposed to himself the task of continuing Boïardo's "Orlando Inamorato." He was followed by Francisco Ludovico, who chanted the glories of Charlemagne; Cataneo, author of "The Loves of Marfisa;" and Bernardo Tasso, author of "Amadis of Gaul."

The latter was neither deficient in imagination nor poetic talent, but his greatest gift to the world was his son, Torquato Tasso, the immortal author of the "Jerusalem Delivered."

Torquato was born at Sorrento, and educated at Padua. Venice, therefore, cannot lay claim to him as one of her worthies; yet it is certain that he has ever been the favourite poet of the Venetians, and for more than two centuries the gondoliers sang no other songs than the strophes of his immortal epic. And though silence long ago fell upon them, and the traveller now vainly waits to hear

> "The voice of Adria's gondolier
> Along the blue and moonlit waters sweep,"—

Tasso is still read, and studied, and loved in the city of the Adriatic.

The Venetian theatre is illustrated by no great names; at least, by none which have acquired a world-wide reputation. It should be recorded, however, that the first regular Italian tragedy, written in verse, and on the classical model, was the "Sophonisba" of Trissino (1514), afterwards reproduced on the French stage by Voltaire. The Venetian dramatists thenceforward continued a close and lifeless imitation of the ancients, until the Marquis Scipio Maffei, courageously trusting to his own resources, produced the modern play of "Mérope,"—a masterpiece of what is called the romantic style. Maffei also attempted to strip comedy of its ancient rags, but this new honour was reserved for Goldoni. Before we speak of the latter illustrious artist, a few words on Italian comedy may prove interesting to the reader.

Its early aspect was that of a satirical pantomime, in which the characters were masked and fantastically costumed, and explained the incidents and object of the piece by lively gestures. These characters were limited in number, and never changed; like the clown, columbine, and harlequin of our Christmas pieces; which are, in fact, only a poor modification of the Venetian mimes.

These mimes were the natural offspring of the Roman *pantomimi*, and their characters were borrowed from Roman originals. The Italian *Zanni* (our English *Zany*) comes direct from *Sannio*, a buffoon; and a passage in Cicero, *De Oratore*, eloquently depicts harlequin and his brother gesticulators, with the perpetual trembling motion of their limbs, their ludicrous and flexible gestures, and all the mimicry of their speaking countenances.* "Quid enim potest tam ridiculum quam Sannio esse? Qui ore, vultu, imitandis motibus, voce, denique corpore ridetur ipso." [For what can be more absurd than Sannio? who, with his mouth, his face, imitating every motion, with his voice and, indeed, with his whole body, breaks out into laughter.]

The attire of the Zannis was composed of pieces of red, blue, orange, and violet cloth, cut in a triangular shape, and patched together so as to seem one and the same stuff. A small cap scarcely covered their denuded head; the face was entirely concealed by a short black mask, pierced with a couple of eye-holes. The Zanni excited the amusement of the spectators by the sound of his voice, his grimaces, and his gestures. Originally, his character was that of a hungry idiot, but in course of

* I. D'Israeli, "Curiosities of Literature:" On the Pantomimical Characters.

time he was invested with some degree of wit and courage.

His companions in the mimic scene were the *Grazziano Dottore;* the Captain Spavento ;* Pedrolino (the French *Pierrot*) ; Pantalone (or Pantaloon) ; Pulcinella (the English *Punch*, the French *Polichinelle*) ; the Scaramucci (*Scaramouch*) ; Giangurgello ; Don Pasquale ; and a crowd of other types, which embodied the peculiarities and absurdities of all classes of society and all the districts of Italy.

The *Zanni* played the part now filled by the modern harlequin, and spoke the Bergamasque dialect, from the pretended resemblance of his character to that of the people of Bergamo, who were popularly supposed to consist of two classes only—complete idiots and thorough knaves. The *Grazziano Dottore*, furnished with a tremendous nose, spoke Bolognese, in allusion to his country: it was his privilege to utter the most monstrous absurdities with a perfectly grave air. The *Captain Spavento's* language was a mixture of Spanish, Milanese, and Neapolitan, and he was intended as a caricature of the Spanish conquerors of Italy. The *Pantaloon* used the Venetian dialect; *Pulcinella* (or "hen-chicken"), the Calabrian. "He spoke," says Baretti, "with a squeaking voice through his nose, to express a weak and timid fellow, who is always thrashed by the other actors, and always boasts of victory after they are gone." The Neapolitans were personified by *Scaramuccio*, a shrewd, active, mischievous busy-body; and *Tartaglia*, "a spectacled dotard, a stammerer, and usually in a passion."

* Literally, "a horrid fright."

Calabria furnished the braggart and booby *Giangurgello;* while *Don Pasquale* was a Roman, filled with devout reverence for the Pope, as well as for the whole college of cardinals.

The Venetian pantomime occasionally permitted the introduction of dialogue, and thus afforded to clever actors an excellent opportunity for satirical allusion and humorous criticism. By degrees, this extemporal comedy was grossly abused, and became a vehicle for the introduction of licentious buffoonery. It was then that Charles Goldoni arose as a reformer, and illustrated the Italian drama with the splendour of his truly original genius.

Goldoni was born at Venice in 1707. A life of duels, adventures, and escapades compelled him to quit his native city, where he had practised as an advocate, and he then embraced the dramatic career. He made his débût in 1732, with the tragedy of *Belisarius,* the worst of his numerous compositions; but discovering the true bent of his talents, he adopted the comedy of character, and gave to the world a succession of lively, humorous, and original dramas, which faithfully reflected the manners and habits of all classes of his countrymen. Italy in the eighteenth century can only be fairly studied in the one hundred and fifty plays of Goldoni.

Before we conclude this brief sketch of Venetian literature, we find ourselves constrained to notice the names of Algarotti (died in 1764), who popularized the system of Newton; Césarotti, the translator of Ossian, Homer, and Demosthenes (died in 1808); Tiraboschi of Bergamo, the illustrious historian of Italian letters; and Ugo Foscolo, the last of the heroes, a great writer and an earnest patriot.

Nicolo Ugo Foscolo was descended from a noble Venetian family, and born in the island of Zante in 1778. He early manifested a powerful intellect, and an intense enthusiasm in the cause of liberty. He mourned bitterly over the degradation of his country, and opposed the despotism of Napoleon with a dauntless eloquence. By his tragedies, and odes, and patriotic addresses he endeavoured to keep alive the spirit of freedom. When the treaty of Vienna handed over Venetian Lombardy to Austria, and crushed out his hopes of a free and united Italy, he abandoned his country in despair, and retiring to England, with whose language and literature he was well acquainted, he thenceforth gained a livelihood by constant literary exertion. He contributed some admirable articles to the Edinburgh and Quarterly Reviews, and published an edition of Dante which will always be held in high esteem. Spent with fatigue of heart, mind, and body, the noble-hearted patriot died in September 1827, at the early age of forty-nine. His was the last illustrious name of which Venice can boast. Misfortune clouded his brief career, but his example and his life-work have not been without fruit. And we may say with Nicolini, that "whoever does not imitate Foscolo, ready to perish on a pallet of straw, rather than abandon his principles, will not live blessed in the memory of man."

III.

Glimpses of Venetian Life.

All the delusion of the dizzy scene,
Its false and true enchantments. . . .
the dash
Phosphoric of the oar, or rapid twinkle
Of the far lights of skimming gondolas.

BYRON, *Marino Faliero.*

HE Venice of the poet and the dramatist is, as Mr. Ruskin observes,* a thing of yesterday, a mere efflorescence of decay, a stage-dream which the first ray of daylight must dissipate into dust. That Bridge of Sighs, which has been the source of so much sentiment, was never crossed by any prisoner whose name is worth remembering, or whose sorrows deserved sympathy; no great merchant of Venice ever saw that Rialto under whose noble arch the traveller now pauses with breathless interest; and the statue which Byron's Faliero apostrophizes as one of his famous ancestors was erected to a soldier of fortune a hundred and fifty years after Faliero's death.

In like manner, it is true that though the streets of

* Ruskin, "Stones of Venice."

THE BRIDGE OF THE RIALTO.

Venice are canals, the pedestrian may fare on foot to any part of the city; nor do its inhabitants eternally move about in gondolas, as is popularly supposed. Much that must be pronounced mere sham and melodramatic emotion is mixed up with the customary descriptions of Venice; yet would the reader err wofully if, rebounding to the other extreme, he concluded it was either a prosaic or commonplace deception. It is, on the contrary, a city of singular and picturesque beauty; clothed in those rich and intense colours which inspired the genius of Titian and Tintoretto, and radiant in the lustre of a thousand associations of noble names and noble deeds, crowning it with an imperishable glory; with

> "The light that never was on land or sea,
> The consecration and the poet's dream."

It is a city wealthy in glorious pictures and magnificent memorials of the grandest architecture; the city of Shylock, and Childe Harold, and the Ghost Seer, of Belvidera, Desdemona, and Faliero. I pity the man for whom Venice is not a marvellous poem, replete with suggestive touches and tender fancies, for whose sensibility it has not a magical and ever-living attraction.

VENICE BY NIGHT.

He who would see fair Venice aright should see it, as Scott would have us see the ruined Abbey of Melrose, by the "pale moonlight." Its haunting aspect, under such a condition, has been described by a poet and a prose-writer—both men of genius, and of quick appreciation—and their different impressions will interest the reader more than any detailed inventory of palaces or churches. First, take the poet's animated lines: *—

"How light we go, how softly skim,
And all in moonlight seem to swim!
The south side † rises o'er our bark,
A wall impenetrably dark;
The north is seen profusely bright;
The water, is it shade or light?
Say, gentle moon, which conquers now,
The flood, those massy hulls, or thou?

"How light we go, how softly skim,
And all in moonlight seem to swim!
Reclining, that white dome I mark
Against bright clouds projected dark,
And catch, by brilliant lamps displayed,
The Doge's columns and arcade;
Over smooth waters mildly come
The distant laughter and the hum."

Now for the description of a traveller, who writes in prose, but with the spirit of poetry: ‡—

"O you!" he exclaims, "whoever you are, that journey towards this enchanted city for the first time, let me tell you how happy I count you! There lies before you, for your pleasure, the spectacle of such singular beauty as no picture can ever show you nor book tell you; beauty which you shall feel perfectly but once, and regret for ever.

* Arthur Hugh Clough, "Poems," p. 50.

† Of the Grand Canal.

‡ W. D. Howells, "Venetian Life," pp. 21-23.—To these descriptions we may add the remarks of Longfellow:—"I first saw Venice by moonlight," he says, "as we skimmed by the island of St. George in a felucca, and entered the Grand Canal. A thousand lamps glittered from the square of St. Mark, and along the water's edge. Above rose the cloudy shapes of spires, domes, and palaces emerging from the sea; and occasionally the twinkling lamp of a gondola darted across the water like a shooting star, and suddenly disappeared, as if quenched in the wave. There was something so unearthly in the scene—so visionary and fairy-like—that I almost expected to see the city float away like a cloud and dissolve into thin air."—LONGFELLOW, "Outre-Mer."

"As the gondola slipped down the gloom and silence of the broad canal, I could at first feel nothing but the beautiful silence, broken only by the star-silvered dip of the oars. Then, on either hand, I saw stately palaces rise gray and lofty from the dark waters, holding here and there a lamp against their faces, which brought balconies, and columns, and carven arches into momentary relief, and threw long streams of crimson into the canal. I could see by the uncertain glimmer how fair was all, but not how sad and old; and so, unhaunted by any pang for the decay that afterwards saddened me amid the forlorn beauty of Venice, I glided on.

"Dark funereal barges like my own went flitting by, and the gondoliers warned each other at every turning with hoarse lugubrious cries; the lines of balconied palaces seemed unending; here and there at their doors larger craft were moored, with dim figures of men moving uncertainly about on them. At last we passed abruptly out of the Grand Canal into one of the smaller channels, and from comparative light into a darkness only remotely affected by some far-streaming corner lamp. But always the pallid stately palaces; always the dark heaven with its trembling stars above, and the dark water with its trembling stars below; but now innumerable bridges, and an utter lonesomeness, and ceaseless sudden turns and windings. One could not resist a vague feeling of anxiety, in these strait and solitary passages, which was part of the strange enjoyment of the time, and which was referable to the novelty, the hush, the darkness, and the piratical appearance, and unaccountable pauses of the gondoliers. Was not this

Venice, and is not Venice for ever associated with bravoes and unexpected dagger-thrusts?"

The first thing which strikes the stranger on setting foot in Venice is its silence. In the very heart of the city—in the centre of the Piazza di San Marco, the rendezvous of merchants and idlers, citizens and patricians—only a low hoarse hum reveals the life of a hundred thousand men. Away from this centre silence prevails, the silence of the desert. For at Venice there are neither carriages, nor carts, nor horses. Thousands of Venetians have never seen any other specimens of the equine race than the brazen steeds which adorn the portal of St. Mark's. There are few pedestrians; for though you may easily traverse the whole town dry-footed along the little quays which border the various canals, and through the scores of tiny lanes which blend together in an almost inextricable labyrinth, these channels of circulation are too narrow and tortuous to admit of the passage of any considerable number of promenaders at once, and indulge, moreover, in so many circuits and détours as to double and even triple the distances from point to point. It is, therefore, by the canals and in the gondolas that the Venetians travel about their city, a gentle and peaceful mode of transport, whose light ripple, far from troubling the silence, seems to render it only the more impressive and more solemn.

And here the question naturally arises, What is a gondola? We turn to Byron for a reply:—

"Didst ever see a gondola? for fear
You should not, I'll describe it you exactly:
'Tis a long covered boat that's common here,
Carved at the prow, built lightly but compactly;

Rowed by two rowers, each called 'gondolier,'
  It glides along the water looking blackly,
Just like a coffin clapt in a canoe,
  Where none can make out what you say or do.
And up and down the long canals they go,
  And under the Rialto shoot along,
By night and day, all paces, swift or slow,
  And round the theatres, a sable throng,
They wait in their dusk livery of woe." *

Mr. Laing describes the gondola as a wherry, less neatly built than the Thames wherry, with the upper half of a mourning hackney-coach, such as our undertakers send out in the rear of a burial train, stuck midships. In this the passengers sit, or recline, on cushions, and may shut themselves up as in a couch with the glass windows or the blinds. Two fellows at opposite ends and sides of the boats, stand shoving the oars from them, and paddle along pretty quickly, avoiding the running foul of other gondolas with great dexterity. In turning corners they might possibly bump against each other, and they give a short cry to warn those coming down the water-street to keep to the right or left.†

GONDOLA.

The skill, says Mr. Howells,‡ with which the gondoliers

* Byron, "Beppo" (Poetical Works). † Laing, "Notes of a Traveller."
‡ W. D. Howells, "Venetian Life."

manage their graceful craft is always admired by strangers who come to Venice, and is certainly remarkable. He describes the gondola as very long and slender, and rising high from the water at either end. Both bow and stern are sharp, the former being ornamented with a deeply-serrated beak of steel, which the gondolier polishes as painfully as an English groom his horse's harness; and the poop having a small platform, not far behind the cabin, on which the gondolier stands when he rows. The danger of collision has always compelled Venetian boatmen to face the bow, and the stroke with the oar is made by pushing, not pulling. It is, consequently, a matter of much difficulty to keep the gondola's head straight, all the strokes being made on one side; and much skill is required to effect the return of the oar blade, preparatory for each new stroke.

Under the hands of the gondolier the gondola becomes a living thing, full of life and winning movement. The wood-work of the little cabins is richly carved, and it is finished with mirrors and luxuriously cushioned seats. The sensation of the gondola's progress, says Mr. Howells, felt by the occupant of the cabin, as he reclines upon these cushions, may be described, to the female apprehension at least, as *too* divine. The cabin is removable at pleasure, and in summer is generally replaced by awnings. But in the evening, when the fair Venetians go out in their gondolas to take the air, even this awning is dispensed with, and the long slender boat glides darkly down the Grand Canal, bearing a dazzling freight of white *tulle*, pale-faced, black-eyed beauty, and flashing jewels.

Is not Venice the very home of the picturesque? Who does not remember the glowing canvas of Titian, Bellini, Tintoretto, and Bassano, and the lively and gorgeous scenes which they represent — the stately personages whom they so admirably depict, the quaint rich costume which seems so worthy of these reverend signors? Let the imagination, aided by these eloquent memorials, carry us over the gulf of two centuries, and place before us a Venetian gentleman in all his bravery.*

A man of tall stature, wrapped in a long black cloak, disembarks from his gondola, and with slow and dignified step traverses the quay of the Piazzetta. The silver insignia flashing upon his girdle of black velvet shows that he is a person of high rank; and, in truth, despite his youthful bearing, he is one of the conscript fathers of the republic—a senator—aged twenty-five years, the legal age for admission to the Grand Council. His long toga droops upon the ground, in defiance of the sumptuary laws which prescribe its proper length; and his ample sleeves, instead of falling, as they should do, below the hand, are clasped tightly about the wrists. The collar stands upright; it is open in front, where it reveals that of a black silver pourpoint; a diamond button, or one of gold, or of wrought silver, fastens the shirt. Contrary to official etiquette, which requires the patricians to wear their own hair, his head is covered with a peruke, on which is perched a small cap of black wool, with a pad of the same material. A stola of the same cloth and colour as the robe, and about an ell in length, is flung over the left shoulder. Stockings and shoes of a bright

* Galibert, "Histoire de Venise," p. 493.

scarlet red complete the costume of this noble personage. When walking, he raises his long robe with his left hand, while his right draws back the folds of the robe a little over the chest, so as to display the glittering jewelled handle of a dagger, thrust in the belt of his pourpoint.

This dignified and handsome costume never underwent any important modifications. But the colour frequently varied. Blue was the favourite for five centuries; it was then replaced by black, which continued in vogue until the downfal of the Republic. Violet, however, was affected for certain public functions; and under solemn circumstances the black official toga gave way to mantles of costly stuffs and dazzling hues. Scarlet, proscribed by the modern taste, which rejects all lively and sparkling tints, was long the favourite colour with Venetians of every class; and the use of the red cloak became so general in the last two centuries that it might be regarded as the national costume. Little children were oppressed with it so soon as they could walk; and not a beggar thought himself fit to appear in public till he had flung some red rags across his shoulders. Visitors called upon their friends wearing the mantle; and the most flattering speech that could be made to a stranger assured him that he wore his cloak like a Venetian.

At the epoch when the young patrician flourished whom we have just seen disembarking from his gondola, with his black toga, his peruke, his cap, and his red stockings, we might have watched him under the porticoes of St. Mark paying elaborate homage to a handsome lady, seven feet high, advancing with slow and painful steps, supporting herself on either side on the shoulder of an attendant. Observe her closely, for she is a lady of high birth, the wife of a knight of the golden étole, of a procurator of St. Mark, of perhaps a member of the Council of Ten. She is mounted on pattens nearly two feet high, and balances herself majestically on these stilts. Since the suppression of these pedestals the noble Venetian ladies have resumed the ordinary stature of the women of their country, and what they have lost in height they have gained in lightness and grace. The use of pattens was, they say, an ingenious invention of the Venetian husbands, to prevent their ladies from going abroad without their knowledge. It is to the daughters of the Doge Contarini, who first rebelled against this ancient fashion towards the middle of the seventeenth century, that the Venetian ladies owe the release of their pretty feet.*

The feminine costume is always and infinitely more diversified and more changeable than that of man. And in this branch of industrial art the Venetian ladies have displayed a fertility of invention fully equal to that of the Parisians. Let us glance at a few of the principal phases. In the eleventh century—the heroic age of Venice—they wore mantles descending to the waist. These, in the twelfth century, were transformed into a sort of cape with large fur-trimmed sleeves, called the Ducal, because resembling that worn by the Doge. The rage for costly furs increased to such an extent as to menace the ruin of the Venetian husbands, and a sumptuary law was passed in 1303 which abridged in every way these extravagant sleeves. The ladies retaliated by lengthening their trains, but these luxurious appendages were retrenched by another

*Galibert, "Histoire de Venise," p. 495.

edict. The extent of stuff being thus reduced, they fell back upon an excess of ornament, and covered their dresses with gold and jewellery, a dangerous extreme of sumptuousness, which provoked another enactment. Then came the fashion of silken robes, confined close to the body by a girdle, to which a golden chain suspended a carving-knife in a rich sheath, a symbol of woman's authority in her most important domain. About the same time the sleeves began to steal beyond the limits fixed by law, and were soon elongated to such an extent that they hugged the ground, while they were covered with a complete network of gems and golden buttons, excesses against which the senate once more fulminated its decrees.

The latter half of the sixteenth century was, perhaps, the most brilliant period of the costume of high-born Venetian dames. One of the occasions on which they displayed themselves in their completest splendour was the solemn entry into Venice of the new Dogaressa, Cecilia Dandolo, wife of the Doge Geronimo Priuli. The procession was arranged on a scale of unusual magnificence, for the Venetians were fully sensible of the value of ceremonies. Some toilettes chosen from among those which were considered the most successful will give the reader an idea of the costly fashions of the time.

First, let us take that of the Dogaressa. Under her regal mantle, with its long-flowing train, she wore a robe of gold brocade, trimmed with ermine, open in front, and garnished with golden buttons. Her head-dress consisted of a curved Phrygian cap, enclosed within the *corno ducale*, or ducal crown. Round her snowy neck shone a collar of the finest pearls—"orient pearls," but not "at random strung"—and a chain of gold, starred with jewels, from which depended a costly bijou, fresh from the workshop of the skilfullest goldsmith on the Rialto. Her waist was encircled by a second chain, whose ends descended to the ground. Her fair hair, plaited behind, and in front gathered up over the brow in two spiral points, completed a surpassingly magnificent *ensemble*, except that in her right hand she carried a small flag, or pennon, which she fluttered to and fro like a fan.

One of the ladies of her suite wore a mantilla of black lace, sown with silver stars, and attached to the summit of the head-dress by golden pins. An ample robe of brocade displayed the sleeves and skirts of the dress beneath, which was made of an exquisitely fine blue stuff; like the Dogaressa, and all the other ladies, she carried a flag in her hand.

These, however, must be taken as specimens of court and ceremonial attire, and it is due to the ladies of Venice to admit that, under ordinary circumstances, they were contented with a more modest garb. Moreover, all luxuriousness and choice of attire was permitted only to married females. The unmarried formed a class apart. Closely confined in the paternal mansion, they held no intercourse with men, not even with their nearest kin, who only saw them on their marriage-day. On the few occasions they went abroad, or when they attended mass, they were enveloped in a long white veil of a very delicate and shining gauze (*gaze*), called *fazzuolo*, which just permitted the skirt of a brown stuff robe to be visible. At a marriageable age they were dressed entirely in black, with an ample mantilla of fine and thickly-woven silk, which was thrown over the head, and descended to the waist, enabling them to see without being seen. Sometimes a small black apron, trimmed with an edging of rich lace, was added to this elegant and yet modest costume. But on the day of marriage, and even of betrothal, all constraint ceased. The maidenly veil was thrown aside, and the loosened tresses poured freely over the snowy shoulder, or were gathered up above the forehead in numerous knots, blended with jewels and golden beads. The fair blonde locks were so highly prized in Venice, as amongst the ancient Greeks, that the hair of the newly-married bride, when necessary, was dyed of this colour. She wore for a whole year the splendid attire of her wedding-day.

Into the lax morality of Venetian society, one of the principal causes of the decline and fall of the Republic, it is not our province here to enter. Nor need we describe the peculiar institution of the *cicisbeo*, or the *cavaliere servente*—two characters which figured conspicuously in Venice for three centuries, and have hardly yet disappeared.

Another Venetian institution, which helped the downfal of the state, was the *bravo*. These assassins and professional murderers, at the disposal of any person prepared to pay for their services and protect them afterwards, formed a numerous class at Venice. They have been rendered familiar to us by the part they have played in the drama and the romance. Occasions for the exercise of their hired bravery were not infrequent. To lodge a ball from an arquebus in the head of an unfortunate rival, to plant a dagger in the throat of an enemy, to disfigure with gashes the countenance of some lovely but imprudent woman, were the noble exploits to which they devoted their career. Their mode of procedure varied according to the circumstances under which, and the persons against whom, they were called to act. This professional brigandage had its acknowledged rules. If their intended victim was a citizen, or of low degree, they despatched him treacherously, like a dog, in an ambuscade. Were he a man of rank, a noble, or a cavalier, who carried a sword, the bravo pretended to attack him like a man of honour, *da uomo onorato*. In this case he donned a coat of almost impenetrable mail, over which he wore a leathern jerkin, covered his head with an iron helmet, and armed himself with a short but broad-bladed sword. An ample cloak, almost concealing his person, completed his equipment. Thus caparisoned, the bravo posted himself in some solitary court or obscure corner, by which he had learned that his intended victim would pass. As soon as he perceived him approaching he threw off his cloak, fastened his helmet securely on his head, and drew his sword. He was thus "on guard" before his surprised adversary had time to collect himself, and the issue of a combat thus perfidiously arranged may easily be divined.

In these "affairs of honour," ordinarily terminating in the death of the man so treacherously assaulted, no charge of murder could be sustained by the officers of justice. How compare to a common assassin the gallant bravo, who fought openly and in "fair" fight? Moreover, the influence of the person by whom he was hired came to his assistance, and he almost invariably escaped punishment. It is not to be wondered at that the trade of the bravo flourished; that assassination was rife in Venice; that not even the best or noblest were safe from the secret knife. As late as 1785, a certain Count of Brescia, who had escaped from prison, found means, thanks to his bravoes, to rid himself of more than a score of his enemies at Venice. Ladies of high rank, too, made use of these assassins, either to gratify their vengeance, to remove a person who held their dangerous secrets, or for services of a less terrible character; for the bravo lent himself willingly to all kinds of enterprises in which money could be gained; at need he would undertake the defence of persons whose lives were imperilled; and assumed the office, and faithfully fulfilled the duties, of a body-guard. Sometimes they were employed in this capacity even by Justice herself. An artisan, having respectfully solicited from a patrician creditor the discharge of a long-standing debt, the latter, weary of his importunity, brutally dashed him headlong from his door; and when he renewed his entreaties, aimed a pistol at him, which it was with difficulty he tore from his grasp. Having escaped this danger, the artisan betook himself to one of the Inquisitors of State, to whom he related what had just transpired. The Inquisitor immediately summoned before him the patrician, ordered him to discharge the debt, and to deposit a sum of money in guarantee of the artisan's life. He was also ordered to support at his own expense, until further orders, a *bravo*, who was thenceforth to follow the creditor everywhere, and see that no accident happened to him; for, in case of misfortune, the noble would have been held accountable, though no blame might really have attached to him.

The cicisbeo and the bravo no longer exist in Venice; except in the pages of dramatist and romancist, they have altogether vanished. Who will regret their disappearance? Unfortunately, many other traits of the ancient life of Venice have been effaced, whose loss we cannot recall without regret, and whose bright and picturesque images the imagination delights to revive.

Venice was the city of fêtes, spectacles, and pleasures; the mysterious and terrible hand of a suspicious, pitiless government appeared to give the reins willingly to all public manifestations which gave no umbrage to its sombre policy; and in this city of universal apprehension, where every one dreaded the sword suspended by a hair, and were uncertain of the morrow's doom, the outward life resembled a perpetual carnival.

The public fêtes of Venice, says M. Galibert, so pompous, so numerous, and so religiously observed, were nearly all devoted to the great object of eternizing the memory of some grand national event—a victory, a deliverance from the plague, the capture of a town, a public revolution.

Thus, to every Venetian the history of his country was always present. He was never allowed to forget its past triumphs or its heroic achievements, and their contemplation, entering intimately into his daily life, was well adapted to keep alive the spirit of patriotism and stimulate him to preserve unimpaired the glorious heritage he had received from his ancestors.

The most solemn and significant of these public festivals was that which occurred annually on Ascension Day, in commemoration of Ziani's victory over the fleet of Frederick Barbarossa.*

On that day was celebrated the famous ceremony of the Marriage of the Adriatic.

> "Then what so gay as Venice? Every gale
> Breathed music! and who flocked not, while she reigned,
> To celebrate her Nuptials with the Sea." †

On the Piazza di San Marco the national industry displayed its immense riches; the commerce of the known world there exposed its countless products; and the Republic at one and the same time demonstrated the wide range of its external power and the brilliant reality of its internal prosperity.

These Espousals of Venice and the Sea were the symbol of the supremacy which she arrogated as Queen of the Adriatic, and of which she was prouder and more jealous than of all her other pretensions. Not unwisely so, for her safety depended on her undisputed sway over the Adriatic. By land she was impregnable; to strike a fatal blow at her heart the enemy must break through her ocean defences. The *Bucentaur*, or *Bucentoro*, ‡ a magnificent vessel used exclusively for this solemnity, was, without any poetical figure, the Ship of the State, the Vessel of the Republic. Originally this national fête was designed to commemorate the conquest of Dalmatia, and

* See *ante*, p. 59.

† Rogers, "Poetical Works:" *Italy*.

‡ The decree of 1311, ordering the construction of this vessel, speaks of it as "*navilium Ducentorum hominum*" (a ship for 200 men), and the word "Bucentaur" is probably a corruption of "Ducentorum."

THE BUCENTAUR.

the victories won over the Narentine pirates in 997, during the reign of the Doge Pietro Orseolo II. They repaired on Ascension Day to visit the sea, beyond the harbour of Lido, and performed certain ceremonies in accordance with the taste of the age. For a hundred and eighty years the custom survived unchanged. But in 1170, after the reconciliation between the Emperor Frederick Barbarossa and Pope Alexander III., that pontiff having, according to some doubtful witnesses, invested the Venetians with the sovereignty of the Adriatic, and consecrated the concession by the gift of a ring of gold, to the ancient ceremonies was added that of the marriage of the Doge with the Sea.

On that day all was gaiety and rejoicing in Venice. At dawn, the silver bells clashed their music from every spire and tower, and all the cannons of the arsenal and the forts of Lido thundered forth simultaneously. Venice, in its richest bravery, poured towards the Piazza di San Marco, and streamed along the quays; or embarking in thousands of gondolas and boats fluttering gaily-coloured flags, gathered around the *Bucentaur*, which had been brought from the arsenal on the previous evening, and moored at the foot of the two columns of the Piazzetta.

The *Bucentaur* was a galley one hundred feet in length. It consisted of two decks, the lower one occupied by a hundred and sixty picked rowers, selected from the most skilful and robust sailors in the fleet, who, seated four by four along each bench, wait, with oar in hand, the signal of departure; forty sailors standing near them complete the crew. The upper deck, divided throughout its whole length by an open partition of nine arcades, each seven feet wide, whose pillars are ornamented with gilded figures, thus consists of two galleries, each sixty feet in length. Along the sides ninety seats are arranged for the Doge's retinue; in the stern is arranged a state-saloon, raised on a couple of steps, and glittering with the ducal throne.

The prow is armed with two spurs or projections, one above the other, and both enriched with gigantic allegorical figures of Justice, Peace, the Earth, and the Sea, and other carvings blazing with gold; while numberless ornaments of sphinxes, marine monsters, ocean shells, and scrolls, decorate the broadsides and poop of this magnificent naval edifice. The upper deck is covered for nearly its whole extent with a roof or awning (in Venetian, *tierno*), supported along either side by pilasters carved in imitation of caryatides; in the middle, by the longitudinal partition of the deck; and draped by an immense hanging of cramoisy velvet glowing with embroidery of gold. Above the ducal saloon floats the resplendent banner of St. Mark.*

The bells strike noon. The Doge, accompanied by the ambassadors of foreign states, by the Papal nuncio, and the members of the Signiory, issues from the ducal palace by the Porta della Carta, attended by a splendid cortége, and preceded by eight standard-bearers, in couples, carrying the standards of the Republic, red, blue, white and violet; and by six trumpeters, whose shrill notes rival the keen chimes of the multitudinous bells. With these sounding musicians advance two children, covered with ribbons, and enveloped in enormous frills. The servants in the suite of the ambassadors, dressed in their richest attire, follow in due order; followed by a

* The *Bucentaur* here described was built in 1727, and burnt by the French in 1797. The sculptures were designed by Antonio Corradini.—GALIBERT, "Histoire de Venise," p. 503.

band of fife-players (*pifferari*), escorted by the ducal equerries. Then come the Doge's secretary, a deacon carrying a wax-taper presented by the Pope Alexander, and the chaplain of the palace, followed by two men supporting on their interlinked arms the footstool and cushion of the Doge. Behind this crowd march the more illustrious actors in the pageant; first, the great captain of the city, in a robe of scarlet—open at the sides and in front, and ornamented with silk girdles and tassels—and in a cassock of cramoisy velvet, fastened at the waist by a velvet belt with velvet buckles, to which is attached a long sabre, that clinks against the ground; his stockings and sandals are red, like the rest of his costume, and he wears a black cap.

Next to this eminently brilliant personage comes the grand chancellor, dressed in senatorial garb; then the little *ballotino*, a richly attired child, whose innocent hand is employed to extract the balls from the urn of scrutiny on the election of the Doge. Finally appears the Doge himself, in a long mantle of ermine, fastened by golden buttons, a blue cassock, and a simar (or long robe) of cloth of gold. His head is covered with a ducal bonnet, also of cloth of gold—a conical head-gear, whose rounded top is slightly curved backward after the ancient Phrygian fashion, and which is surrounded by a golden crown blazing with jewels. His sandals, like the bonnet, are of a woven golden stuff. On the right hand of the prince advances the Papal legate, easily recognized by his square cap, his surcoat buttoned from top to bottom, and his lace-embroidered alb, covered with a *camail* or short cloak; and on his left, the imperial ambassador

(*Cesareo*), clothed in a mantle with an upright collar, surmounted by a gorgeously expanded ruff, and in a velvet bonnet. The other ambassadors, attired according to the mode of their respective courts, paraded in their rear. After them two officers follow—one bearing the Doge's umbrella, the other the royal sword, with the point upwards; and the procession is closed by the members of the Signiory and the Grand Council.*

Slowly and stately moves the glittering train towards the extremity of the mole of the Piazzetta, where the *Bucentaur*, like some magnificent ocean-bird, reposes on the bosom of the waters. The embarkation immediately commences, to the blare of the silver trumpets and the shouts of the excited multitudes. Each person takes his allotted seat: the patricians on the four rows of benches arranged in the double gallery of the deck; the Doge, his councillors, and the ambassadors, under the dais erected on the poop. In the prow are posted the admiral of the arsenal and that of Lido, charged with the guidance of the *Bucentaur*, while the admiral of Malamocco places himself at the helm; the masters, mates, and a hundred of the arsenal workmen (*arsenaloti*) surround these officers, on the alert to execute their orders. Now the anchor is weighed! All the bells of the city ring out a jubilant peal, to which the ships of war, the arsenal, and the fort, respond by salvos of artillery; and with this far-rolling thunder the musicians on board the *Bucentaur* and the surrounding boats

* An amusing description of this ceremony is given by quaint old Howell in his "Epistolæ Ho-Elianæ," book i., letter 31; but the minute account in the text is adopted from M. Galibert.

mingle the strains of a joyous music. Majestically over the shining wave glides the King of the Adriatic, to the regular cadence of the long red oars; and around it, like butterflies around a gorgeous rose, hover thousands of gaily-decorated barks and skiffs,—barks and skiffs of all kinds and all dimensions—the slender rapid galliot; the richly-ornamented wherry; the gilded barges of the ambassadors, fringed with gold and silver; the private and public gondolas, loaded with passengers in festal costume, and with women brilliantly attired and masked.

Still with the sound of music and rejoicing, and under a luminous Italian sky, the radiant fleet advances towards the island of Santa Elmo, where it is met by a great gilded galley, bearing the patriarch of Venice and his clergy. He proceeds on board the *Bucentaur*, and blesses a vase of water which is handed to him, afterwards throwing it into the sea as a supposed preventative of tempests. Having arrived at the Port of San Nicolas, the ducal vessel crosses the strait amid the thunders of a hundred cannon, and proceeding a short distance out to sea, she puts about. At this moment a door behind the sovereign's throne is suddenly thrown open; the Doge steps into a small gallery, and from thence flings into the waves a golden ring, accompanying the action with these sacramental words:—

"Desponsamus te, mare, in signum veri perpetuique dominii."

[We wed thee, O sea, in token of our true and perpetual sovereignty.]

Then breaks from the assembled thousands a loud

hoarse cry of joy and triumph. The marriage-ceremony is terminated.

After a solemn mass, which the Doge and all his retinue, disembarking, attend at the church of San Nicolas of Lido, the gay fleet returns to Venice in the same well-ordered pomp. Then the great dignitaries, the ambassadors, and the members of the Government, repair to the ducal palace, and assist at a sumptuous banquet presided over by the Doge; while the populace pour headlong into the Piazza di San Marco and abandon themselves to all kinds of revelry.

Ascension Day was, in fact, the inauguration of the great yearly fair of Venice, which commenced on the preceding evening and lasted a fortnight. All round the Piazza wooden booths were rapidly run up, which, far from presenting the miserable aspect of the impoverished sheds in use at ordinary fairs, were substantial edifices, constructed on an uniform plan, and of considerable architectural pretensions.

It was at these annual expositions that Venetian industry displayed all the variety and fertility of its products: its stuffs of silk, and wool, and velvet; its exquisite lace (*merletu*) known as *Point de Venise;* its chains of gold, delicate and supple as silken threads; its renowned Murano crystal; the brilliant glass-ware (*conterie, margherita*), of which the Venetians alone possessed the secret of manufacture; bracelets of gold, and luxuriously ornamented arms and armour. Art also had its allotted place, where the painter and the sculptor sometimes exhibited their latest masterpieces; where occasionally glowed the dazzling colours of a Titian, a Tintoretto, and a Giorgione; where Canova for the first time exposed to the public one of his earlier works, the marble group of Dædalus and Icarus.

Under another aspect, the fair of the *Sensa* (Ascension) was the Hyde Park—the Rotten Row—the Derby—the Ascot of Venice. For its hilarious fortnight, the Piazza di San Marco became the general rendezvous, the favourite promenade. It was there the exquisites and the fine ladies of the time fluttered in the sunshine, and displayed the latest achievements of capricious Fashion. And there, too, the milliners and the modistes, in unconscious ridicule of their patrons, exhibited in the most advantageous position a gigantic doll, attired in the style which they wished to puff into popularity as the *mode* for the ensuing year. In the morning the women made their appearance clad in the graceful veil—or *zendaletto*—of black taffeta, which covered their head and shoulders, was crossed around the neck and waist, and fell upon the ground in elegant simplicity. In the evening they were arrayed in the customary carnival attire; wearing the *tabura* and the *bauta*—the former a long mantle of black or coloured silk; the latter a kind of black silk hood, trimmed with lace, on which was coquettishly perched a little man's hat, three-cornered, and decked with plume and cockade. Of this costume the mask was an indispensable adjunct. The Sensa fortnight was considered—and so were all fête-days in general—as a demi-carnival. Al fresco spectacles, singers, dancers, marionettes, buffoons of every kind, attracted on these occasions the applause, and received the largesse, of the

Venetian populace, which sought no greater boon than to promenade in the Piazza like its masters, devouring some savoury *frittola*, or some of those sweets or preserves to which the Venetians have always been so partial.

But let us direct our glances, for a moment, to the real Carnival, the Carnival of Venice, which, with the clash of bells and the clink of rattles, agitates and swells the surging currents of the masquerade for four months. *Speaking* masks and *silent* masks advance now in dense groups, now in single files, like the fantastic apparitions of the magic lantern. A lawyer encumbered with a gigantic wig—in a robe of black, and with a paper portfolio under his arm—pleads in a ridiculously squeaking voice, accompanying and enforcing his observations with oratorical gestures which are rendered absurd by the truth concealed in their exaggeration. By the side of this everlasting babbler, a group of French simpletons, ridiculously attired, display the eccentricities of foppish gallantry, and attack a laughing Venetian damsel with the artillery of grotesque and high-flown compliments. Close at hand a would-be Englishman displays his insular reserve and haughty pride, or a pseudo-American bustles about with well-feigned inquisitiveness. Here, the universal Punch is the centre of an admiring audience, who applaud his old jokes as if they had never heard them before, and burst into fits of shrill laughter when he mimics the Neapolitan *patois*. There Harlequin, brandishing his wooden sword, bounds and pirouettes to the delight of an attentive crowd, blowing kisses to every fair girl who passes, and lavishing smart accolades on the shoulders of impertinent admirers, who press too closely upon him. And now he goes in quest of nimble Columbine, from whom he has been sundered by the sudden irruption of a band of peasants traversing the Piazza with their asses, their dogs, and their baggage. Will he find her standing, with down-dropped eyes and half-concealed smiles, among the group gathered round yonder Dominican, whose portly figure and double chin are a pregnant commentary on his text of abstinence and self-sacrifice? Or will she not rather have been attracted by this company of pretended Spanish soldiers, who, with more than Castilian gravity, go through a series of improvized military exercises? No; he will seek her among the open-mouthed and open-eyed admirers of yonder quack, who, in portentous peruke and spangled coat, liberally gives away his "Elixir of Love," his "Wine of Everlasting Youth," and his "Infallible Remedy" for all the ills that flesh is heir to. But she is not there, and discomfited Harlequin is off with a leap to the spectacled magician, with pointed cap and white beard, who has established his astrological consulting-office at the foot of the Campanile. Or will she have been captivated by some one of those peripatetic rhapsodists, those improvisatores, who, with eloquently passionate gestures, and accompanying themselves on a cracked violin in lieu of a lyre, pour out verse upon verse of bald but sonorous declamation? Poor Harlequin! he would hunt his missing fair one far and wide if his old friend the Clown did not inform him, with a malicious smile, that he had just seen his Columbine, in the company of a radiant foreign stranger, entering the theatre of San Cassiano, where the new opera is being represented.

The *Giovedi grasso* (*Le Jeudi gras*, Shrove Tuesday) was one of the most important days of the Venetian carnival, for then was presented in the Piazza di San Marco a rude and curious spectacle, strikingly illustrative of the coarse, grotesque taste of the age.

In 1162, Ulrich, the patriarch of Aquileja, seized, by a treacherous stratagem, the city of Grado, then subject to Venice. The Venetians, however, quickly recovered it, and made prisoners the patriarch and twelve of his canons. As the turbulent patriarchs of Aquileja had long been a thorn in the side of the Republic, the Venetians now determined to indulge in an appropriate revenge. Accordingly, they refused to release the patriarch unless he agreed to send to Venice a bull and twelve fat hogs. What meaning the patriarch attached to this singular condition is unknown; but the Venetians understood the bull as typical of himself, and the swine of his portly canons; and it was the great event of the Giovedi grasso for these animals to be slaughtered in the Piazza San Marco, in the presence of the Doge, the senators, and the people.

The locksmiths, and other workers in iron, having distinguished themselves in the recapture of Grado, to their guild was allotted the honour of immolating the typical animals. Great skill was shown in decapitating the bull at a blow, without suffering the sword to touch the ground after passing through the animal's neck. The swine were slain with lances. Athletic games ensued for the delectation of the people; and the Doge and his senators attacked and destroyed with staves some lightly-built timber castles, symbolical of the triumph of the Republic over the feudal power.

As the centuries advanced, this part of the ceremony, as well as the slaughter of the swine, was discontinued; a fact in which Mr. Ruskin sees evidence of a corrupt disdain on the part of the Doges of wholesome and simple allegory; but in which most people, as Mr. Howells remarks, will discern nothing more than a natural wish to discontinue, in more civilized times, a childish barbarity.*

Another kind of spectacle perpetuated the memory of the ancient quarrels of the inhabitants of San Nicolo and Castello—two districts situated on the opposite banks of the Grand Canal—who were formerly engaged in continual strife. From time immemorial, on the Giovedi grasso, the two factions of Castellani and Nicolotti, represented by volunteers, and clothed in distinctive costumes, engaged upon a bridge in mimic battle. The bridge being without parapets, more than one of the combatants went headlong into the water. Whichever band succeeded in crossing the bridge on the bodies of its adversaries, was declared victorious; but most frequently, in these fictitious encounters, as in real combats, both parties might with equal justice claim the laurel of triumph.

The Nicolotti and the Castellani had also, on this same day, another and more amusing method of testing their strength and competing with each other. Certain men were selected to give a representation of what was called the Labours of Hercules (*le Forze d'Ercole*); these being human pyramids composed of six, seven, or eight men

* W. D. Howells, "Venetian Life," p. 227.

GRAND CANAL, FROM THE RIALTO.

mounted one upon another; the base was formed of sixteen to twenty men, and the number diminished gradually to the summit of the pyramid, terminated by a child who stood there on his head, with his legs in the air, and after various movements of his arms and legs, resumed his feet, bowed to the Doge, and leaped from an elevation of more than thirty feet to some mattresses spread upon the ground. The men who had supported him leaped after him, then the third, and so on to the base or last tier. The victory belonged to the party who had reared their pyramid highest, or had longest preserved their equilibrium.

The last scene of the Carnival was the burial of the Carnival itself. An immense procession of the most extravagant and grotesque masks, accompanied an effigy, or stuffed figure, intended to emblematize the Carnival; they were armed with whistles, rattles, pipes, and bells—the whole producing a monstrous *charivari*—and carried paper lanterns in their hands, or small tapers attached to their heads. From time to time they hissed the defunct, exclaiming, "For the death of the Carnival." At midnight the clocks of St. Mark and the other churches "clashed and hammered" throughout the city the last hour of Carnival and the first of Lent.

Two only of the national *religious* festivals, says Mr. Howells,* now shadowly survive the Republic—that of the Church of the Redentore on the Guidecca, and that of the Church of the Salute on the Grand Canal—both votive churches, and built in grateful acknowledgment of the deliverance of Venice from the plague in 1578 and 1630. The celebration of these two *festas*, in all their general features, bear a close resemblance; but that of the Salute is less important, though in character the more religious. A bridge of boats is annually thrown across the Canalazzo, and on the day of the Purification

* W. D. Howells, "Venetian Life," p. 235.

the people throng to the Virgin's shrine to express their gratitude for her protection. And so strong was this gratitude immediately after the disappearance of the pest, that the senate built a wooden church while the architects were preparing their designs for the present building, and consecrated it with unusual pomp (1630). On the Festa del Redentore (the third Sunday of July) a bridge of boats is thrown over the canal of the Guidecca, and vast throngs incessantly traverse it day and night. But though the small tradesmen, says Mr. Howells, who deal in fried cakes, in apples, peaches, pears, and other fruits, make intolerable uproar behind their booths on the long quay before the church; though the vendors of mulberries (for which the gardens of Guidecca are famous) fill the air with their sweet jargoning (for their cries are like the shrill notes of so many singing-birds); though thousands of people meander to and fro, and saunter along the bridge,—yet the Festa del Redentore has now none of the old-time gaiety it wore when the Venetians thronged the gardens, and feasted, sung, danced, and flirted the night away, and at dawn went in their fleets of many-lanterned boats, covering the lagoon with fairy light, to behold the sunrise on the Adriatic Sea.

The most imposing, however, and the most curious of the shows or sports which lent life and animation to the fêtes of Venice, were those nautical races called *regattas* —the Olympian games of the Adriatic capital—instituted, it is said, to commemorate the deliverance of the young Venetian brides carried off by the Triestine pirates.*

* See *antè*, p. 45.

A REGATTA IN VENICE.

Confined at first to simple trials of speed between the galleys of the State, and intended to exercise their crews, these races acquired, after awhile, the importance and splendour of a public solemnity. It was the spectacle to which the people looked forward every year with the greatest impatience, and in which they participated with the highest enthusiasm; it was, in effect, tnat most flattering to these islanders, born and living in the bosom of the waters. The gondoliers who intended to figure on these occasions went into training a long time beforehand; for them the regatta was a day of triumph or shame, and not infrequently the happiness of their whole life depended on the issue of this trial of strength and skill. The loved maiden whom they sought in marriage would not give any decided answer to their prayers until the great event was decided. When the day approached, the relations of the gondoliers named to take part in the race exhorted them to do their best, and reminded them of the prowess of their fathers, their brothers, or some of their kinsmen. They pointed out the prizes gained in these tourneys proudly suspended against the walls of their humble dwellings, trophies of which the gondoliers were as proud as the patricians of their blazoned escutcheons. Masses were celebrated, and the images of their favourite saints decorated with garlands, to secure the success of the competitor.*

At early morn the Grand Canal was covered with gondolas, barks, wherries, boats of every kind, large and small, unadorned or richly ornamented, and loaded with spectators who found their eyes and ears regaled even before the commencement of the regatta. For on this occasion the Grand Canal and its double range of palatial edifices presented a fairylike spectacle. Magnificent hangings of velvet, satin, and damask of the liveliest colours decorated the walls and floated from the bal-

* We condense this graphic description from M. Galibert's "Histoire de Venise," pp. 509-512.

conies of the palaces; terraces, and windows, and quays, and canal, invaded by a curious multitude, displayed in the most picturesque confusion all the varieties of foreign and Venetian costume, while numerous orchestras, posted upon stages along the canal-bank, rent the air with their loud exultant strains.

The race-course (if we may use the expression) was about four Venetian miles, or upwards of five and a quarter English miles in length. The starting-point was at Castello, at the eastern extremity of the city; thence the barks glided along the Quai des Esclavons into the Great Canal, which they traversed for nearly its entire length towards the churches of Santa Lucia and Corpus Domini, where in the midst of the water was planted the turning-post; in wheeling round this goal the gondoliers displayed all their vigour and address to avoid running foul of a rival boat, or to gain the lead. The post turned, the *bateletti* re-ascended the canal as far as the palazzo Foscari, in whose vicinity rose a magnificent architectural construction representing a temple, a mountain, a fortress, or a triumphal arch. Here the gondoliers halted, and here the distribution of prizes took place. The conquerors received from the hands of the magistrates a small flag on which was inscribed the value of the prize gained; moreover, the colour of the flag—red, green, blue, and yellow—indicated its relative importance. The smallest prize was only ten ducats, to which was added a live sucking pig; and hence originated the insulting term of "lowest prize of the regatta," freely hurled at one another in their quarrels by the gondoliers.

The first race was run by small boats (*bateletti*) with only one oar; it lasted an hour. In the second figured gondolas also impelled by a single oar; then the two-oared bateletti and gondolas entered into competition. A fifth race was sometimes made up with the same boats equipped and rowed by women belonging to the fisher-folk of Chioggia, de Mestre, and the islands of the Lagoon.

These exercises were protracted over five or six hours; the distance was generally accomplished in less than forty minutes. According to a calculation made at the regatta held in 1846, in honour of the Empress of Russia, the usual rate of speed in calm water was one thousand yards in four minutes. It is not probable that the gondoliers of old were less skilful or less robust than those who displayed their energies on this occasion.

The most brilliant race was that in which the gondola was managed by one man with one oar. Standing in the stern of his swift galley, bending over his long oar, his countenance beaded with sweat, his eyes inflamed with the ardour of the strife, the gondolier swept past the spectators with the speed of a horse at full gallop, and flew like an arrow between a double tier of long boats, called *bissoni* or *malgherotti*, with eight or ten oars, manned by young patricians, whose gondoliers took part in the regatta. These show-barks were magnificently decorated,—gold, silver, hangings, feathers, and flowers were lavished upon them. Their prow was adorned with figures representing the mythological divinities: Juno with her peacock, Neptune on his shell drawn by marine horses, and Venus with her doves, mingled among a motley group of savages, Chinese, and Moors. The company on board the bissones, kneeling upon cushions, and armed with a cross-bow, discharged small pellets of gilded or silvered plaster at any boat which threatened to obstruct the passage of the gondoliers whom they patronized. When the regatta was given in honour of some illustrious personage on a visit to Venice, the noble guest was placed in a bissona outshining every other in magnificence, and equipped at the cost of the Republic. At the regatta of May 1846, in which all the traditional usages were closely observed, the Empress of Russia and her daughter, the Grand Duchess Olga, were embarked in a sumptuously decorated bissona, and escorted by gondolas in black and white, bearing their attendants.

The regatta was always preceded by another nautical exercise, which took place on the Eve of the Ascension, on the canal of the Guidecca, and was called the *Corso*, in reference, we suppose, to the horse-races in vogue in several Italian towns. Some hundreds of small canoes, each carrying one man, described, with the rapidity of a whirlwind, an immense ellipse. In this movement they seemed to pursue or avoid each other with all their might, so that at times the mobile chain formed an unbroken line, as if the gondolas had been all attached by chains, and appeared to move *en masse* by the impulse of a common force. In the interior of the area thus marked out, young cavaliers, four or six in each *batelli*, performed various evolutions and feats of skill and strength. They wore a loose white pourpoint, white breeches, and a black scarf. During these exercises, the quays of the canal of the Guidecca, and the canal itself, and the windows of the houses looking out upon it, were crowded with spectators.

We must not omit an allusion to a spectacle of frequent occurrence even now-a-days in the city of the isles.

The *Fresco*, or Water-Pageant, is simply a procession of boats, with lights and music. Two immense barges, lit up with hundreds of twinkling paper lanterns, carry the military bands; then come the barges of the civil and military dignitaries, followed by the gondolas of such citizens as choose to share in the display. No gondola shows less than two lanterns, and many exhibit eight or ten, shedding a mellow radiance of blue and red and purple over gay uniforms and rich silken robes.

"The soldiers of the bands," says Mr. Howells,* "breathe from their instruments the most perfect and exquisite music of its kind in the world; and as the procession takes the width of the Grand Canal in its magnificent course, soft crimson flashes play upon the time-worn marble of the palaces, and tenderly die away, giving to light and then to shadow the opulent sculptures of arch, and pillar, and spandril, and weirdly illuminating the grim and bearded visages of stone that peer down from doorway and window. It is a sight more gracious and fairy than ever poet dreamed; and I feel that the lights and the music have only got into my description by name, and that you would not know them, when you saw and heard them, from anything I say."

The principal actors, the heroes of these spectacles,

* W. D. Howells, "Venetian Life," p. 125.

were always the *barcarolli*, or gondoliers, who formed at Venice the most numerous and the most interesting class of the population. The majority of the members of this corporation were in the service of the patricians; and preserved with jealous care the ancient privilege of exclusively serving their *padroni* in the gondola. But, in addition to this special service, they were employed in receiving visitors, and executing commissions which their masters were unwilling to intrust to other domestics. Participating in the secrets of their patrons, their fidelity and discretion were the qualities of which they boasted. They were not less remarkable, however, for their shrewd wit and quick intelligence. Many of their *bons mots*, and the lively repartees, often trembling on the verge of insolence, which they exchanged with one another, or even addressed to their masters, are still remembered. Who has not heard tell, moreover, how the Venetian gondoliers charmed the weariness of their solitary hours by chanting strophes of Tasso's "Jerusalem Delivered," and echoing from bark to bark the lamentations of Erminia and the sighs of Tancred! Undoubtedly these poetical habits formerly existed, but the race of rhapsodists long ago died out.

> "In Venice Tasso's echoes are no more,
> And silent rows the songless gondolier." *

It is true that among the gondoliers stationed at the door of the hotels, or on the mole of the Piazzetta, you may still meet with some miserable creatures who, for thirty sous and a cup of wine, will undertake to deafen

* Byron, "Childe Harold," canto iii.

you with some unrecognizable rags and tatters of Tasso, shouted in a hoarse guttural voice; but there is nothing in common between these frightful croakers and their ancestors of poetic and melancholy memory.

But if you can no longer hear

> "The voice of Adria's gondolier
> Along the blue and moonlit waters sweep,"

you may amuse yourself with the three tragic legends which form their stock in trade as *raconteurs*, and which they relate with true Italian liveliness.

The first of these legends, according to Mr. Howells,* is that of a sausage-maker, who flourished in Venice some centuries ago, and who improved the quality of the broth which the *luganegheri* make of their scraps and sell to the gondoliers, by now and then mincing up into it a neighbour's child! Having been detected by a gondolier who found a little finger in his broth, he was brought to justice, and dragged through the city at the heels of a wild horse.

The second relates to an innocent baker-boy, who was put to death on suspicion of having murdered a noble, because in the dead man's heart was discovered a dagger fitting a sheath picked up by the baker on the morning of the murder, and by him retained. Many years afterwards a malefactor, who died in Padua, confessed the murder, and thereupon two lamps were lighted before a shrine in the southern façade of St. Mark's Church,—one for the murdered nobleman's soul, and the other for that of the innocent boy.

* W. D. Howells, "Venetian Life," pp. 288–290.

The fact of the murder, and of the punishment of the unfortunate victim, is an incident of Venetian history, and the Council of Ten never pronounced a sentence of death thereafter, till one of their number had repeated the solemn warning: "*Ricordatevi del povero Fornaretto!*" (Remember the poor Baker-Boy!)

This touching story has been woven by the poet, Dall 'Ongaro, into a no less touching tragedy; but as yet poetical honours have been denied to Veneranda Porta, the heroine of the gondoliers' third legend.

Veneranda Porta was a lady of the days of the Republic, who had been unfaithful to her husband, and plotted with her paramour to remove him by the secret knife. The head of the murdered man, however, being discovered, and exposed, according to custom, on the granite pedestal at the tower of St. Mark's Church, it was recognized by his brother, and the inquiries thereupon instituted brought to light the crime and its authors. They were brought before the Ten, and condemned to be hanged between the columns of the Piazzetta. The gondoliers relate that when the sentence was pronounced, Veneranda said to the chief of the Ten, "But as for me, this sentence will never be carried out. You cannot hang a woman. Consider the impropriety!" The Venetian rulers were not to be diverted from their course by any such question of delicacy, and the chief replied, "Madam, you shall be hanged in my breeches!"

Among the gondoliers certain acknowledged distinctions of rank exist; a kind of hierarchy founded on merits and honours, personal, or transmitted from generation to generation. Before all are the crowns gained in the regattas. These trophies are bequeathed by father to son; and the families which can exhibit the greatest number are considered as the worthiest, the most distinguished, as invested with a kind of nobility. They intermarry, when possible, among themselves; and for the victor, or son or grandson of a victor, in the regatta, to marry a girl whose father or relations had won no prizes at any of these triumphs, would be a fatally derogatory act, an ineffaceable blot upon his escutcheon.

The private life of the Venetians, especially of those of the patrician class, is to-day, as it has ever been, very exclusive and retired. Society, as it is understood in France and in most parts of Italy, has never existed at Venice. With political liberty, or the manners which supply its place, the *salon* and the *conversazione* seldom flourish. The Venetian house is always closed; not even our English *home* is, in this respect, more severe or apparently more inhospitable. There is, however, this characteristic difference; the English gentleman shuns the intrusion of strangers, because he loves to live in the bosom of his family, and to enjoy the pleasures of domestic peace; while the Venetian nobleman or citizen receives no one because he is never at home, or never wishes to be; he lives out of his house, which is for him not so much a dwelling as a secure asylum, where he can find, at need, his wife, his children, and his servants. Formerly, society existed, as even to-day it exists, only at the theatre, the café, and the casino. It is in these various centres of reunion that the patricians and wealthy citizens do congregate at all hours of the day, or night, to discuss their business or their pleasures.

The *casini* were either private or public. The former were in no respects like our English clubs, but separate residences, where the nobles spent the leisure not employed in their various functions. As many of them resided at a distance from St. Mark, and yet were required to visit the palace almost daily, they found it convenient to have close at hand a place of retirement, which afterwards became a second dwelling. By degrees these supplementary mansions multiplied, until, in the latter days of the Republic, each noble had his own. Here they spent the greater part of the day in brooding over their political projects, in receiving visits, in gambling, or entertaining their friends.

As for the public *casini*, social life at Venice was intimately bound up with them. You would meet under their roofs from fifty to sixty persons of both sexes, who dissipated the night in conversation and various amusements, and even in games of chance, which they could here engage in without any fear of being denounced by the police. Strangers were admitted on the presentation of one of the members, and once admitted, might return whenever they pleased without any fresh invitation. Each casino was under the protection of a patrician, for the Government tolerated no numerous assemblages unless they were superintended by one of its members. Its administration was intrusted to a president and treasurer, annually elected from the members. These casini have been represented by ill-informed authorities as nurseries of vice and debauchery, but this is an error or a calumny.

The gravest statesmen, the most eminent personages of the Republic, and women of the highest rank and most spotless character, supported them. Unquestionably a terrible license of manners prevailed at Venice, but the casino had no share in it. We must seek its causes in the tolerance of the Government, the neglect and inefficacy of the clergy, the influx of strangers, and the uncontrolled dissipation of the masses, who enjoyed an almost continual carnival.

Thus have we glanced with all brevity at the principal features of the private and public life of the Venetians. The perpetual fêtes which we have hinted at, the endless spectacles, the animated and joyous scenes incessantly renewed, made Venice the rendezvous of the idle and opulent of every country; while its vast commerce and restless industry attracted from all corners of the world a busy and active population. But under the brilliant exterior of this city of palaces, theatres, and masquerades, what deadly wounds were festering! These outbursts of noisy gaiety—what a heart-sorrow and fatal melancholy did they most miserably conceal! At the Venetian banquet a skeleton was ever present; an eternal shadow, like the ghost of Banquo, chilled every reveller with its ice-cold hand; the ominous phantom of the State Inquisition! It mingled in business and pleasure—in the private and public relations of the Venetians; it dogged them in the piazza, the church, the casino; it followed them to the inmost chambers of their gloomy palaces. It seemed to realize the old pagan idea of a supreme divinity, which was ubiquitous, omniscient, inexorable, and remorseless!

The theatres and the canals were asylums for criminals, and there, under no circumstances, might the sbirri seize them. But even in these places, every disorder, every menace, every insult or commotion, was pursued and punished with an extreme rigour. To the Council of Ten and the State Inquisitors belonged the police supervision of these public haunts, as well as the discovery and punishment of the crimes committed therein. Take as an example of the merciless cruelty of this famous tribunal, the terrible decree which struck down, towards the middle of the last century, a young noble of one of the most illustrious and powerful Venetian houses. Giovanni Mocenigo, one evening, in the Theatre of San Salvatore, for some unknown cause, fired a couple of pistol-shots in the box of the Foscarini, and wounded the two brothers, Nicolo and Sebastian. He took to flight, and succeeded in effecting his escape. But soon afterwards the Council of Ten published a *bando*, which, in its incredible rigour and ingenious cruelty, fully realized Shakspeare's idea of the "bloody book of the law." We quote a few of its provisions.

Mocenigo was degraded of his rank, provisionally banished, and condemned, if arrested, to be beheaded between the columns of St. Mark.

To him who should give him up, alive or dead, was promised a sum of two thousand ducats, and the privilege of procuring the pardon of any other criminal.

All his property, present and to come, was confiscated; all contracts negotiated by him six months before his condemnation were declared null and void.

All towns, villages, hamlets, communes, and places subject to the Venetian signory, whither he might flee for refuge, were ordered to surrender him immediately, living or dead, under the penalty of their public functionaries, if the decree were neglected, being sent to the galleys.

His parents and friends, and every Venetian, under penalty of losing their entire possessions and suffering ten years at the galleys, were forbidden to correspond with him by letter or otherwise, or to render him any assistance.

His punishment was never to be adjourned, modified, diminished, or suspended, even at the intercession of foreign sovereigns.

No man was allowed to speak in his favour, under a penalty of two thousand ducats for every time he so offended.

And yet the victim of this ruthless decree was of an illustrious family, which had given four Doges to the Republic; was only twenty-one years old; and had been fully and freely forgiven by the Foscarini.

With respect to strangers, the State Inquisitors had various methods of procedure, according to their rank. If the suspected individual were a man of mark, the official and officious monitors contented themselves with warning him that "the air of Venice was unhealthy" (*che l'aria e cattiva*). If he did not, or would not, comprehend the meaning of these words, he was openly invited to quit the territory of the Republic within eight-and-forty hours. If he showed himself in no haste to obey this admonition, he was despatched to the frontier under a strong escort of sbirri armed to the teeth. If the grounds on which he were suspected were of real validity, and implicated him in grave offences, the unfortunate man was, without any scruple, pointed out to the cordon of the sbirri of the tribunal, who secretly put him to death. The rule of the Inquisitors was the old tyrannical maxim: *Sit divus, modo non vivus;* and the death of a man appeared to them perfectly justifiable for reasons of public policy.

Sometimes they invested their acts of authority with a curious air of ostentation and singularity. Thus, on one occasion, a Genoese painter, while labouring at his art inside a Venetian church, quarrelled with a couple of Frenchmen who inveighed bitterly against the Government. The conversation was overheard and reported. Next day the painter was summoned before the Inquisitors, who asked him if he could recognize the two men with whom he had held a discussion on the preceding evening. The poor man, trembling in every limb, replied that, as far as he was concerned, he had spoken only in praise of the Government. A curtain was then drawn aside, and he beheld the two unfortunate Frenchmen suspended to the ceiling; after which he was dismissed, with an injunction not to express in future any opinion on the Government, good or bad; for, added the Inquisitors, the Government needs no one's apology.

The Prince de Craon was exposed to an ordeal of almost equal severity. During his sojourn at Venice he had been robbed, and had openly and energetically complained of his loss in the public places which he frequented. He was nevertheless allowed to depart, but when his gondola had reached about the middle of the lagoon, a signal given by the Inquisitors of State compelled its *padrone* to stop.

"What means that signal?" said the astonished prince.

"Nothing good," replied the gondolier.

He had scarcely spoken before they were boarded by a boat displaying a red flag, and manned by the sbirri of police.

"Pass into our boat," said their chief to the prince, who, somewhat intimidated by the lugubrious show, immediately complied. Then commenced a rapid and energetic interrogatory:—

"You were robbed on Friday last; were you not?"

"Yes."

"Of what amount?"

"Five hundred ducats."

"In what contained?"

"A green purse."

"Do you suspect any person of the theft?"

"Yes; one of my late domestics."

"Would you know him again?"

"Undoubtedly."

At this moment the chief of the sbirri uncovered a corpse, which lay at the bottom of the boat, holding in its hand a green purse, containing five hundred ducats.

"This is your robber, and this is your money. Go, your highness, and do not again set foot in a country whose institutions you have so ill appreciated!"

During the later days of the Republic, the Inquisition of State, as well as its other institutions and powers, had lost much of its prestige; there remained only the weak shadow of that mysterious Government whose ruthless energy and surpassing ability men had admired, while detesting its abominable principles and the terrible secrets of its policy.

Part Third.

PUBLIC BUILDINGS AND MEMORABLE PLACES.

Column, tower, and dome, and spire,
Shine like obelisks of fire.

SHELLEY.

I.

Memorable Places.

Shall we go see the relics of this town?

SHAKSPEARE.

SITUATION OF THE CITY.

ENICE is built upon seventy-two low level islands, the foundations for the buildings being formed with masonry and piles. It is divided into two unequal portions by the Canalazzo, or Grand Canal, which winds through the city in a double curve like an ꙅ, and it is intersected in every direction by one hundred and forty-six smaller canals, spanned by three hundred and six bridges. Most of these bridges are steep, and they are not, like some of our railway bridges, graduated into easy steps. Over the Grand Canal only three bridges have been thrown—the Rialto, of stone; and two of iron, one opposite the railway-station, and the other between the Campo di San Stefano and the Academia delle Belli Arti.

The small canals are called Rii, and form the water-highways of Venice. They are crossed by such numerous bridges that there is no part of Venice to which the stranger cannot walk if he chooses, passing through narrow alleys or passages, known as *calli.* There are also several small squares or *campi.*

The most considerable of the Venetian houses have each a door opening inland, and another towards the canal; but many, built in the interior of the islands, can have no immediate access by water. Along the banks of the Rii sometimes extends a wharf or quay, called a *riva,* and usually secured by a parapet, bored for a wicket; but more often the Rii only stretch from house to house, and these, in such a case, will rise on either side straight from the water's edge. Several of the finest palaces, especially on the Grand Canal, can only be seen from the water; and the stranger, therefore, who wishes to explore the city thoroughly, will do well to charter for his use a gondola.

THE PIAZZA DI SAN MARCO.

To gain a general idea of Venetian life, the traveller should first visit the great gathering-place of the citizens, the Piazza di San Marco. He will approach it through the Calle Luna San Moisè, a paved alley, nowhere more than seven feet wide, full of people, and echoing with the discordant and brazen shouts of itinerant salesmen. Overhead he will observe an inextricable confusion of rugged shutters, and iron balconies, and chimney-flues pushed out on brackets to save room, and arched windows with projecting sills of Istrian stone, and gleams of green leaves here and there where a fig-tree branch escapes over a lower wall from some garden-court, leading the eye up to the narrow stream of blue sky high over all. "On each side"—to use the words of an eloquent writer—"a row of shops, as densely set as may be,

PIAZZA OF SAN MARCO, AND THE CAMPANILE

occupying, in fact, intervals between the square stone shafts, about eight feet high, which carry the first floors; intervals of which one is narrow and serves as a door; the other is, in the more respectable shops, wainscoted to the height of the counter and glazed above, but in those of the poorer tradesmen left open to the ground, and the wares laid on benches and tables in the open air, the light in all cases entering at the front only, and fading away at a few feet from the threshold into a gloom which the eye from without cannot penetrate, but which is generally broken by a ray or two from a feeble lamp at the back of the shop, suspended before a print of the Virgin.

"The less pious shopkeeper sometimes leaves his lamp unlighted, and is contented with a penny print; the more religious one has his print coloured and set in a little shrine with a gilded or figured fringe, with perhaps a faded flower or two on each side, and his lamp burning brilliantly. Here at the fruiterer's, where the dark-green water-melons are heaped upon the counter like cannon balls, the Madonna has a tabernacle of fresh laurel-leaves; but the fruiterer next door has let his lamp out, and there is nothing to be seen in his shop but the dull gleam of the studded patterns on the copper pans, hanging from his roof in the darkness. Next comes a 'Vendita Frittole e Liquori,' where the Virgin, enthroned in a very humble manner beside a tallow candle on a back shelf, presides over certain ambrosial morsels of a nature too ambiguous to be defined or enumerated. But a few steps further on, at the regular wine-shop of the Calle, where we are offered 'Vino Nostrani a Soldi 28.32,' the Madonna is in great glory, enthroned above ten or a dozen large red casks of three-year-old vintage, and flanked by goodly ranks of bottles of maraschino, and two crimson lamps; and for the evening when the gondoliers will come to drink out, under her auspices, the money they have gained during the day, she will have a whole chandelier." *

* J. Ruskin, "Stones of Venice," vol. ii., c. iv., sect. 10, *et seq.*

Emerging on the bridge, we pass into the Campo San Moisè, whence to the entrance into St. Mark's Place, called the *Bocca di Piazza* (Mouth of the Piazza), we see less of the true Venetian character, and more of the modern semi-Parisian air. Now before us rises the vast tower of St. Mark's, of which we shall speak hereafter; and all around are shops gay with many wares, and beneath the pillars of the great cathedral are seated vendors of toys, sweetmeats, and caricatures. The open space is crowded with loungers listening to the music of a military band, and round the whole square stretches a line of cafés, which are seldom empty; and in the recesses of the porches, all day long, knots of men of the lowest classes bask, lizard-like, in the sun, while the children shriek and curse, and snarl and sleep, or gamble away the few centesimi earned by occasional toil, or thrown by the hand of charity.

VENETIAN HOUSES.

The Venetian climate alternates between four months of winter and eight months of summer—and such a summer! Cloudless skies, and a broad bright sun shining pitilessly overhead, and waters gleaming and glowing everywhere like brazen mirrors. Venetian houses, therefore, are built for a summer-life; for those days of languor when one loves to lie on a soft couch, fanned by balmy airs which steal through the open window, with a romance of Goldoni's in one's hand, and listless eyes ever and anon turned upon the marble palaces without, and the glitter of the canals. The rooms not upon the ground floor are consequently large, lofty, airy, and in winter cold. In the palaces there are, it is true, two suites of apartments; a small, warm, and cozy suite on the first floor for winter; and the grander, cooler chambers and *salons* above, whither, when spent and summer-worn, you may retire for refuge from the hot breath of the *scirocco.* But mostly people occupy the same room in summer and in winter, marking the change of season by laying down a small strip of carpet before the sofa. The floors are of stone or marble, oiled and tastefully polished, and sometimes adorned with marvellous designs in mosaic-work. You seldom meet with a stove in a Venetian house, though the winter has so raw and bleak a breath that it seems to strike to the very soul; seldom a stove, and never a cheery, blazing fire—a fire of good glowing coal, which is the very eye of an Englishman's home. The Venetians, poor souls! content themselves with the *scaldino*, a small earthenware pot of bristling charcoal, which may be carried on the arm.

A house in Venice, as in Glasgow or Edinburgh, means a flat; that is, a whole story in a building, or part of it only, which is always completely separate from the story above and below, or from the other rooms on the same floor. Each house has its own entrance from the street, or by a common stair from the ground floor, which is entirely devoted to cellars and magazines, the kitchen being on a level with the other rooms of the house to which it belongs. Each "house" has its private door, but the street entrance is in common, and provided with bells for the different stories. When a stranger rings, a servant appears at some upper window, with the interrogation, "*Chi xe?*" (Who is it?) He replies, not with his name, but "*Amici!*" (Friends!) Whereupon the servant draws the latch of the door by an apparatus of wire, and the stranger, entering, wanders up the gloomy, comfortless staircase until he discovers the place he is in quest of. But should neither master nor mistress be at home, the servant answers your "Amici" with "*No ghe ne xe!*" (Nobody here), and lets down a basket by a string outside the window, in which you deposit your card.

No man possessed with an English idea of comfort can relish a Venetian house. "The lower windows are heavily barred with iron; the wood-work is rude, even in most of the palaces; the walls are not papered, though they are sometimes painted; the most pleasing and inviting feature of the interior is the frescoed ceiling of the better rooms. The windows shut imperfectly, the heavy wooden blinds imperviously (is it worth while to observe that there are no Venetian blinds in Venice?), the doors lift slantingly from the floor, in which their lower hinges are embedded; the stoves are of plaster, and consume fuel without return of heat; the balconies alone are always charming, whether they hang high over the streets, or look out upon the canals, and, with the gaily-painted ceilings, go far to make Venetian houses habitable."

The best houses in Venice are situated on the Grand Canal, which holds much the same relation to the City of the Adriatic as Grosvenor Place, let us say, to London. At the eastern end it begins near the Piazzetta, a common landing-place and quay, where lie dozens of hearse-like gondolas, and where vociferous gondoliers tout for fares. Nearly opposite you may see the Island and Church of San Giorgio; and adjoining this, and enclosed by a sort of mole with a lantern-tower at each end, is the original Porto Franco, or Free Port, whose limits now extend to a considerable distance round Venice. To the westward lie the Long Canal and the Island of La Guidecca.

THE GRAND CANAL AND ITS PALACES.

Pushing our way through the crowd of Greeks, Armenians, and Venetians, we hail one of the gondolas, agree about our fares, double ourselves up in the awkward little cabin, and with one gondolier at the stern and another at the prow, proceed upon a voyage of exploration.

On our left hand stands the Custom House, or *Dogana del Mare*, a building of small architectural merit, and surmounted by a huge globe, on which an allegorical figure of Fortune stands erect, while two kneeling figures support it, one on either side. The Dogana was erected in 1682. Its style is the later Renaissance. Beyond this we reach the Church of Santa Maria della Salute; its lofty porch crowned with statues, and its entire mass with enormous cupolas. On the right, after passing the gardens of the Royal Palace, and the Greek Pavilion, built by Napoleon, we arrive at the *Palazzo Giustiniani*, now the *Albergo dell' Europa*, an edifice in the Gothic style of the fourteenth century. Beyond it stands the *Palazzo Trevio*, formerly Emo, which contains a good collection of modern pictures. Most of the Venetian

THE DOGANA.

palaces have a strong family likeness. They rise abruptly from the water, with a flight of steps at the grand entrance, and numerous tall posts, painted in stripes, to serve as mooring-points for the gondolas. They are very lofty; some are six stories high. The windows and balconies are heavily enriched with carvings of little lions and dogs in marble, and between them vases of flowers. Generally they have a faded and worn appearance, like that of a poor noble.

The *Palazzo Contarini Fasan*, off which our gondoliers pause for awhile, is built in the richest Venetian Gothic of the fifteenth century. The sculptures belong to the Renaissance period. Remember that the Contarinis gave no less than eight doges, and I know not how many beautiful women, to Venice. It was a prince of this family that ruled over the state during its last desperate struggle with Genoa, and it may have been from the marble steps of his stately mansion that he embarked, under the silent stars, to attack the Genoese fleet at Chiozzia. The *Palazzo Cornaro*, on the same side of the Canalazzo, was erected by Sansovino in 1532. The façade presents the three orders—Doric, Ionic, and Composite.

Continuing our voyage, we notice,—

On the right, the *Palazzo Cavalli*, of some interest as the residence of the last of the elder branch of the Bourbons, the Count de Chambord, or Henri Cinq, as the French Legitimists call him. Its architectural style is Renaissance Gothic.

On the left, the *Palazzo Foscari*, built towards the end of the fifteenth century by, it is said, Bartolommeo Bon, the architect of the Ducal Palace. It is formed of a triple gallery, with corridors covered by acute arches, the whole having a Saracenic air. Here died, of an excess of agony, the unhappy Doge whose son was done to death with such merciless cruelty by the Ten:—

> "Here Foscari's noble heart at length gave way."

The palace was the usual residence of foreign princes

THE DOGANA—ANOTHER VIEW.

PALAZZO CORNARO.

on their occasional visits to Venice. Henry III. and Francis I. of France here spent joyous days under its roof, as well as Casimir of Poland, and the Kings of Bohemia and Hungary. The Austrians converted it into a barrack, and damaged the interior greatly.

Passing the entrance of the Rio di San Pantaleone,

we arrive at the *Palazzo Balbi*, built by Alessandro Vittoria in 1582. It exhibits the architectural features of three orders—Rustic, Ionic, and Composite. Then come several large and stately mansions,—the Palazzi Grassi, Morosini, Contarini, Pisani, and Grimani. In the *Pisani Palace* (of the latest Venetian Gothic) was the famous "Family of Darius," by Paolo Veronese, purchased for our National Gallery at the price of £13,560. To the Pisanis belonged the great sea-hero whose deeds we have narrated in a preceding section.

The noblest of all the public buildings of Venice, next to the Ducal Palace, is that appropriated to the business of the Post-Office, anciently known as the *Casa Grimani.* It consists of three stories of the Corinthian order, at once "simple, delicate, and sublime;" but is constructed on a scale so gigantic, that the three-storied palaces on its right and left only rise to the cornice which marks the level of its first floor. The finish of its details is equal to the colossal perfection of its whole, and though the decoration is sparing it is of such exquisite delicacy as instantly to rivet the eye. It is, in truth, one of the finest specimens in Europe of the Renaissance architecture; belonging to the middle (or what Mr. Ruskin calls the Roman) period of that noble school. The architect was Sanmicheli; the founder, Girolamo Grimani, father of the Doge Marino Grimani. On the election of the latter, in 1595, his duchess, a lady of the Morosini family, was inaugurated with singular magnificence, as was the Venetian custom in the case of a Dogaressa. In glittering gold brocade, and with a crown of gold upon her head, she was conducted to the

Church of St. Mark, amidst the roar of cannon and the blare of triumphal music. Afterwards, in the gilded Bucentaur, she was brought back to the Ducal Palace, where she sat enthroned among the haughty Venetian ladies. Then for several weeks, the days were occupied with fêtes and processions; the nights, with balls and banquets.

The next mansion we pause at has a peculiar interest for Englishmen. The *Palazzo Moncenigo* was the residence, in 1818–1820, of Lord Byron, who wrote here his "Beppo," and other poems. Some curious glimpses of the life he led in the Venetian capital may be obtained from the biographical pages of Thomas Moore.

The *Palazzo Bembo* is a noteworthy building, erected about 1360. The doors of the sea-story are Byzantine, and above the entresol a beautiful Byzantine cornice is built into the wall. On the site behind stood the palace built by "blind old Dandolo,"

"Byzantium's conquering foe,"

of which a small and interesting thirteenth-century Gothic edifice may possibly have formed a part. Last of all, before reaching the Rialto, we come to the *Palazzo Manin*, built by the great Venetian architect Sansovino. It has a mournful fame as the residence of the last of the doges of Venice.

The *Rialto*, rendered immortal by the genius of Shakspeare, derives its name from that of the island where Venice first sprung into existence—which it connects with the opposite isle of St. Mark. The original bridge, of wood, was built in 1264. Several structures, also of wood, succeeded it, and were successively destroyed by fire, until the present Renaissance edifice, of marble, was begun in 1588, and completed within two years, all the stonemasons in Venice being employed on the works. It was designed by Antonio da Ponte, and cost 250,000 sequins. Sansovino affirms that 12,000 piles of elm timber, each six feet long, were used in forming the foundation. The bridge consists of a single arch, whose span is about 91 feet, and whose height, from the level of the water, is 24½ feet. The southern side is enriched with a sculpture of the Annunciation, and the keystone is the dove flying towards the Madonna. The two figures on the other side, St. Mark and St. Theodore, are by the same sculptor, Girolamo Campagna. The width of the bridge is 72 feet, and this width is divided longitudinally into five parts; that is, into three streets or passages, and two rows of shops. The central street, or passage, measures 21 feet 8 inches in width, and the two side ones about 11 feet. The number of shops upon it is 24, and they are always tastefully set out with dainty wares. The bridge, indeed, and the Merceria, or street of shops, which leads to it, are what Londoners would call "the greatest business thoroughfares in Venice."

Immediately on passing through the bridge, you see, on the left, the *Palazzo de' Camerlinghi*, or Palace of the Treasurers; and on the right, the *Fondaco de' Tedeschi*, dating from 1525. This was one of the factories or marts of the foreign nations, whose merchants dwelt here under their respective domestic jurisdictions, as do our British merchants, now-a-days, in their factories at Canton. It was built early in the sixteenth century by a certain Girolamo Tedesco, who has made no other sign of his existence and career as an architect. It exhibits, in style, a period of transition from the Venetian-Gothic to the classical. Its walls were once enriched with frescoes by Titian, Giorgione, Carpaccio, and others.

On the left observe the *Fabbriche Nuove di Rialto*, built by Sansovino in 1555. They form a series of buildings, partly connected by arcades, and anciently employed as warehouses and custom-houses. The whole place was the resort of the merchant-princes of Venice in the palmy days of its commercial greatness; and the traveller may please his fancy with the idea that here Shylock lent out his moneys at exorbitant usance, and here Antonio conversed with his friends Bassanio and Gratiano.

Passing on the right some thirteenth-century buildings, quaint enough to delight the most fantastic artist, we arrive at

The *Casa*, or *Ca d' Oro*, which, not long ago, belonged to Mademoiselle Taglioni, the celebrated danseuse, and which is one of the most interesting architectural monuments in Venice, though it has suffered severely from merciless depredations. According to Fergusson, it was built about 1350, and in the richest style of Venetian-Gothic. It was gilded, and hence, according to some authorities, its name; others say it was called after the Doro family. "It has no traces of the high roofs or aspiring tendencies of the northern buildings of the same age, no boldly-marked buttresses in strong vertical lines; but, on the contrary, flat roofs and horizontal divisions pervade the design, and every part is ornamented with a fanciful richness far more characteristic of the luxurious refinement of the East than of the manlier appreciation of the higher qualities of art that distinguished the contemporary erections on this side of the Alps."

The *Palazzo Vendramin Calerghi* was built in 1481, for the Doge Andrew Loredano, by Pietro Lombardo, and is a fine specimen of the Renaissance style. The decay of the family compelled its sale, in 1681, to the Duke of Brunswick for 60,000 ducats. It afterwards passed to the Calerghis, the Vendramins, and the Duchesse de Berri. There is a garden beside it, rich in evergreens, and decorated by gilded railings and white statues.

The *Fondaco de' Turchi*, or Turkish Factory, an eleventh-century building, is now the Government tobacco-warehouse.*

Marbles and pictures, and coins and medals, painted glass, enamels, and majolica, are among the treasures of

* We borrow the following eloquent description from Mr. Ruskin:—"It is," he says, "a ghastly ruin; whatever is venerable or sad in its wreck being disguised by attempts to put it to present uses of the basest kind. It has been composed of arcades borne by marble shafts, and walls of brick faced with marble; but the covering stones have been torn away from it, like the shroud from a corpse; and its walls, rent into a thousand chasms, are filled and refilled with fresh brickwork, and the seams and hollows are choked with clay and whitewash, oozing and trickling over the marble—itself blanched into dusty decay by the frosts of centuries. Soft grass and wandering leafage have rooted themselves in the rents, but they are not suffered to grow in their own wild and gentle way, for the place is in a sort inhabited; rotten partitions are nailed across its corridors, and miserable rooms contrived in its western wing; and here and there the weeds are indolently torn down, leaving their haggard fibres to struggle again into unwholesome growth when the spring next stirs them; and then, in contest between death and life, the unsightly heap is festering to its fall."—"*Stones of Venice*," ii. pp. 119, 120. It once belonged to the Dukes of Ferrara, but was purchased from them in the sixteenth century, to be used as a warehouse for the goods of the Turkish merchants. Its architecture is Byzantine.

THE CASA D'ORO.

the *Museo Correr*, or Municipal Museum. They are all of high interest and value; but scarcely of less interest or value is its historical relic, the tarnished red flag of the Bucentaur, embroidered with figures of the Virgin and the Lion of St. Mark.

The *Palazzo Manfrini*, on the left, next attracts our notice. Its picture-gallery has been dispersed, but the halls, staircases, saloons, and other apartments in the interior, present many details worthy of investigation; and from some of the windows delightful glimpses may be obtained of the garden—a rare enjoyment in Venice—blooming with beds of flowers.

The *Palazzo Pesaro* is a very noble and imposing pile, belonging to the third period or later style of the Renaissance school of architecture; what Mr. Ruskin, in allusion to the peculiar character of its ornamentation, calls the *Grotesque* Renaissance. The heads sculptured over this massive edifice are, in very truth, of the grotesquest kind; and remind one of the grinning masques of imps, demons, and fantastic animals introduced in the corbels of their churches by the old Gothic artists. Some of them are instinct with life and spirit.

SOME MEMORABLE PLACES.

Here our tour of the Grand Canal closes. But we have not seen half "the sights of Venice" yet. The churches and public buildings, it is true, we shall examine more particularly by-and-by, but there are many shrines not less worthy of the stranger's pilgrim-homage. The *Palazzo Moro*, a modernized building, shares in the immortal fame of Shakspeare; it occupies the site of the residence of Cristoforo Moro, a lieutenant of the Republic at Cyprus in 1508, whose history furnished the idea of "Othello," and without whom the world would have lacked that sweetest example of womanly tenderness and conjugal devotion, Desdemona. Or if you will stroll into the Corte del Sabbion, you will see a rich, quaint, walled-up doorway, in a semi-Moorish, semi-Byzantine style. What of it? inquires the pilgrim. Why, mark it well; it is nearly all that remains of the house where the great traveller, Marco Polo—he who visited Cathay and the "Sultan" of China—resided after his forty years' wanderings, and died in 1323. Come with me, too, and inspect the old Servite Convent, with its vast walls embracing several acres of ground. It derives its interest from its association with the great name of Paolo Sarpi,* the intrepid monk who laughed at excommunication, and dealt the temporal power of the Pope a blow from which it has never since recovered. Unable to foil him with the lawful weapons of logic and argument, Rome resorted to her old and accursed method of silencing a dangerous opponent with the bravo's dagger. Sarpi was severely wounded, but not slain; and he lived on, loved and protected by the Republic, to the ripe old age of seventy, when he died with a pathetic saying on his lips: "I must go to St. Mark; for it is already late, and I have much to do." †

The house of Tintoretto the painter, who seems to have dipped his pencil in the hues of a summer-sunset,

* See *ante*, pp. 149-157.

† T. A. Trollope, "Paul the Pope and Paul the Friar," p. 378.

PALAZZO PESARO.

stands on the Quay of the Campo dei Mori; it is large, and has a carved and balconied front, in which are set a now illegible tablet describing it as the great master's dwelling, and his medallion portrait.

TITIAN'S HOUSE.

Titian's house is situated at a place called Berigrande, opposite to the island of Murano. He removed hither in 1531, and at that time a more delightful situation for the residence of a painter can hardly be conceived. An adjoining piece of land he fenced in, and converted into a pleasant garden of flowers and trees. The view was then unimpeded on every side. He looked over the wide canal, says Mrs. Jameson,* which is the thoroughfare between the city of Venice and the island of Murano; in front the two smaller islands of San Cristoforo (now a cemetery) and San Michele; and beyond them Murano, rising on the right, with all its swelling domes and lofty campanili, like another Venice. Far off extended the level line of the mainland; and, in the distance, the towering chain of the Friuli Alps, sublime, half-defined, with jagged snow-peaks soaring against the sky; and more to the left, the Euganean Hills, Petrarch's home, and Shelley's inspiration, melting, like visions, into a soft mysterious light. Who does not remember—

"The dell 'mid lawny hills,
Which the wild sea-murmur fills,
And soft sunshine, and the sound
Of old forests echoing round,
And the light and smell divine
Of all flowers that breathe and shine?"—SHELLEY.

* Mrs. Jameson, "Miscellaneous Essays," pp. 38-41.

Then, in the purple evening, gondolas filled with ladies and cavaliers, and resounding with music, were seen skimming over the crimson waves of the Lagoon, till the purple darkness came on rapidly—not, as in our colder north, like a gray and sombre veil, which even in summer saddens the attentive spirit—but "like a gemmed and embroidered curtain suddenly let down," which is scarcely less beautiful or less inspiring than the gay scenes it covers!

Such was the view from Titian's garden; the garden with the famous bushy tree which the great artist, it is said, painted in his picture, *the Death of St. Peter the Martyr*. Here he spent the last glorious years of a glorious life, and here he executed some of his finest works; such as the Florentine Venus, the Ecce Homo, the Entombment, the Venus and Adonis, the Last Supper, and the Martyrdom of St. Lawrence. The day's labour done, his well-spread table was placed in the balmy and blooming garden; and wise and witty talk seasoned the meal—the talk of Aretino, Sansovino, Ludovico Dolce, Sperone Speroni, and Cardinal Bembo. The conversations at his table, to quote again from Mrs. Jameson, gave rise to Dolce's "Dialogo della Pittura," and neither music nor good cheer was wanting to the feast. No, nor the charm of beauty; for among the guests were La Franceschini, Paola Sansovino, and the superb Violante, the daughter of Palma the painter, and Titian's love-queen. Who would not wish to have been present at those garden-suppers, as at the wit-feasts of the Mermaid Tavern—immortal *symposia*, whose memories shall surely be imperishable? Alas! would that the world had been richer in Boswells!

There was a strange contrast between the life and death of Titian, reminding one of those strains of Mendelssohn, which begin so gaily, flow on so joyously, and terminate after all in a sad and tender minor. In this same house, the scene of so many mirthful nights, Titian lay dying of the pestilence which had decimated Venice; on a bed near him, his son Orazio. The latter was borne by the curators of the sick to the plague-hospital; but the old man, his beard white with the snows of ninety winters, was left to die alone. For him there could be no hope; the death-damps were already standing thick upon his brow. It appears that, before he could have ceased to breathe, "some of those wretches who come as surely in the train of such horrors as vultures in the rear of carnage—robbers, who went about spoiling the dead and dying—entered his room, ransacked it, carried off his jewels, the gifts of princes, valuable cups and vases chased in gold and silver; and, worse than all, some of his most precious pictures." The compassionate pilgrim will hope that the painter's eyes, dim with the mists of death, could not see the profanation. He died on the 27th of August 1576, and the Senate, putting aside the law which ordered the incremation of plague-stricken corpses, permitted the remains of the illustrious master to be embalmed. They were honoured with a public funeral, and deposited with great pomp at the foot of the Altar of the Crucifix in the Church of the Frari.

On a small canal, near the same church, stands the pleasant old Gothic palace where was born Goldoni, the immortal dramatist, who has left us so many vivid pictures of mediæval Venetian manners. The house is indicated by an inscription and medallion of the dramatist above the land-door.

FUNERAL OF TITIAN.

II.

The Churches of Venice.

> The church was open ; it perchance might be
> That there to offer thanks I might essay :
> All silence and all shade
> It seemed, save only for the rippling flow . . .
> . . . when the sunset air
> Sighed through the casement of the house of prayer.
>
> JEAN INGELOW.

THE PIAZZA DI SAN MARCO.

HE spot in Venice most frequently visited by the stranger, who returns to it again and again, like a lover to his mistress's bower, is the Piazza di San Marco.

Here the first thing that will arrest his attention is the flock of pigeons that fill the air with their murmur. They are fed daily at two o'clock, and at the expense of the Government.* They have been settled in the city since 877. After the religious services of Palm Sunday, it was anciently the custom of the sacristans of St. Mark's to

* Such, at least, was the case before the downfal of the Republic ; but the cost is now defrayed from a bequest left by some charitable lady.

release some birds with their wings clipped, which the people in the Piazza scrambled for. The pigeons that escaped took refuge in the roof of the church, where they gradually increased to an enormous number, and assumed a certain sanctity of character.

The principal edifices in the Piazza are, the great Church and Cathedral of St. Mark; on the right, the Procuratie Nuove and the Libreria Vecchia; on the left, the Procuratie Vecchie and the Torre dell' Orologio (or Clock Tower). Its length is 576 feet; its greatest width, on the east, 269 feet; its least, on the west, 185 feet. At right angles with the Piazza lies the Piazzètta, extending to the mole or quay; and on the mole, near the southern end of the Piazzetta, stand the two famous granite columns, crowned by the Lion of St. Mark, and by a statue of St. Theodore, the patron-saints of the Republic.

It was formerly the custom to carry the newly-elected doge round the Piazza in triumphal procession; and again, on his death, its circuit was made in solemn pomp by his funeral train.

> "Now in a chair of state, now on his bier;
> They were his first appearance, and his last!"

To tell of all the magnificent spectacles it has witnessed would require a volume; but we may refer to one of the most interesting—the great two days' festival in celebration of the Candian victory in 1364, when a tournament was held on a scale of unrivalled magnificence—because on that occasion, by the side of the doge, sat Francesco Petrarch, the poet.

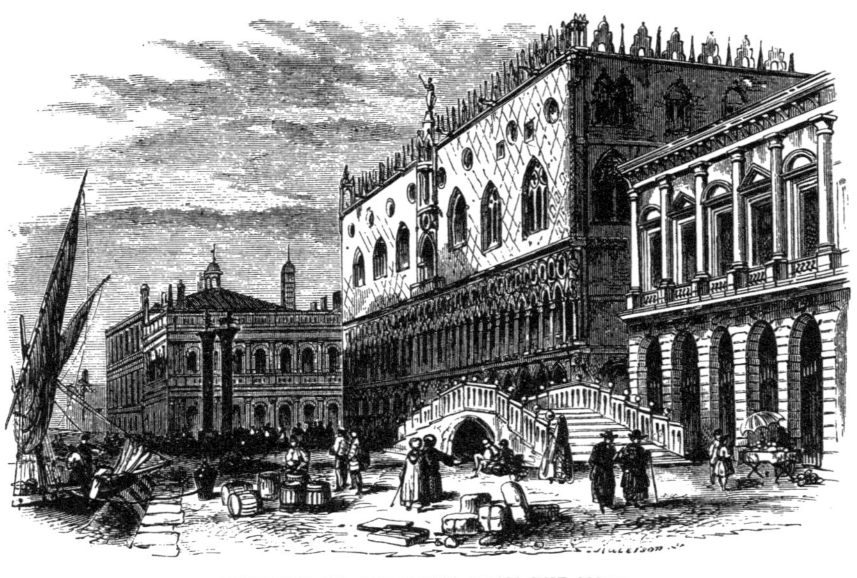

PIAZZETTA DI SAN MARCO FROM THE MOLE.

THE CATHEDRAL OF ST. MARK.

St. Mark's Church is the "crowning glory" of Venice—that is, if you look at it with educated eyes and in a reverent spirit. It was not made the cathedral until 1507, that honour having formerly been worn by the Church of San Pietro di Castello. Previously, it was the ducal chapel, founded in 828 by the Doge Giustiniani Participazio to receive the relics of St. Mark which two Venetian merchants had carried off from Alexandria.* Destroyed by fire in 976, on its site the present edifice was erected by the great Doge, Pietro Orseolo I., surnamed "The Holy," and completed more than a century later, by Domenico Contarini, in 1041. The mosaics and other embellishments were added by the Doge Domenico Salvo, 1071; and the church was finally consecrated in the reign of Vitale Faliero, October 8, 1085.†

* See p. 21.

† Such is the statement of Sansovino, though Lazari gives 1094 as the date. At all events, every care was taken to render the consecration an event of peculiar solemnity, and recourse was had to what Ruskin justly calls "one of the best arranged and most successful impostures ever attempted by the clergy of the Romish Church." The body of St. Mark, whose removal from Alexandria we have described elsewhere, had perished in the conflagration of 976; but the revenues of the church depended too much on the homage rendered to these relics to permit the confession of their loss. They were therefore miraculously re-discovered under circumstances thus related by the historian Corner or Cornaro:—"After the repairs undertaken by the Doge Orseolo, the place in which the body of the Holy Evangelist rested had been altogether forgotten; so that the Doge, Vitale Faliero, was entirely ignorant of the place of the venerable deposit. This was no light affliction, not only to the pious doge, but to all the citizens and people; so that at last, moved by confidence in the Divine mercy, they determined to implore, with prayer and fasting, the manifestation of so great a treasure, which did not now depend upon any human effort. A general fast being proclaimed, and a solemn procession appointed for the 25th day of June, while the people assembled in church interceded with God in fervent prayers for the

The plan is that of a Greek cross, with the addition of spacious porticoes. The centre is surmounted by a noble dome, and a smaller cupola rises over the centre of each of the arms of the cross. The façade exhibits two rows of columns, of various kinds of marble, of various styles, and various dimensions. Quaint inscriptions in quaint characters cover them from base to capital. Evidently they are the remains of older buildings, and their incongruous character would shock a strict classical taste. But where they are they seem eminently appropriate, and the general picturesque effect loses nothing from the ancient sculptured tablets inserted in the walls. The recesses over the five doorways are filled with large mosaics: the subject of the first and second is, the removal of St. Mark's body from the tomb at Alexandria, executed by Pietro Vecchio, in 1650; of the third, the Last Judgment, by Liborio Salandri; of the fourth, the Venetian magistrates adoring the Evangelist's body, by Sebastian Rizzi, 1728; and of the last, the Basilica of St. Mark, by some architect of the fourteenth century.

It seems useless to attempt a description of St. Mark's, either externally or internally, without availing oneself of the richly-coloured language of Ruskin, who has entered more deeply than any other writer into the spirit of Venetian architecture. He speaks of its sculpture, fantastic and involved, of palm leaves and lilies, and grapes and pomegranates, and birds clinging and flutter-

desired boon, they beheld, with as much amazement as joy, a slight shaking in the marbles of a pillar (near the place where the Altar of the Cross is now), which, presently falling to the earth, exposed to the view of the rejoicing people the chest of bronze in which the body of the Evangelist was laid."

CATHEDRAL OF ST. MARK.

ing among the branches, all twined together into an endless network of buds and plumes; and in the midst of it the solemn forms of angels, sceptred and robed to the feet, and leaning to each other across the gates, their figures indistinct among the gleaming of the golden ground through the leaves beside them, interrupted and dim, like the morning light as it faded back among the branches of Eden when first its gates were angel-guarded long ago.

And round the walls of the porches (continues this artist-in-words) there are set pillars of variegated stones, jasper and porphyry, and deep green serpentine spotted with flakes of snow, and marbles, that half refuse and half yield to the sunshine, Cleopatra like, "their bluest veins to kiss,"—the shadow, as it steals back from them, revealing line after line of pleasant undulation, as a receding tide leaves the waved sand; their capitals rich with interwoven tracery, rooted knots of herbage, and drifting leaves of acanthus and vine, and mystical signs, all beginning and ending in the cross; and above them, in the broad archivolts, a continuous change of language and of life—angels, and the signs of heaven and the labours of men, each in its appointed season upon the earth; and above these another range of glittering pinnacles, mixed with white arches edged with scarlet flowers—a confusion of delight, amidst which the breasts of the Greek horses are seen blazing in their breadth of golden strength, and the St. Mark's Lion, lifted on a blue field covered with stars, until at last, as if in ecstasy, the crests of the arches break into a marble foam, and toss themselves far into the blue sky in flashes and wreaths of sculptured spray, as if the breakers on the Lido shore had been frost-bound before they fell, and the sea-nymphs had inlaid them with gold and amethyst.*

The famous bronze horses,

> "Their gilded collars glittering in the sun,"

surmount the central portal of the vestibule. The Venetians brought them from the Hippodrome at Constantinople, after the capture of that city by Enrico Dandolo and the Crusaders in 1204. Antiquaries have ascribed them to the Greeks of Chios, and the school of Lysippus; but all that seems certain is, that the Emperor Augustus removed them from Alexandria to Rome, and placed them on a triumphal arch; that they were successively transferred to arches of their own by Nero, Domitian, Trajan, and Constantine—the latter translating them to his new capital on the Bosphorus. The weight of each steed is computed at 1932 pounds.

The vestibule extends along the entire front of the cathedral. A diamond-shaped slab of red and white marble, visible in the pavement close by the centre portal, marks the scene of the reconciliation between Pope Alexander III. and the Emperor Frederic Barbarossa, July 23, 1177. Here, too, the Doge Dandolo, gray-headed and bent with age, offered himself as leader of the Venetian host in the fourth Crusade. And here, in 1364, beside the prince of the Republic, sat the poet Petrarch, and witnessed a tournament of surpassing splendour.

> "In that temple porch
> (The brass is gone, the porphyry remains)

* Ruskin, "Stones of Venice," ii., sect. 13, 14, 15.

FRONT VIEW OF ST. MARK.

Did Barbarossa fling his mantle off,
And, kneeling, on his neck receive the foot
Of the proud Pontiff—thus at last consoled
For flight, disguise, and many an aguish shake
On his stone pillow.
In that temple porch,
Old as he was, so near his hundredth year,
And blind—his eyes put out—did Dandolo
Stand forth, displaying on his crown the cross.
He went to die;
But of his trophies four arrived ere long,
Snatched from destruction—the four steeds divine,
That strike the ground, resounding with their feet,
And from their nostrils snort ethereal flame
Over that very porch; and in the place
Where in an after-time, beside the Doge,
Sate one yet greater, one whose verse shall live,
When the wave rolls o'er Venice. High he sate,
High over all, close by the ducal chair,
At the right hand of his illustrious host,
Amid the noblest daughters of the realm,
Their beauty shaded from the western ray
By many-coloured hangings; while, beneath,
Knights of all nations, some of fair renown
From England, from victorious Edward's court,
Their lances in the rest, charged for the prize."*

The nave is separated from the aisles in each of the four compartments by graceful colonnades and round arches, supporting lofty galleries. The capitals of the pillars are enriched with delicately carven sculptures emulous of the foliage with which Nature decks her shapely trees. Within and without, the columns, all of marble, number upwards of five hundred, and in design and execution betray the hand and fancy of Greek architects. During the erection of the building, every vessel that cleared out of Venice for the East was ordered to bring back pillars and marbles for the holy work,

* Rogers, Poetical Works—"Italy."

which was in some respects a type of the wealth, power, and religious zeal of the Republic.

The interior is very rich, but the richness is subdued by the gloom, and all the opulence that surrounds the stranger does not distract or annoy. The walls gleam with precious marbles; the vaulting is adorned with mosaics upon a ground of gold; the pavement is of tesselated marble. Under foot and over head there is "a continual succession of crowded imagery, one picture passing into another, as in a dream; forms of beauty and shapes of terror blend in fantastic combinations; in the midst of dragons, serpents, and ravening beasts ot prey, bright birds drink out of running fountains and crystal vases; here you see the symbols of life, and its chance and change, hear of its redemption and future purification; and always and everywhere, by cunning device and graceful contrivance, the eye is led to the emblem of divine love and human salvation—the cross, lifted and carved in every place, and upon every stone; "sometimes with the serpent of eternity wrapt round it, sometimes with doves beneath its arms, and sweet herbage growing forth from its foot; but conspicuous most of all on the great rood that crosses the church before the altar, raised in bright blazonry against the shadow of the apse."

Over the central archway is placed a rich eleventh-century mosaic, the Virgin and St. Mark. Entering by this door, you will observe, on the right hand, a porphyry basin for holy water: it is supported by an old Greek altar, with bas-reliefs of children and dolphins—a curious commentary on the downfal of the ancient creed of Hellas.

Further to the right is the *Baptistery*, all aglow with gleaming marbles, rich mosaics, and bas-reliefs, dating from the fourteenth century. The altar-table is formed of a massive granite slab, brought from Tyre in 1126, and reputed to have supported the feet of our Lord when he preached to the inhabitants of the doomed city. A monument against the wall commemorates Andrea Dandolo, who died in 1354—the last doge buried in St. Mark's. He was the friend of Petrarch, and the chronicler of the state, which he ruled during a period of suffering and disaster.

The tomb of the great doge has been compared to a narrow couch, from which two angels are drawing the curtain back, and looking in upon the silent sleeper. His face is that of a man in middle life, with two deep furrows cloven right across the forehead, which is crowned by the fillet of the ducal cap. The rest of the features are small and delicate, and a grand solemnity rests upon the entire countenance. The roof of the canopy above is azure, sown with stars; beneath, in the centre of the tomb, sits a sweet semblance of the Virgin Mother, and all around stretches a soft, sweet border of flowers and leaves, growing rich and deep, as if in a field in summer.

The ceiling of the Baptistery is blazoned with two great circles of figures, radiating from a central Christ: the first circle is that of the apostles; the second is filled with the "thrones, dominations, princedoms, virtues, powers" of heaven; and upon the walls, again and again repeated, the gaunt figure of the Baptist is seen in every circumstance of his life and death.

The choir and its divisions are described as rising in a triple ascent. They are separated from the nave by a rich Byzantine screen, surmounted by fourteen statues, with a cross in the centre, and a silver image of the Saviour. The high altar, supported by four columns, which are wreathed with bands of sculpture and covered with Latin inscriptions, is supposed to date from the eleventh century. The bands, nine upon each column, portray the principal events and traditions of Gospel history, from the marriage of St. Anna to the Ascension. Eight bronze statues, grouped on either side of the altar, represent the four Evangelists and the four Doctors of the Church. As a whole, the effect of the choir is wonderfully gorgeous, and cannot fail to excite the admiration of all who

"Value the giddy pleasure of the eyes."

The treasury of St. Mark's is remarkable for its fine collection of ancient Byzantine jewellery, and its store of invaluable relics. To the artist and the English traveller, the former will prove most interesting, though the latter includes among its precious things such curiosities as "a bit of the dress of our Saviour, a small quantity of earth soaked with his blood, a fragment of the pillar to which he was bound, and a portion of the genuine cross." The hard-hearted heretic will, we fear, be inclined to doubt the authenticity of these precious remains! At all events, he will examine with greater interest the treasures brought from the Church of San Sophia in Constantinople; the diamond and sapphire cross given by the Emperor of Austria to the Patriarch of Venice; the sumptuous candelabra wrought by Benvenuto Cellini; and the golden rose presented by Pope Gregory to one of the dogaressas.

The bronze door of the sacristy is a marvel of art. It is covered with vigorous bas-reliefs, whose execution occupied Sansovino for a period of twenty-two years.

The dimensions of St. Mark's externally, are 260 feet from east to west, and 215 feet at the transepts; internally, 205 feet in length, and 164 feet in breadth. It covers 46,000 square feet.

Its great glory *within*, says Mr. Fergusson, is the truly Byzantine profusion of gold mosaics which cover every part of the walls above the height of the capitals of the columns, and are spread over every part of the vaults and domes, being, in fact, the real and essential decoration of the church, to which the architecture is entirely subordinate. *Without*, its great beauty consists in the number of marble columns which surround and fill all the front and lateral porches. Like those in the interior, they fill no constructive office, but are in themselves rich and beautiful, and dispersed in most admired disorder. Mr. Fergusson is of opinion that the design was copied from the original Church of St. Mark at Alexandria, from whence the Evangelist's body was translated to Venice. And it is probable that many of the columns now standing at Venice were at the same time brought from the church at Alexandria.*

* Fergusson, "Illustrated Handbook of Architecture," ii. 963, 964.

SANTA MARIA GLORIOSA DE' FRARI;

or, as the Venetians more briefly name it, the Frari, is next, in point of antiquity, to St. Mark's. It was built —or, at all events, designed—by Nicolo Pisani, in 1250, and consists of a nave and aisles, with two transepts. The general character of its architecture is early Gothic, and each aisle is separated from the nave by six Gothic arches, but the details are Byzantine. In the interior there is much to interest the thoughtful stranger. The choir is enclosed by a fine fifteenth-century screen of marble, and is fitted up with carved wooden stalls, and a pulpit at each end. A broad passage, uniting the transepts, separates the choir from the high altar. Near the second altar stands the costly monument erected by the Emperor Ferdinand I. of Austria to Titian. It was inaugurated in 1853, with great pomp, and consists of an elaborate Corinthian canopy, crowning a sitting statue of the great master, and supported by a massive basement. Several allegorical statues adorn it. To the right of the huge mausoleum may be seen the simple tablet, inscribed,—

"Qui giace il gran Tiziano de' Vecelli,
Emulator de' Zeusi e degli Apelli,"

which for centuries indicated the last resting-place of the famous painter.

A brother in art, Canova the great sculptor, lies not far from the rival of Zeuxis and Apelles. His tomb, with some few alterations, is from a model by Canova himself, originally designed to cover the dust of Titian. It is built of white marble. In the centre of a pyramid is a half-closed door, into which enters a female figure. She carries an urn, and is all grace and sadness. On the opposite side rests a couchant lion, his eye vigilantly guarding the sacred portal. A large figure, emblematical of Sculpture, lies as if dead. His torch is reversed, and a hammer and chisel are thrown useless at his feet. Above, two angels hover, who hold with outstretched arms the sculptured profile of Canova.*

Over the fourth altar hangs a fine painting, by Palma Giovane, representing the martyrdom of St. Catherine; but of far higher merit is the altar-piece in the sacristy — a Madonna, enthroned with two angels, and four saints in the sides, who contemplate the infant with deep emotion. The two little angels, says Kugler, are of the utmost beauty: the one is playing on the lute, and listens, with head inclined, to hear whether the instrument be in tune; the other is blowing a pipe. The whole is perfectly finished, and of a splendid effect of colour.†

There are also paintings by Licinio, Luigi Vivarini, and others, but the Frari is more celebrated for its monuments. In the Tribune the stranger's attention is at once arrested by Rizzo's memorial to the ill-fated Doge Francesco Foscari (died 1457), whose tragic story has been told by Byron and Samuel Rogers.‡ It was erected by the doge's grandson, Nicolo; and is the first important example, says Ruskin, of Renaissance art. Under a canopy which this writer compares to an

* Mrs. Newman Hall, "Through the Tyrol to Venice," p. 282.

† Kugler, "Schools of Painting in Italy," edited by Sir C. Eastlake, i. 238.

‡ See pp. 108–113.

enormous French bed, sustained at the flanks by two diminutive figures in Roman armour, is placed a sarcophagus with the recumbent figure of the doge. Its panels are filled with half-length figures of Faith, Hope, and Charity; while at the doge's head stand Justice and Prudence; at his feet, Temperance and Fortitude. These figures, however, convey no allegorical expression, but are nothing more "than handsome Venetian women, in rather full and costly dresses, and tolerably well thrown into postures for effect from below." Opposite is the tomb of the Doge Nicolo Tron (died 1472), also by Antonio Rizzo, measuring 50 feet in width, 70 feet in height, consisting of five stories, and adorned with nineteen full-length figures, and an abundance of sculptures. Melchior Trevisano is commemorated by a statue in complete armour—the work of Dentone, which stands forth as a vigorous presentment of one of the olden knights. The monument of Bishop Jacopo Pesaro glows with a profusion of rare Oriental marbles. The epitaph is curious:—

"James Pesaro, Bishop of Paphos, who conquered the Turks in war, himself in peace; transported from a noble family among the Venetians to a nobler among the angels; laid here, expects the noblest crown, which the just Judge shall give to him in that Day. He lived the years of Plato. He died 26th March 1547."

The mingled classicism and carnal pride of this epitaph, says Ruskin, surely need no comment. The crown is expected as a right from the justice of the Judge, and the nobility of the Venetian family is only a little lower than that of the angels. The quaint childishness of the

"Vixit annos Platonicos" is also very notable. Rather curious than artistic is the colossal monument of another of the Pesaro family—the Doge Giovanni, who died in 1659. Huge Moors, in black marble, with their drapery of white marble, sustain the first story; above this, two monsters, long-necked—half dog, half dragon—support an ornamental sarcophagus, on whose summit the full-length statue of the doge in robes of state stands forward, with its arms expanded, like an actor courting applause, under a huge gilded canopy of metal; on each side of him are sitting figures of genii, and meaningless allegories in Roman armour; below, between the negro caryatides, two ghastly figures in bronze—half corpse, half skeleton—carry labels inscribed with an elaborate eulogium; but in large letters, graven in gold, the following words are the first and last that strike the eye: "Vixit annos LXX. Devixit anno MDCLIX. Hic Revixit anno MDCLXXIX." [He lived 70 years. He died in the year 1659. Here he lived again in 1679.] It is surely impossible for false taste and base feeling to sink lower.* It seems a sculptor's nightmare—the reproduction of some horrible dream; and embodies neither lofty sentiment, exalted thought, nor pure feeling.

Over the Pesaro altar hangs a magnificent Titian—a votive picture, known as the *Pala dei Pesari.* It is (or was) the private property of the Pesaro family. The Virgin is represented as enthroned in an elevated situation, and within a noble architectural framework. In her arms rests the Saviour, with his face turned towards St. Francis. St. George and St. Peter are also pro-

* Ruskin, "Stones of Venice," iii. 91, 92.

minent; and, below, five members of the Pesaro family kneel in adoration before the Virgin. For this picture, which Kugler describes as full of the finest truth and life, Titian received one hundred and two golden ducats.

The sacristy contains a fine specimen of Giovane Bellini.

The archives of Venice are preserved in the conventual buildings attached to this interesting church.

Three churches, built by the architect Palladio, are briefly noticed by Mr. Forsyth, a judicious critic, in words which, with some modification, we may adopt.*

IL REDENTORE,

in the island of La Guidecca, is admirable in plan and elevation. The interior is, perhaps, perfect in its proportions, simple, grand, harmonious. It consists of one broad and noble nave.

This church was erected by the Republic as a thanksgiving offering, after the cessation of the terrible pestilence of 1576.

The altar-pieces are by Bassano, Tintoretto, and Palma. Three interesting works by Giovane Bellini, and a Paul Veronese, enrich the sacristy.†

* Forsyth, "An Excursion in Italy," pp. 364, 365.

† Critics differ. Mr. Ruskin describes this church as "small and contemptible, and only becoming an object of interest because it contains three small pictures!"

SAN GIORGIO,

opposite to the Piazzetta—generally called San Giorgio Maggiore, to distinguish it from the Greek church, San Giorgio dei Greci—was built by Palladio in 1556–1610. It is not so pure in design as Il Redentore, but still worthy of its architect. The transepts seem too long for the nave, and the cupola too small. The marbles are finely assembled on the walls. The chief cloister, though supported by coupled columns, is nobly elevated; the windows exhibit a surprising grandeur of design. In this church lies interred the Doge Dominico Michieli (died 1128), who exhorted his countrymen to co-operate with the Crusaders in their war against the Infidels.

The interior contains some most precious pictures: as, Tintoretto's "Gathering the Manna," a remarkable landscape, full of interest and power; "The Last Supper," "Martyrdom of Various Saints," "Coronation of the Virgin," "Resurrection of Christ," and "Martyrdom of St. Stephen,"—all by the same great master.

SAN FRANCESCO DELLA VIGNA

is another of Palladio's churches, but not one of his most admirable. Its front, like San Giorgio's, has two wings, each covered with half a pediment. The pediment in the middle is entire, and contains an eagle cooped in a circle. But why did not the sacred bird fill the whole tympanum with his expanded wings? The Greeks were so accustomed to assimilate the one figure to the other, that the very name for pediment is, in Greek, an eagle.

It was built at the expense of the Doge Andrea Gritti,

SANTI GIOVANNI E PAOLO.

who laid the foundation-stone August 15, 1554. It contains seventeen chapels, some good paintings (especially one by Giovane Bellini), and tombs of several doges.

SANTI GIOVANNI E PAOLO,

popularly known as San Zanipolo, was begun by the Dominicans about 1234, under the immediate patronage of the Senate and Doge Giacomo Tiepolo,* but not completed until 1390. It measures 330 feet 6 inches in length, 123 feet in height, 142 feet 6 inches in width at the transepts, and 91 feet in width in the body of the church. The interior—Venetian-Gothic in style—has a noble and impressive air. The monuments, in their workmanship and their associations, claim the stranger's notice. Yonder, for instance, from the chisels of the Lombardis, father and sons, is the memorial of Doge Pietro Moncenigo (died 1476). Those of Dionigi Naldo (1510), and Orsini, Count of Pittigliano (1509), recall the memory of the League of Cambray; for these trusty generals led the armies of the Republic in the struggle inaugurated by that nefarious compact. The fine statue, by Campagna, of the Doge Leonardo Loredano (1521), again reminds us of the League of Cambray, which was baffled by the sagacity and patient energy of this illustrious prince. Various epochs in Venetian history are recalled to the mind of the spectator by a long succession of tombs and statues: Doge Corner, or Cornaro (1367); Doge Giovanni Dolfino (1361); Doge Antonio Veniero

* The popular tradition is: that in the year 1226 the doge dreamed a dream; that in his dream he saw the little oratory of the Dominicans, and, behold, the ground all around it (now occupied by the church) was covered with vermilion-coloured roses, which filled the air with perfume. And in their midst hovered a throng of white doves, with golden crosses upon their heads. And while the prince gazed, wondering, two angels stooped down from heaven with golden censers, and passing through the oratory, and among the flowers, spread everywhere abroad the smoke of their celestial incense. Then the doge heard suddenly the utterance of a loud, clear, melodious voice, and it said: "This is the place that I have chosen for my preachers." Whereupon he awoke, and repairing to the Senate declared to them his vision. The Senate accordingly decreed that forty paces of ground should be given to enlarge the monastery; and the doge himself made afterwards a larger grant.

(1400); Doge Pascale Malipieri (1461); Doge Michele Steno (1413), in whose reign the unfortunate Carraras were murdered; Doge Giovanni Dandolo (1289); and many others;—so many, that the church has somewhat inappropriately been termed "the Westminster Abbey of Venice."

That of Jacopo Cavalli is worthy of note for several reasons. And first, because he was a gallant Veronese soldier, who served the state well and faithfully, was therefore ennobled by it, and became the founder of the Cavalli family. It is recorded of him that at the siege of Fettro, in the war against Leopold of Austria, he refused to assault the city until the Senate promised the spoil of it to his soldiers. He died in 1384. Next, because it is singularly rich in religious imagery, which is boldly and finely sculptured. The sculptor was proud of the labour of his hands, and below the epitaph inscribed his name. Thus:—

> "QST OPERA DINTALGIO E FACTO IN PIERA,
> UN VENICIAN LAFE CHANOME POLO,
> NATO DI SACHOMEL CHATAIAPIERA."
>
> This work of sculpture is done in stone;
> A Venetian did it, named Paul,
> Son of Sachomel the stone-cutter.

The tomb of the Doge Marco Cornaro, already named, is rich and fully developed Gothic; in the same style, but more elaborate, is that of the Doge Michele Morosini (died 1382). Ruskin characterizes the latter as the richest monument of the Gothic period in Venice. The recumbent figure of the doge is particularly noble and impressive.

The Doge Andrea Vendramin is commemorated by a monument (date 1480) which attracts general attention, partly from its costliness, and partly from the delicacy and precision of its chiselling. It is one of those works in which the execution is far superior to the design.

In a purer and higher style is that to the great Doge Michele Morosini (died 1382), the first Venetian tomb adorned with allegorical figures of the Virtues. The prince, with a serene, resolute, and thoughtful face, is represented kneeling before the Cross, as if brought to the feet of the suffering Saviour by the Madonna. The sarcophagus is adorned with elaborate foliage, and the whole surmounted by a highly florid Gothic canopy.

The tomb of Doge Tomaso Mocenigo, characterized by Sansovino as a man who before all things desired peace —"Huomo altre modo desideroso della pace"—is the last in Venice which can be considered purely Gothic. The recumbent figure is very beautiful. It was carved by two Florentine sculptors in 1423.

Among the fine paintings here enshrined, the noblest was Titian's Martyrdom of St. Peter;* esteemed by many the third picture in the world—the first being Raffaelle's Transfiguration, and the second, Domenichino's St. Jerome. "The saint is looking up to heaven," says Kugler, describing it as in his time it existed, "in expectation of death. His sufferings are seen most in the furious spring of the murderer, and in the terrified action of the disciple. The landscape—the border of a dark wood, with fine clouds, and the mountains seen behind

* Not the apostle, but a Dominican monk of Verona, who was murdered in a wood on his return from a council of his order. The picture was so highly esteemed that the Venetian Senate passed a decree forbidding the Dominicans to sell it *under pain of death*.

in bright twilight—is one of Titian's invariably masterly scenes." In form, in colour, in expression, the work exhibited the painter's highest qualities.*

In the interesting Gothic church of

SAN STEFANO

lies buried the wretched Francesco Carrara, last Lord of Padua—the victim of the subtle policy of Venice. For Protestants, San Stefano has a peculiar interest: here Martin Luther once said mass on his journey to Rome, before he had inaugurated the German Reformation. He lodged in the adjoining Augustinian convent, whose cloister is adorned with frescoes by Pordenone, painted at the period of his fierce rivalry with Titian. It is said that while at work upon them, he always wore his sword and buckler, in readiness to contend with that great master, *vi et armis*, should the necessity arise. The Venetians flock to San Stefano, during Lent, to hear the powerful sermons of the so-called "preacher-monks."

The church, built 1294–1320, is a good example of the Venetian pointed style. The interior has a fine wooden roof. The Doge Andrea Contarini (died 1367) has a sarcophagus in the adjoining cloister, which is now a public thoroughfare and mart for old clothes!

* Since the above was written, the church has suffered severely from fire, and Titian's great picture been destroyed. An old and excellent copy, however, has been presented to the church by the authorities of the Museum of Florence.

LA MADONNA DELL' ORTO

is a building in the Renaissance Gothic, built in the fourteenth century, very rich in design, and profuse in sculptured details. A large effigy of St. Christopher—the "Christ-bearer"—is preserved in the choir; and the same saint figures, with the Twelve Apostles, over the church door. Here were buried Ramusio, the geographer; Alessandro Leopardi, the architect; and the great artist Tintoretto, whose pencil has embellished the church with four important paintings.

These are, The Last Judgment, The Worship of the Golden Calf, The Presentation of the Virgin, and Martyrdom of St. Agnes. Of the two former, Ruskin observes that no pictures will better reward a resolute study; and of the Last Judgment he gives a powerful description in his "Modern Painters:"—"Bat-like, out of the holes and caverns and shadows of the earth, the bones gather, and the clay-heaps heave, rattling and adhering into half-kneaded anatomies, that crawl, and startle, and struggle up among the putrid weeds, with the clay clinging to their clotted hair, and their heavy eyes sealed by the earth darkness yet, like his of old who went his way unseeing to the Siloam Pool; shaking off one by one the dreams of the prison-house, hardly hearing the clangour of the trumpets of the armies of God, blinded yet more, as they awake, by the white light of the new Heaven, until the great vortex of the four winds bears up their bodies to the judgment-seat."

SAN PIETRO DI CASTELLO,

the mother-church and cathedral of Venice, has been modernized into a Palladian building of the seventeenth century, and necessarily deprived of nearly all its interest. The fine campanile was erected in 1674. The church contains a curious relic; an ancient Episcopal seat, or throne, traditionally reputed to have been that of St. Peter at Antioch, and given, in 1310, by the Emperor Michael Palæologus to the Doge Gradenigo. The Oriental inscriptions on the back form a well-known antiquarian puzzle.

SAN SEBASTIANO,

built, in the classical style, by Castiglione and Sansovino, 1506–1548, is the burial-place of Paolo Veronese, and the appropriate monument of that illustrious painter, whose finest productions embellish its walls. The roof he enriched with subjects from the Book of Esther; the Capella Maggiore, with pictures of the Virgin, of various saints, and of the Martyrdom of St. Sebastian. At the first altar is a St. Nicholas, by Titian, painted by the master in his eighty-sixth year.

A recent traveller has described, in graphic terms, the famous fane of

SANTA MARIA DELLA SALUTE,*

founded by the Republic in 1631, as a thanksgiving offering after the plague was stayed—the great plague,

* This is the principal object in Turner's celebrated picture of the Grand Canal.

which slew 60,000 men, women, and children, in the capital alone! "It is a cold, superb church," says Mr. Howells, "lording it over the noblest breadth of the Grand Canal: and I do not know what it is saves it from being as hateful to the eye as other temples of the Renaissance architecture. But it has certainly a fine effect, with its twin *campanili* and single massive dome, its majestic breadth of steps from the water's edge, and the many-statued sculpture of its façade. Strangers go there to see the splendour of its high altar (where the melodramatic Madonna responds to the prayer of the operatic Venezia, and drives away the haggard, theatrical Pest—all in Campagna's manner), and the excellent Titians, and the Tintoretto in the sacristy."*

It is an octagonal building, crowned with a dome, which, internally, is supported on eight pillars. A continuous aisle is carried round it; and there are eight recesses, one of which forms the entrance, and the other seven are chapels. The disposition, says Mr. Woods, produces a degree of intricacy, without confusion; that is, without rendering it at all difficult to understand the design, which is very favourable to the expression of richness and splendour, and presents some very picturesque and even beautiful combinations; but the windows, disposed two on each side over the arches of the central octagon, have a bad effect. The architect, or at least the presiding genius, was Baldassare Longhena.

Santa Maria is enriched with three Titians—one, "The Descent of the Holy Spirit," a fine example of his brilliant genius. Luco Giordano, Tintoretto ("The Marriage

* Howells, "Venetian Life," pp. 155, 156.

in Cana," 20 feet long by 15 feet high), Palma Vecchio, and Salviati, are also seen to advantage. The tomb of Sansovino, the great Venetian architect, occupies a conspicuous place in the oratory of the adjacent conventual buildings. His remains were removed hither from San Geminiano in 1820. The tomb of the Doge Francesco Dandolo, formerly in the chapter-house, has been broken up into three portions, of which the canopy alone retains its original position.

This fine church is eminently worthy of a visit. It stands near the Dogana, on a tongue of land which juts out opposite St. Mark's Place, and is frequently represented by artists in their views of Venice. The foundation consists of 1,200,000 stakes or piles.

SAN SALVATORE,

near the Ponte di Rialto, a "base Renaissance building," was begun by Spavento and Julius Lombardo, in 1506, and completed by Sansovino about 1534.* The façade, by Sardi, was added in 1663. It presents a mixture of styles, but the general character is Italian. The plan is that of a patriarchal cross, consisting of a nave and three transepts, each point of intersection being crowned with a dome.

Among its remarkable monuments are one by Sansovino to the Doge Francesco Venier (died 1556), a

* Occupies the place of the ancient church under whose porch Pope Alexander III. is said to have passed the night on his flight to Venice in 1176. The story runs that he was discovered in his disguise by the doge, who received him into his own palace. The Republic then espoused his cause.

stately mass, with columnar façade, like that of a temple. Over the altar, also designed by Sansovino—what a life of incessant labour must his have been, you meet his handiwork everywhere in Venice!—is placed a picture of the Annunciation, by Titian, executed when the artist was nearly ninety years of age, and exhibiting decadent powers both of conception and execution. The story runs that a critic pointed out to him its inferiority, and hazarded the suggestion that posterity would not believe it to have proceeded from his pencil; whereupon the impetuous master energetically wrote in the margin, "Titianus *fecit*, FECIT!"

Catarina Corner, or Cornaro, Queen of Cyprus, is buried in this church, and commemorated by a monument, whose bas-relief represents her resigning her crown into the hands of the Doge Barberigo. She was a lady of surpassing beauty; and her uncle, Andrea Corner, while an exile at Cyprus, showing her portrait to the young Prince Lusignan, that inflammatory youth fell in love with the pictured charms. He was then Archbishop of Nicosia; but, supported by Venice, by the Pope, and by the Sultan of Egypt, he won the crown of Cyprus, originally bestowed on his house by Richard I. of England. Catarina, solemnly adopted as the daughter of the Republic, was given, with a rich dowry, to King James Lusignan, but in two years became a widow, and their only child, James III., died in 1475. The beautiful Catarina reigned over Cyprus, under the protection of Venice, for a period of fourteen years, when her beauty and her opulence attracting numerous suitors, the State grew apprehensive that the fertile island might pass into other hands. The Venetian government, therefore, boldly claimed the sovereignty, and Catarina's brother, Giorgio, was instructed to arrange the details of her deposition. She resigned the crown reluctantly, but her woman's spirit was soothed by many signs of honour. She was received in Venice with all the ceremonies given to a crowned head, and, sole among all her country-women, before or since, was accorded a triumphal entrance into the city in the gilded Bucentaur. With a yearly revenue of 8000 ducats she retired to Asola, among the Trevisan Mountains, where she assembled a brilliant court of wits, poets, and men of letters. Titian immortalized her beauty on his canvas, and Cardinal Bembo, in his "Asolani," has perpetuated the memory of her talents and virtues.

OTHER CHURCHES.

As these pages are not intended to answer the purpose of a handbook, it will be unnecessary for us to enter into a detailed description of every Venetian church. They are very numerous, but generally range themselves into four principal styles: the Venetian-Gothic; the Lombardic, or Renaissance; the Paladian Italian; and what may be termed the Decorated Italian. In addition to those particularly described, we may mention—and only mention—the following:—

S. Andrea, "well worth visiting," says Ruskin, "for the sake of the peculiarly sweet and melancholy effect of its little grass-grown *campo*, opening to the Lagoon and the Alps." The church is of the later Gothic period, much defaced, but still picturesque.

SS. Apostoli, rebuilt in 1575, by Guglielmo Bergamasco. Contains a picture by Paolo Veronese, "The Fall of Manna."

La Chiesa de' Carmini, or of La Virgine del Carmelo, a late thirteenth century building. The cloister is full of interesting monuments. In the interior of the church, over the first altar on the right, is a glorious Tintoretto—"The Circumcision of Christ."

San Cassano, with three superb Tintorettos; namely, "The Crucifixion," "The Descent into Hell," and "The Resurrection."

San Fesca, worth visiting for the sake of its exceedingly picturesque campanile, of late Gothic, crowned by a cupola.

San Giacomo de' Lurio, an interesting building of the thirteenth century, said to contain four works of Paolo Veronese.

San Giacomo de' Rialto, a picturesque structure, containing some portions of eleventh century work. It stands on the site, and retains the name, of the first church ever built on that Rialto "which formed the nucleus of future Venice, and became afterwards the mart of her merchants." Restored in 1531.

San Giovanni Crisostomo, built by Tullio Lombardo, 1489. The style is early Renaissance, and the church contains some good sculpture, besides a noble Sebastian del Piombo and a fine Giovane Bellini.

San Giorgio de' Greci, built by Sansovino.

Chiesa de' Jesuiti, built by Fattoretto and Rossi (1715–1730), where lies interred the last of the Venetian doges, Manini, who, when required to take the oath of allegiance to the Austrian emperor, and thereby recognize the destruction of his country's independence, dropped senseless to the ground, overwhelmed with grief. It contains a Tintoretto—"The Assumption;" and a Titian—"The Martyrdom of St. Lawrence."

Santa Maria Formosa, the scene, in the old days, of the procession on February 2nd, which commemorated the rape of the Brides of Venice—

> "Ever to preserve
> The memory of a day so full of change—
> From joy to grief, from grief to joy again—
> Through many an age, as oft as it came round,
> 'Twas held religiously. The doge resigned
> His crimson for pure ermine, visiting,
> At earliest dawn, St. Mary's silver shrine."—ROGERS.

According to tradition, a church was erected here about 639 by a certain Bishop of Uderzo, who, having been driven from his bishopric by the Lombards, beheld, while he was praying, the Virgin Mary in a vision, and was ordered by her to build a church in her honour wherever he should see a white cloud rest. And when he went out the white cloud sailed before him, like the pillar of fire before the Israelites; and on the spot where it finally reposed he raised a church, and, from the loveliness of the form revealed to him in his vision, called it the Church of St. Mary the Beautiful (*Formosa*). This building was reconstructed in 864, and some half century later enriched with relics of St. Nicodemus—destroyed along with the church by fire in 1105. It was then rebuilt on a magnificent scale, and, according to Corner, remained untouched for four centuries, until destroyed by an earthquake in 1689. A rich merchant, named Turrin Toroni, then erected the present edifice, in the style of Sansovino, and embellished it with two façades of marble. The principal of these consists of a pediment, supported by four Corinthian pilasters, and is remarkable for its lack of all religious symbols or sculpture; being, in fact, a monument to the Admiral Venenigo Cappello, who died in 1642. Over the door is his statue in Roman armour.

Madonna dei Miracoli, built about 1480–90, an interesting example of what is called the Cinquecento style.

San Moisè, where rest the remains of the able but adventurous projector, John Law, who died at Venice in 1729. The building is a bad specimen of the worst style of the Renaissance, but contains an important picture of Tintoretto's—"Christ washing the Disciples' Feet."

San Pantaleone, built in 1668.

San Rocco, enriched with paintings by Titian, Tintoretto, and Pordenone. Those of Tintoretto are—"San Rocco before the Pope," "The Annunciation," "The Pool of Bethesda," "San Rocco in the Desert," "San Rocco in the Hospital," "A Landscape with Cattle and Figures," "Finding of the Body of San Rocco," and "San Rocco in the Campo d' Armata."

The *Scuola di San Rocco*, an interesting Renaissance building of the date of 1517, is embellished with no less than two and sixty paintings by Tintoretto, forming an admirable study of that great master's style.

Gli Scalzi, a Renaissance building, built by Longhena in 1680, and all ablaze with glowing marbles, rich mosaics, gilding, bas-reliefs, and statues; the altar-piece is a Madonna and Child, by Giovane Bellini.

De' Tolentini, by Scamozzi, a specimen of the later Renaissance.

San Trovasio, a Palladian building, dating from 1583, contains two Tintorettos.

San Zaccaria, a beautiful early Renaissance building, with some fine carvings and paintings, erected by Antonio di Marco, 1456–1515. It contains a superb Giovane Bellini—"The Virgin, with four Saints."

Santa Maria Zobenigo, a Renaissance building, which is little more than a pretentious monument to the Barbaro family. It possesses, however, a Tintoretto of great beauty—"Christ with Santa Justine and San Agostino."

The church and Armenian convent of San Lazaro, where Lord Byron studied—or pretended to study—Armenian, are worth a visit. The library is good, and the convent may be considered a "centre of Armenian literature."

III.

Public Buildings of Venice.

Rose, like an exhalation from the deep,
A vast metropolis, with glistering spires,
With theatres, basilicas adorned;
A scene of light and glory, a dominion,
That has endured the longest among men.

SAMUEL ROGERS.

WE must once more invite the reader to visit the *Piazza di San Marco.*

Dickens has aptly described it as "anchored in the deep ocean," and extolled it as "a place of surpassing beauty and grandeur." On its broad bosom, he continues,* is a palace, more majestic and magnificent in its old age than all the buildings of the earth in the high prime and fulness of their youth. Cloisters and galleries—so light, they might have been the work of fairy hands; so strong, that centuries have battered them in vain — wind round and round this palace, and enfold it with a cathedral, gorgeous in the wild luxuriant fancies of the East. At no great distance

* Charles Dickens, "Pictures from Italy," p. 75.

from its porch, a lofty tower, standing by itself, and rearing its proud head, alone, into the sky, looks out upon the Adriatic Sea. Near to the margin of the stream rise two ill-omened pillars of red granite; one having on its top a figure with a sword and shield, the other a winged lion. Not far from these again a second tower—richest of the rich in all its decorations, even here, where all is rich—sustains aloft a great orb, gleaming with gold and deepest blue, the twelve signs painted on it, and a mimic sun revolving in its course around them; while above, two bronze giants hammer out the hours upon a sounding bell. An oblong square of lofty houses, of the whitest stone, surrounded by a light and beautiful arcade, forms part of this enchanted scene; and here and there gay masts for flags rise, tapering, from the pavement of the unsubstantial ground.

The Place of St. Mark's, exclaimed Napoleon, is a saloon of which the sky is worthy to serve for a ceiling. Scarcely any other city in the world can show, in so limited an area, such a number of stately and beautiful buildings. Critics may differ as to their relative merits; but at least none are mean, tawdry, or commonplace.

Beginning at the north-east corner, the stranger successively notices the Torre dell' Orologio, the Procuratie Vecchie, the Procuratie Nuove, the Campanile of St. Mark, the gorgeous Cathedral, the Ducal Palace, the Zecca or Mint, and the two granite Pillars. The Cathedral we have already portrayed; of each of the others we shall have something to say: but instead of describing them in the above order, we prefer to consider their relative interest and importance, and shall therefore begin with

THE DUCAL PALACE.

> "Statues of glass—all shivered—the long file
> Of her dead doges are declined to dust;
> But where they dwelt, the vast and sumptuous pile
> Bespeaks the pageant of their splendid trust."—BYRON.

It is situated on the eastern side of the Piazzetta, in the immediate vicinity of the Campanile, with its southern point looking out upon the Canale della Guidecca. The front on the piazzetta is composed of two rows of arcades, one above the other; the lower a colonnade, the upper a gallery, surmounted by a very large and lofty wall of a pale reddish marble, pierced by five great windows, and covered with luxuriant coloured ornamentation.

Mr. Ruskin, looking at this strange creation with a poet's eye, pronounces it "a piece of rich and fantastic colour—as lovely a dream as ever filled the imagination."* Even Mr. Fergusson, a soberer critic, admits that it is difficult to judge it calmly. "It is the centre," he says, "of the most beautiful architectural group that adorns any city of Europe, or of the world—richer than almost any other building in historical associations, and hallowed, especially to an Englishman, by the noblest poetry in the world. All this spreads a halo over and around it, that may furnish ample excuses for those who blindly praise even its deformities." † But, while giving credit

* Ruskin, "Stones of Venice," ii. *in loc.*

† Fergusson, "Illustrated Handbook of Architecture," ii. 796, 797.

to its picturesque situation, and a certain grandeur of design, Mr. Fergusson wholly condemns the execution of it. The two arcades, which constitute the base, are, from their extent and the beauty of their details, as fine as anything of their class executed during the middle ages. "There is also a just and pleasing proportion between the simple solidity of the lower, and the airy—perhaps slightly fantastic—lightness of the upper of these arcades. Had what appears to have been the original design been carried out, the building would rank high with the Alhambra and the palaces of Persia and India; but in an evil hour it was discovered that larger rooms were required for the meetings of the Council and for State occasions than were originally contemplated, and the upper wall, which was intended to stand on the back wall of the arcades, was brought forward even with the front, overpowering the part below by its ill-proportioned mass."

This western front belongs to the palace as rebuilt by the Doge Marino Faliero. The original building was erected in 813 by the Doge Angelo or Agnello Participazio, and seriously injured by fire in a popular revolt during the reign of Candiano IV. It was then repaired, and richly embellished by Pietro Orseolo II., who entertained the Emperor Otho the Great under its roof. For a second time injured by fire in 1106, it was restored before 1116, when it received the Emperor Henry V., and extorted his imperial admiration. Further decoration and restoration were undertaken by Doge Sebastian Ziani, who enlarged it "in every direction;" and thus enlarged, it remained untouched until the dogeship of

Pietro Gradenigo, who, in 1301–9, engrafted on the old Byzantine palace a new saloon in the Venetian-Gothic style. Other additions in the same elaborate style were made by succeeding princes; notably by Francesco Dandolo and Michale Steno, the latter of whom completed the great Council-chamber, and covered its ceiling with a starry firmament, in allusion to his armorial bearings (A.D. 1400). It had been begun in 1341, pursuant to a decree of the Grand Council; but the work was interrupted by the conspiracy of Faliero, and the violent end of Calendario, its master-builder. I have said that Doge Steno completed it; the whole of the decorations, however, occupied a total period of sixty years, and, with other portions of the building, did not receive the final touches of the artist until 1423. Then was perfected the Gothic Ducal Palace of Venice, or, as it was then called, the *Palazzo Nuovo;* standing side by side with the *Palazzo Vecchio,* or Byzantine Palace.

To prevent the Republic from being involved in heavy cost, the Senate had decreed that no person, under a penalty of one thousand ducats, should be allowed to propose the rebuilding of this ancient structure, inharmonious as it manifestly was with the gorgeous modern pile. But a fire which occurred in 1419 gave occasion for the Doge Tomaso Mocenigo to disregard the prohibition. Carrying a thousand ducats into the Senate-chamber, he accordingly proposed that the palace should be rebuilt; not, he said, for his own convenience, since he was old, and could not expect to live to see the walls raised a pace above the ground, but for the honour of the dukedom and the dignity of the state. The Senate, says Sanudo, could not oppose the duke's desire, and unanimously devoted the one thousand ducats to the expenses of the work.

Mocenigo, as he had predicted, did not live to see it begun; and the demolition of the old Byzantine Palace and the commencement of the new Renaissance structure were events which distinguished the reign of Francesco Foscari. The existing façade to the piazzetta was finished about 1441; the interior buildings connected with it were added by Doge Cristofero Moro (the Othello of Shakspeare) in 1462. The façades towards the canal and court were next constructed, under the superintendence of the best Renaissance artists of the time; the Giant's Staircase being executed by Antonio Ricci, and after he had absconded with a large sum of the public money, by Pietro Lombardo.

Thus was the magnificent pile wrought to perfection. But fire seems to have been its persistent enemy. In the conflagrations of 1574 and 1577 its principal apartments were destroyed, with, unhappily, the glorious masterpieces of Bellini, Pordenone, Carpaccio, and Titian, illustrating the heroes and victories of the Republic. The work of restoration was undertaken by Palladio, and successfully carried out. The prisons, formerly at the top of the palace, were removed to the other side of the Rio del Palazzo; and the Bridge of Sighs, to connect them with the palace, was built by Antonio da Ponte.*

* See Sansovino, "Venezia Descritta;" and Ruskin, "Stones of Venice," *in loc.*

The mean level of the sea at Venice has risen every century about three inches. It has, therefore, been necessary to raise in a corresponding manner the pavement of the quay and piazzetta, so that part of the columns of the lower tier of arches has been covered up, giving them a dwarf and clumsy appearance never intended by the architect.

In the palmy days of the Republic, the walk in the lower gallery, or arcade, which was called the Broglio, became a favourite resort of the Venetian merchants. "In this," says Dr. Moore, "the noble Venetians walk and converse; it is only here and at council where they have opportunities of meeting together, for they seldom visit openly or in a family way at each other's houses, and secret meetings would give umbrage to the state inquisitors; they choose, therefore, to transact their business on this public walk. People of inferior rank seldom remain on the Broglio for any length of time when the nobility are there."

The principal entrance to the Palazzo is the Porta della Carta, erected by Bartolommeo Bon. Both its design and its sculptures are admirable. You pass through it into a noble quadrangle—the Grand Court—and, lo, on the west side, frowns the stern Byzantine façade of Faliero's palace; on the eastern, the elaborate classical front of Palladio. In the centre two superb fountains of sculptured bronze are placed, one by Nicolò de Conti (1556), the other by Alfonso Alborghetti (1559). Opposite to you rises the famous *Scala dei Giganti*—the Giant's Staircase—built of exquisite marbles, delicately carved and richly inlaid, by Antonio Rizzo, about 1483.

GRAND STAIRCASE IN THE DUCAL PALACE.

The two huge statues which crown the ascent on either hand, and give it its distinctive name, are by Francesco Sansovino, and represent Mars and Neptune. The coronation of the doges took place on the upper platform ; * and here, by a strange and unnecessary anachronism, Byron represents Marino Faliero as being divested of his dignity and suffering execution.

> " One has approached the doge, and now they strip
> The ducal bonnet from his head—and now
> He raises his keen eyes to heaven ; I see
> Them glitter, and his lips move. Hush ! hush !—no ;
> 'Twas but a murmur. Curse upon the distance !
> His words are inarticulate, but the voice
> Swells up like muttered thunder ; would we could
> But gather a sole sentence !
> 'Tis vain ;
> I cannot hear him. How his hoary hair
> Streams on the wind, like foam upon the wave !
> Now—now—he kneels ; and now they form a circle
> Round him, and all is hidden ; but I see
> The lifted sword in air—ah ! hark ! it falls !
> . . . . The gory head rolls down the Giant's Steps !"
>
> BYRON, *Marino Faliero.*

Proceeding along the loggia, or gallery, to the right, we notice an inscription commemorating the visit of Henry III. of France, in 1574 ; busts of the two greatest seamen of Venice, Pisani and Carlo Zeno, equals in genius, valour, patriotism, and fortune ; and the opening of the once celebrated Lion's Mouth, which was provided for the reception of secret charges against supposed enemies of the state, and placed a powerful engine of persecution in the hands of Malice and Envy.

Returning to the platform, and proceeding towards the left, the stranger reaches the great staircase—the Scala d' Oro—of marble and gold, the ceiling embossed and

* This was intended to typify that the highest dignity of the state could only be reached by those who had climbed to it by gradual and successive steps.

enriched with fine bas-relief and exquisite arabesques. It was built in 1577, and partly designed by Sansovino. It seems a portion of some fairy palace in the lands of wonder and enchantment, and one could almost believe it to have been the work of genii.

Through an antechamber filled with books we pass into the

SALA DEL GRAN CONSIGLIO,

or Hall of the Grand Council, 175½ feet long, 84⅓ feet broad, and 51⅓ feet high. It was begun in 1341, and completed in 1365, but the Grand Council first assembled beneath its roof in 1423. Here, in former times, the Venetian nobles discussed the foreign relations of the Republic; but its walls have long ceased to re-echo the voices of other than grave bookworms, or curious strangers. It is now the depository of the library of St. Mark, including a great number of printed works, as well as the valuable manuscripts bequeathed by Petrarch. The walls are covered with huge historical paintings; those on the north wall, eleven in number—by Cagliari, Bassano, Tintoretto, Francesco Bassano, Fiammingo, Vicentino, Jacopo Palma, Zucchero, and Gamberato — illustrate incidents in the visit of Pope Alexander III. and the Emperor Barbarossa to Venice; on the west side are three, and on the south seven—by Guilio del Moro, Paolo Veronese, L'Aliense, Il Vicentino, Tintoretto, Palma Giovane, and Le Clerc—in commemoration of certain noteworthy historical events. Looking on the eloquent canvas, the Venetian must have felt all its stir and inspiration, and inly have sworn that he would not be unworthy of the illustrious spirits whose great deeds were recorded as incentives to a life sublime.

Over these pictures, and forming a frieze round the saloon, are placed the portraits of the seventy-two doges, from A.D. 800, with the blank space covered by a black veil that should have been occupied by Faliero's, but for his treason to his country. Many of these portraits were painted by Tintoretto, but the earlier ones are from imagination.

A corridor leads us into the

SALA DELLO SCRUTINO,

or Hall of Scrutiny, where the scrutineers *audited*, as it were, the election of the doge, but where are now preserved the choicer books, manuscripts, and Aldine editions* of the Library. The portrait frieze of the doges is continued and completed in this chamber. There are also eleven historical paintings by Tintoretto, Bassano, and others; and a grand and impressive painting of the *Last Judgment*, by Palma Giovane.

Passing through the

SALA DELLE QUATTRO PORTE,

so called from the four fine doors in it designed by Palladio, who, in conjunction with Sansovino, embellished the ceiling; and through the Anti-Collegio, or Guard-

* So called from the printer, Aldus Manutius, who established the first printing-press at Venice in 1488, and was liberally encouraged by the State.

GRAND HALL OF THE DUCAL PALACE.

Room, containing some admirable pictures by Tintoretto,* Veronese, and Bassano; we enter the

SALA DEL COLLEGIO,

or Presence Chamber, where the doge and his privy council gave audience to the ambassadors from foreign states. The ceiling glows with allegorical designs and historical episodes by Paolo Veronese; the walls exhibit the rich colouring of the same great master. Tintoretto is also represented by many masterpieces. The ducal throne is preserved here, and the twenty-seven crimson cushioned stalls which accommodated the leading dignitaries of the Republic, whose shadowy presence seems to fill the chamber with a solemn grandeur, and recall to life the stirring days of Venetian glory. "What, ho, there! who waits without?" "The ambassador from his most Christian Majesty the King of Spain." "Admit him to our presence." The doors are thrown open; the guards and pages fall back in silent order; bending low and bowing often, the ambassador enters, followed by his splendid train. Advancing to the throne he pays his courteous homage, to which the doge responds in formal obeisance. The chancellor now steps forward, and

* Mr. Hillard justly remarks that, in these rooms, admiration is especially claimed for the colossal genius of Tintoretto, who grapples with whole acres of canvas. What lavish and exuberant energies were put into the brain and arm of this extraordinary man! "I imagine him to have been one of those in whom activity and endurance are so blended, as to produce a combination which appears hardly less than supernatural to those who are doomed to struggle against frequent invasions of weariness and exhaustion. I suppose him to have been content, like Napoleon and Humboldt, with four hours' sleep in the twenty-four. From the crown of his head to the sole of his foot, he seems to have been filled, pressed down, and running over with condensed and concentrated power."
—HILLARD, *Six Months in Italy.*

receives the letters from the court of Spain, which he duly reads aloud, with grave and measured accent. The doge replies: how hushed the glittering throng while he assures the ambassador of the high esteem in which the Republic holds its trusty ally! Now the first councillor on the prince's right hand rises from his seat, and motions to the ambassador to occupy it, who is thus admitted, as it were, into the council of Venice, and acknowledged worthy to share in its confidence.

But the dream vanishes: doge, and councillors, and ambassador, pages and guards, all disappear; and the wondering visitor passes through a door of rare marble into the

SALA DELLO SENATO,

or Senate Hall, where the "potent, grave, and reverend signiors" of the Venetian senate were wont to assemble in solemn conclave. What mighty debates have been held beneath this roof! What momentous issues of peace and war have here been decided! Clothe the walls with rich and glowing tapestry; cover the seats with crimson cushions; invest the ducal throne with elaborate ornament; fill the hall with the mellow light of innumerable tapers; and then summon on the scene the prince with his councillors, secretaries, and chancellors; the mysterious ten; the inquisitors; the procurators of St. Mark; and the senatorial body. So shall you see the ancient majesty of Venice, and understand why its name is still a power among men.

The most interesting feature of the building is, perhaps, its sculptured ornamentation, whose inner meaning has been developed with so much eloquence and beauty by

Mr. Ruskin. The most ancient portions, at the angles, represent the Fall of Man and the Drunkenness of Noah, surrounded by an abundance of exquisitely chiselled leafage of the vine. The more modern, near the church of St. Mark, depicts the Judgment of Solomon; the former is in the highest and purest Gothic, the latter in admirable Renaissance. Over the angle facing the piazzetta, and above the delicate vine sculpture, which almost seems to rival nature in truth and force, is a figure of the archangel Raphael, with the inscription, "O reverend Raphael, bid the gulf be calm, we beseech thee;" over the representation of the Fall, stands the sword-bearing Michael; and over that of the Wise King's Judgment, Gabriel, holding a lily.

The capitals of all the columns, moreover, are rich in the finest leaf-work conceivable; in emblematical figures of the most various expression, and in diverse symbolism of the most truthful character. Here you may see Temperance, Constancy, Modesty, Patience, Mercy, Piety, Benignity, and Humility; there, the more repellent features of Luxury, Gluttony, Pride, Anger, Avarice, Idleness, Vanity, and Envy. At one point, a bevy of birds seem flying out the foliage; at another, we are confronted by figures of Solomon and Aristotle; at another, by emblems of the craft of shoemaker, smith, and carpenter; and at yet another, by the sun and moon, and the astrological divisions of the Zodiac. The thirty-sixth capital, the last of the piazzetta façade, represents, on its front or first side, Justice enthroned, seated on two lions; and on the seven other sides examples of acts of justice or good government; and is considered typical of the belief of the

Venetian rulers that their sway could only be stable by being based on Justice.*

Adjoining the Hall is the Chapel, with an altar-piece by Scamozzi, and a Madonna by Sansovino. There are also three rooms which were specially appropriated to the use of the Council of Ten ; the *Sala della Bussola*, or antechamber, at whose entrance yawned the famous Lion's Mouth, and whose ceiling was painted by Veronese ; the *Sala del Consiglio dei Dieci*, or Hall of the Council of Ten, enriched with numerous paintings, and rendered sombre and awful by its associations—its memories of the secret body who held in their hands the lives and fortunes of all Venice ; and the *Sala dei Capi del Consiglio dei Dieci*, the Hall of the Three Inquisitors, chosen from the Ten, who were more powerful than the powerful, like the Fate or Demogorgon that in the old Greek legends controls even the gods themselves.

We have not enumerated above one-half of the interesting chambers in this famous palace. Our space forbids further detail. We must visit, however, the *Sotto Piombi*, or prisons at the top of the building, "under the leads," as their name indicates. Here was confined the Venetian Tyrtæus (1820–30), the patriotic bard Silvio Pellico, who, in his book *Le Mie Prigione*, has revealed the secrets of his prison place. They are terrible enough, these dark, close, stifling, miserable cells ; but far more terrible are the *Pozzi*, or dungeons in the lower stories, which can only be reached by obscure and intricate passages.† The

* Ruskin, "Stones of Venice," iii. 364, 365.

† Thus described by Andersen in "The Improvisatore :" "The light of the lamp from the passage alone can force its way between the close iron bars into

lowermost tier are dark as Erebus—dark with a darkness that is almost palpable; and surely no mind could long retain its balance exposed to their unutterable horror. Each is square, with a sort of slab to serve for the prisoner's bed; and here, in a low, dark, noisome hole, the unhappy captive — innocent, perhaps, of every crime except that of misfortune; ignorant, very often, of what offence he was accused—was doomed to linger through the wretched years, until madness deprived him of the power of memory and the bitterness of regret, or death mercifully took him to its blessed repose. Modern defenders of Venice would have us believe that the poor wretches doomed to these awful dungeons were all abandoned criminals; but even were their hypothesis better founded than they can show it to have been, what shall we think of the lenity of a state that inflicted on the vilest the torture of a slow and gradual death?

Ascending from this scene of horror we reach the passage to the famous *Ponte dei Sospiri*, or,

BRIDGE OF SIGHS.

"That deep descent leads to the dripping vaults
Under the flood, where light and warmth were never!
Leads to a covered bridge, the Bridge of Sighs:
And to that fatal closet at the foot,
Lurking for prey."—ROGERS.

This is a structure of marble—covered on both sides and on the top, very narrow and very lofty, and scantily

the uppermost dungeon; and yet this is a cheerful, airy hall compared with those which lie lower down, below the swampy cellars, deeper even than the water outside in the canals; and yet in these unhappy captives have sighed, and inscribed their names on the dripping walls."

BRIDGE OF SIGHS.

lighted by small windows—which connects the Ducal Palace with the *Carceri*, or the public prison, and spans the canal known as the *Rio della Paglia*. The Prison, a large building of sombre character and great strength, was erected, in 1589, from the designs of Antonio da Ponte. The benevolent Howard visited it in one of his tours of philanthropy, and observes : "It is one of the strongest I ever saw. There were between three and four hundred prisoners, many of them confined in loathsome and dark cells for life, executions here being very rare. There was no fever or prevailing disorder in this close prison. None of the prisoners had irons. On weighing the bread allowance I found it fourteen ounces. I asked some of them who had been confined many years in dark cells whether they should prefer the galleys. They all answered in the affirmative, so great a blessing is light and air."

The interior of the bridge is converted into a double passage. Criminals, when taken out of the prisons to suffer death, were led across this bridge—hence its significant name—to hear their sentences, and afterwards were strangled in "the fatal closet at the foot."

THE ARSENAL.

"In the Venetians' arsenal there boils
Through wintry months tenacious pitch, to smear
Their unsound vessels: for the inclement time
Seafaring men restrains, and in that while
His bark one builds anew, another stops
The ribs of his that hath made many a voyage;
One hammers at the prow, one at the poop;
This shapeth oars, that other cables twirls;
The mizzen one repairs, and main-sail rent."

DANTE, *L'Inferno*, Canto xxi. (Cary's Translation).

The arsenal is the next point to which the stranger will direct his footsteps. It is situated at the southern extremity of Venice, and extends two miles in circuit. Its

THE ARSENAL.

gateway, with its huge square towers and machicolated battlements, erected in 1460; its massive crenellated walls; the four colossal marble lions that front the entrance, and were brought from Athens by the Doge Morosini in 1685; its four basins; its dry docks, slips, rope-walk, model-room, all attest the ancient power and splendour of the Republic. A model of the famous Bucentaur is preserved here. The rope-walk, 346 yards long, was erected by the Doge Nicolo da Ponte in 1579. But worthy of special notice is the noble Armoury, which contains many objects of historical interest; things that give life and reality to history, and are, in fact, its most eloquent illustrations. Here you may gaze on the great standard of the Turkish admiral, whose folds of red and yellow silk fluttered in the hot battle-breezes of Lepanto, and which may have been grasped by the unwounded hand of Cervantes. Here may you brandish the sword, and weigh the helm and buckler, of the Doge Sebastiano Ziani. In yonder rich suit of armour once heaved the athletic frame of Henri Quatre, who presented it to the Republic in 1603. Arbalêtes, or cross-bows, you may seek to bend, which were once bent by the sturdy arms of old. Instruments of torture—rude iron helmets, without aperture for eyes or mouth, that closed in upon the miserable victim, and stifled him to death—Francesco da Carrara's spring-pistol, with which he shot his foes by poisoned needles — oriflammes and banners — heavy-swords, spears, battleaxes, and the first rude models of "murderous ordnance" — trophies and specimens of mediæval armour,*—these are memorials of a by-gone age which appeal to the imagination of the very dullest.

* Among other notable objects is the armour of the great admiral, Carlo Zeno, who could not only fight, but speak Latin and French; the Doge Contarini, who, in the war of Chiozzia, mortgaged his estates to equip a fleet against the Genoese; the Doge Mocenigo, who founded the library in the Piazzetta; and the Doge Barberigo, described as "a virtuous and a wise man of great experience in the affaires of Italie, and a courteous and gentle person."

The Arsenal, as an observant traveller remarks,* is the most impressive and characteristic spot in Venice. The Ducal Palace and the Church of St. Mark's are symbols of pride and power, but the strength and the life—the vital power—of Venice resided here. Here her six centuries of history were epitomized; and here, as she rose and fell, the hum of labour also rose and subsided. Here was the index-hand which pointed to her most glorious noon; to the sad decline of her greatness, and her fall from her high estate.

Whither shall we now direct our steps? To the *Scuole*, or Charitable Institutions of Venice? They are more pleasing monuments of the people than the Pozzi and Piombi of their despotic government. Public benevolence founded and has supported them. Architecturally, the most remarkable are the *Scuola di San Marco*, a brilliant Byzantine pile, designed by Martino Lombardo, and erected about 1490; and the *Scuola di San Rocco*, begun in 1517, and completed in 1550 by Scarpagnino, a fine classical edifice, very rich in Titians, Tintorettos, and other "things of beauty."

But, as our space is limited, we hasten from Charity to Art. The

ACADEMICA DELLE BELLE ARTI,

or Academy of the Fine Arts, occupies the old Convent of La Carità, on which Palladio exhausted all the resources of his fertile genius. Unfortunately, it was ravaged by fire in 1630, and the only Palladian portion

* Hillard, "Six Months in Italy," i. 63.

PIAZZA DI SAN MARCO, AND GRANITE COLUMNS.

that escaped destruction was a square hall, now occupied as a drawing-school. The Academy, in design and constitution, resembles all other foundations intended to promote the study of the Fine Arts, and the reader would fail to be interested by any detailed description of it. Nor do we feel inclined to enter upon a catalogue raisonnée of the treasures which it possesses in its *Pinacoteca.* It requires a Ruskin to make eloquent and intelligible an account of the masterpieces of a great painter. A mere enumeration of the subjects which he has treated can originate no just or pleasing ideas in the weary reader's mind. If we tell him that the walls are hung with Titians, and Tintorettos, and Bellinis—with glowing specimens of Paolo Veronese, Padovanino, Bonifacio, Palma Giovane, Vicentino, and others—he will know that the pilgrim who can stand before them, and gaze upon them, and muse on their surpassing beauty, will enjoy an intellectual banquet of the highest and rarest kind. It is supposed there are about six hundred works assembled in this great picture-gallery, but, sooth to say, one-half of them might be consigned to oblivion without inflicting an irreparable loss upon posterity.

The art-treasures of Venice, however, are countless, but they must be sought in the palaces and churches.

Calling to mind, as we write, the famous sights of the city, we remember that we have not yet spoken in detail of the Campanile, the Torre del' Orologio, and the Granite Columns.

THE CAMPANILE,

or Bell Tower of St. Mark, like most of the Italian campaniles, is detached from the cathedral to which it belongs. It was begun in 902, during the dogeship of Domenico Tiepolo, but not carried up to the belfry until 1150, when Morosini wore the ducal "crown of thorns."

The belfry, an open loggia of four arches in each front, dates from 1510; the design, by Maestro Buono, is simple but impressive, and terminates in a lofty pyramid. A glorious view is commanded from this point, embracing the Lagoon, the domes and towers of Venice, the blue line of the Adriatic, and the distant gleam of the snow-peaks of the Alps.

The height of the Campanile is 323 feet; its width at the base, 42 feet. The figure of an angel, which crowns the whole edifice, and serves as a vane, is said to be 30 feet high.

At the foot is a rich and fantastic loggia, by Sansovino (1540), in the Composite style, and adorned with bronze statues of Pax, Pallas, Apollo, and Mercury, with shapely marble columns, and allegorical bas-reliefs. Of these, the central represents Venice as Justice, with two rivers, the Brenta and the Adige, flowing at her feet: she is supported on the one hand by the Cretan god, Jupiter, and on the other by the Cyprian goddess, Venus. The others have for their subjects: Tethys assisting Leander in his love-quest after Hero, and the Fall of Helle from the Ram of Phryxus—two ancient myths whose connection with Venetian history it is difficult to imagine.

THE SCALA ANTICA.

The *Scala Antica* (or "Antique Staircase") forms the external access of the Palazzo Minelli, and is remarkable for the grace and lightness of its architectural details.

THE SCALA ANTICA.

In truth, it is, as a recent traveller* has termed it, one of the most curious and interesting edifices in Venice.

* Adalbert de Beaumont, *Venise*, in "Tour du Monde," 1862, 2nd semestre, p. 33.

Constructed in the style of the fifteenth century, it is generally attributed to one of the Lombardi, who seems to have been desirous of imitating the effect of the Leaning Tower of Pisa. By one of its flanks it is attached to the main body of the palace. In the centre of the spiral it is supported by a marble column consisting of eighty rounded blocks or stages, which are simply the extremities of the different steps or stairs; the other extremities being rested on the outer circumference, composed of arches and pilasters. Consequently, there are as many arcades as steps.

This tower is divided into seven stories; the first supported by six columns, the next five by eight, and the uppermost by fourteen; making sixty columns and 112 steps to the entire building.

Each step is about nine inches high by seven feet long. Hence, the interior diameter, including the thickness of the axis or column which supports the tower, measures 13 feet 6 inches. The total height is about 75 feet.

The palace communicates with each story of the staircase by a gallery with flattened arches, in the Renaissance style. It is situated in the *Corte del Maltero* (or Maltero Court), near the quay called *della Vida.*

THE TORRE DELL' OROLOGIO.

Opposite the superb pile which Venetian piety consecrated to the patron-saint of the Republic stands three beautiful pedestals of bronze, covered with elaborate sculptures of Tritons and Ocean-Nymphs, which, in their exquisite and life-like fidelity, seem to realize the poet's aspiration :—

> " So might I
> Have glimpses that would make me less forlorn,
> Have sight of Proteus coming from the sea,
> Or hear old Triton blow his wreathèd horn."—WORDSWORTH.

From these pedestals—designed by Alessandro Leopardi, and erected, one at the cost of Paolo Barbo, a Procurator of St. Mark, in 1501 ; the others by Doge Loredano, in 1505—once floated in all their glorious pride the three gonfalons, or banners, of silk and gold, which symbolized the three principal territories of the Republic—Venice, Cyprus, and the Morea.

To the left rises the three-storied Clock-Tower, or *Torre dell' Orologio*, the work of Peter Lombard (Pietro Lombardo), and dating from 1494. It is named from its resplendent clock-dial, of gold and azure, which indicates the hours by means of the twelve Zodiacal signs. Over it two quaint Moorish figures strike the hours upon the bell ; and the tradition runs, that one of these bronze Saracens once committed murder, by hurling an unfortunate workman, who stood within sweep of its hammer, off the parapet. A figure of the Virgin, of gilded bronze, and a huge lion holding the Gospel of St. Mark in his paw, adorn the upper stories. The internal machinery, constructed by the two Rinaldis, father and son, of Reggio, is very curious, though not equal to the famous clock of Strasburg. On certain religious anniversaries, and at a certain hour, a door flies open; and the three kings of the East—Melchior, Balthazar, and Caspar—clothed in Oriental magnificence, make their appearance, and after humble obeisance to the Virgin, cross over, and vanish within another door on the opposite side.

In front of the quay and landing-steps of the Piazzetta stand the two memorable

GRANITE COLUMNS,

associated with the fortunes of Venice for so many years. They were transported from the Holy Land in 1127 by the Doge Dominico Michiele. Originally there were three, but in landing them one was lost in the mud of the Lagoon. The two others were safely brought to shore, but remained prostrate on the quay for several years before any one would undertake to raise them. A reward offered by the Doge Sebastiano Ziani at length induced one Nicolo Barratiero, or "Nick the Black-leg," to offer his services. He succeeded, and claimed for his remuneration the privilege of carrying on, in the space between the columns, those games of chance elsewhere prohibited by the Venetian law. The doge could not refuse; but, to neutralize the privilege, it was enacted that all public executions should thenceforth take place on the same spot; and hence, to the imaginative Venetians, it became so ominous that even to cross it was considered indicative of a coming misfortune. When Marino Faliero was made doge, his gondoliers, by some mischance, landed him "between the columns;" a circumstance which, in the minds of the populace, accounted for his sorrows, his treason, and his fate.

We may record another remarkable incident connected with this sinister locality. One of the most successful of the Venetian generals in the middle of the fifteenth century was Francesco Carmagnola, who had formerly served under Visconti, Lord of Milan, and when leading the troops of Venice against his former master, incurred the suspicions of the Venetian government (1431). He was accordingly recalled, under the pretext that they desired his counsel. Invited to a banquet at the Ducal Palace, he was received by the nobles with a courteous appreciation of his great services, but a message arrived from the doge to excuse his presence, and Carmagnola, with the other guests, retired. As he was crossing the inner court to reach the Piazzetta an attendant accosted him, and, pointing towards the prisons, said—"Yonder is your way." He was immediately surrounded by guards, and resistance being hopeless, he entered his dungeon, exclaiming, "I am a dead man." A few weeks later, after he had several times been put to the torture, he was led out to execution,—here, between the granite columns. He was dressed in scarlet, and his mouth was gagged, to prevent him addressing the assembled multitude. After three unsuccessful strokes his head was severed from his body, May 5th, 1432. The opinions of historians are divided as to Carmagnola's guilt or innocence, but none have failed to condemn the needless treachery of the Venetian government.

One of the columns is surmounted by the Lion of St. Mark, holding the Gospel in his paw. During the occupancy of Venice by the French, the evangelist's words were erased, and "*Droits de l'Homme et du Citoyen*," the shibboleth of the French Republic, substituted. Thereupon a gondolier remarked, that St. Mark, like all the rest of the world, had turned over a new leaf! The other column supports a fine figure of St. Theodore, executed by Pietro Guilombardo in 1329. He stands upon a crocodile; a nimbus surrounds his head; his right arm carries a buckler, and his left wields a sword: intimating that Venice took for its motto, "Defence, not defiance," and drew the sword only to shield itself from attack. Venetian history, however, reads a different moral.

THE ZECCA,

or Mint, from whence was derived the name of the well-known Venetian coin, *zecchino*, stands on the Molo, and adjoins the *Libreria Vecchia*, a building erected from the designs of Sansovino, in 1316, for the reception of the library bestowed upon the State by the poet Petrarch. This is a noble structure, consisting of two orders: the lower, a highly-decorated Doric; the upper, a graceful Ionic. But the Zecca is superior in artistic effect. Sansovino has here combined what is called the Italian Rustic with Ionic and Doric, and the whole pile conveys an excellent idea of the strength and richness of his genius.

And now our task is ended. In our perambulation of Venice we have noted its sumptuous churches, its historic memorials, its glorious palaces, its stately public edifices; with such occasional glimpses of Venetian life as time and space permitted us. We have sought to deal with the more prominent points of our subject in such wise as to prepare the student for its further inves-

LIBRERIA VECCHIA.

tigation in the eloquent and elaborate pages of Ruskin, or on the glowing canvas of David Roberts, Prout, Turner, and Canaletti. The pride and grandeur of Venice have vanished for ever, but her name is still a power among men—is still a spell for the imagination—is still, and eternally will be, associated with

> "Otway, Radcliffe, Schiller, Shakspeare's art;"

so that the present writer, who has always felt the absorbing interest of her changeful history, would venture to echo the impassioned words of Byron :—

> "And of the happiest moments which were wrought
> Within the web of my existence, some
> From thee, fair Venice! have their colours caught."

As part and parcel of a regenerated Italy, may she flourish through long years of prosperity and peace, and, in the enjoyment of constitutional freedom, forget the past sorrows of the widowed

QUEEN OF THE ADRIATIC!

NOTE.

GLASS WORKS AT THE ISLAND OF MURANO.

HE Venetian glass has long been celebrated all over Europe, and its choice specimens have at all times obtained high prices from enthusiastic collectors. Anciently, it was highly esteemed by the great and wealthy, from a belief that it immediately broke when brought into contact with poison. Its manufacture was begun at Venice in the seventh century, and in 1291 removed to the island of Murano—its secret being guarded with jealous care, and its manufacturers being esteemed worthy to rank with the patrician class. Their rich-coloured glass was in vogue from 1436 to 1500, when they introduced the exquisite lace-work patterns and mirrors. Reticulated glass came into vogue in the sixteenth, and variegated in the seventeenth century. For a long period the Venetian ware monopolized the supply of Europe; but with the general decline of trade and commerce in the Republic this important manufacture also declined, and France, Germany, and England obtained the command of the market.

At Murano, however, the glass works continued to fashion, as objects of curiosity for the traveller, certain curious little bottles, plates, and vases, in glass coloured with alternate stripes of pink and white, in addition to the ordinary articles. A few years ago Dr. Salviati, a Venetian gentleman of great taste and ability, resolved to improve and develop this branch of Venetian trade, with the view of reviving its ancient glories. In this he so far succeeded, that the objects displayed at the Exhibition of 1862 attracted general admiration. Since that period—we learn from an article in the *Standard*—the work has made rapid strides, though the secrets of the craft are still jealously guarded by the little family band in whose possession they have remained for generations.

The Venetian glass, we may add, is neither very clear nor very bright, but is remarkable for its exquisite colouring and fine artistic character.

From the authority already named we borrow a few particulars of the more prominent varieties. First among these comes the single-tinted glass—the exquisite opal, into whose composition enters the caprice not only of the artist hand, but of the chemical process which it employs, without even as yet fully comprehending. The worker in opal glass can be certain beforehand only of his form. In colour his tazza may vary from the faintest and most delicate blush to a thick creamy opaque, like a prism melted into cloud. It will pass from one to the other in his hands, changing its hues with the rapidity of a dying dolphin, and all that he can be sure of is, that as it cools so it will remain. Then comes the "avventurine," that rich glittering bronze which sparkles in the light with the prismatic brilliancy of diamonds, but which is at least as capricious as the more delicate tint of which we have just spoken. This peculiar glass is formed by the admixture of certain metallic salts, kept for several hours in a state of fusion, and then sealed hermetically in the furnace to cool. If the Fates are propitious, it comes out glittering like ten thousand jewels, and capable of being re-fused as often as may be desired, without fear of further change. If otherwise, all that results from the laborious and costly process is a dull brown mass, fit only to be broken up for the baser uses of mosaic. What are the elements of success, and what of failure, one man only, by name Bigaglia, seems to know, for he alone is almost uniformly successful in the operation, by which he has realized a large fortune, and which he only now practises as an amusement. He is nearly ninety years old, and has as yet told the secret to no one. Very possibly it may die with him, and the production of avventurine remain as much a matter of chance as ever.

Among the other specialities we can but notice the "agato" or vari-coloured glass enclosed between two layers of crystal; the "vario pinto," a modification of the same idea; the old original Venice work, built up, so to speak, of bits of glass of every shape and colour, in forms the most deliciously bizarre that the most grotesque imagination could possibly conceive; the pure white "lattimo," painted like porcelain; the rich marble-like chalcédony; the engraved mirrors, looking into which Narcissus himself might almost forget to admire his own reflected image; and the chandeliers whose grotesque outlines could only have been invented in a dream. Every variety has a peculiar "flavour" of its own, and it is difficult, if not impossible, to determine whether any one can claim a superiority over the others.

INDEX.

LIST OF ILLUSTRATIONS.

www.ingramcontent.com/pod-product-compliance
Lightning Source LLC
LaVergne TN
LVHW020125110826
845151LV00001B/278

* 9 7 8 1 4 2 5 5 4 1 5 6 9 *